# Assembling the Past

# Assembling the Past

**Studies in the Professionalization of Archaeology**

Edited by
Alice B. Kehoe
and Mary Beth Emmerichs

University of New Mexico Press
Albuquerque

Library of Congress Cataloging-in-Publication Data

Assembling the past : studies in the professionalization of
archaeology / edited by Alice B. Kehoe and Mary Beth Emmerichs.—
1st ed.
    p.   cm.
Includes bibliographical references and index.
  ISBN 0-8263-1939-4 (alk. paper)
  I. Kehoe, Alice B.   II. Emmerichs, Mary Beth.  1.
Archaeology—History.  2. Archaeologists—History.  3.
Professional socialization—History.
  CC107   .A77  1999
  930.1—dc21

99-006846

# Contents

## III.  Southwestern Archaeology as Case Example  161

# Acknowledgments

A book like this contains the hard work of many people. I would like to thank the authors of the papers, and give special thanks to Alice Kehoe for responding so positively to my ideas about how to bind the papers together into a social history of the archaeological profession.

Most of all, I would like to thank my husband and computer consultant, Jack Emmerichs, for his technological and moral support, and my wonderful daughter, Sharon Emmerichs, for her expert typing and proofreading. Their energetic participation in this project was invaluable.

Mary Beth Emmerichs
University of Wisconsin-Sheboygan

# Introduction

## Alice B. Kehoe

The 1987 conference "Explaining Archaeology's Past: The Method and Theory of the History of Archaeology" convened by Andrew Christenson (Christenson 1989) catalyzed a surprising range of scholars and quickly spawned an informal committee, the organization of sessions at national meetings, and under the editorial enthusiasm of Douglas R. Givens, a *Bulletin of the History of Archaeology.* Two of the sessions directly inspired by the 1987 conference produced the papers published in this book.

"Mainstreams and Margins" was the title of the session presented by Jane Waldbaum, a Classical archaeologist, and Alice Kehoe on January 6, 1989, at the First Joint Archaeological Congress in Baltimore, and included earlier versions of essays here by William Dever, Stephen Dyson, Lawrence Desmond, James Halporn, and Jonathan Reyman. "Networks of the Past" was organized by Reyman for the American Anthropological Association annual meeting on November 16, 1989, in Washington, D.C., and included the contributions by Elin Danien, Donald McVicker, Mary Ann Levine, Susan Bender, and Don Fowler. We solicited Neil Silberman's essay, presented at another session of the Archaeological Congress, for its relevance to our focus on the broad historical background from which professional archaeology arose. The theme that emerged from such focus is the struggle to professionalize the discipline of archaeology, a struggle that involved the marginalization of the uncredentialed, members of the wrong social class, women, and those with the wrong regional or academic connections.

### From Antiquarians to Archaeologists, from Aristocrats to Academics

In the history of archaeology, a distinction must first be made between the practice of archaeological research and the profession of archaeology. Archaeology, understood as the praxis of systematic scientific collection and excavation of data on past human cultures, has been carried out since antiquity (Trigger 1989:28–30). Collingwood (1956[1946]:58) identified the origins of modern science with the beginning of archaeology as a science in the sixteenth-century research of Francis Bacon's countryman William Camden.

British archaeologist Stuart Piggott describes the early modern phases of scientific archaeology as antiquarianism, inlcuding the 1640s to the 1730s, and the 1730s to the 1830s (Piggott 1976:101).

In the antiquarian phases, British county surveys recorded historical sites, earthworks, megaliths, burials, and finds of ancient coins (and also rocks, fossils, fauna, and flora). That these projects deserve to be seen and understood as early modern science is demonstrated not only by their results but, even more importantly, by their invocation of the methodology of science "instaurated" (to use his term) by Francis Bacon (Piggott 1976:102, 1985:23). The first genuinely professional archaeologist was probably Edward Lhwyd, employed as assistant and then Keeper of the Ashmolean Museum in Oxford. Lhwyd's friend and colleague John Aubrey demanded that historical references be relegated to secondary status in favor of the direct study of field monuments. Aubrey's *Monumenta Britannica* is "the first English book that can be called 'archaeological' in the modern sense" (Hunter 1975:159; see also Atkinson 1975:xi). Concurrent with such British archaeological efforts, Carlos de Sigüenza y Góngora studied Teotihuacán in a scientific manner (Schávelzon 1984).

By the mid-eighteenth century, Enlightenment enthusiasm for armchair reasoning over "mere" amassing of data favored speculative hypotheses. William Stukeley had meticulously mapped Avebury and Stonehenge between 1719 and 1724 (Piggott 1985:50,153), but became better known for creating the myth of the Druids. In his landmark *Ancient Wiltshire* (1810), Richard Colt Hoare challenged the prevailing fashion by proclaiming, "WE SPEAK FROM FACTS, NOT THEORY" (capitals in original, quoted in Cunnington 1975:1, 133–134). (The "we" refers to Colt Hoare and his partner William Cunnington, a tradesman whose outdoor walks led him to systematically record archaeological features that were then tested through excavation.) Thomas Jefferson pioneered scientific archaeological excavation in the United States by investigating mounds on his estate in Virginia in 1784 (Willey and Sabloff 1980:28–29, 31). Jefferson also instructed a series of travelers and explorers of the West to take scientific notes on archaeological manifestations (Kennedy 1994:133–220).

In the nineteenth century, Boucher de Perthes, stimulated by the great biologist Georges Cuvier, began his systematic field research in France (Daniel 1967:61). Egyptology was inaugurated by the discovery of the Rosetta Stone by scientists who accompanied Napoleon's army in 1798. Half a century later, Mesopotamian archaeology began at Nineveh (Trigger 1989:39–40). Field archaeology was initiated in Central Europe by Arnold, with the excavation of the Hallstatt-La Tène barrows (Sklenář 1983:53). Fieldwork in Denmark began rather hesitantly in the 1830s, and was then established in the 1850s with the appointment of Jens Worsaae as Inspector of Ancient Monuments (Kristiansen 1985:15).

In the mid-nineteenth century, governments began financing and otherwise encouraging archaeological research. For example, Ephraim Squier and

E. H. Davis's *Ancient Monuments of the Mississippi Valley* (1848) was chosen to be the Smithsonian's first scientific monograph. Daniel Wilson organized the collections of the Society of Antiquaries of Scotland in preparation for its transition to the National Museum of Scotland in 1851. The Swiss "lake dwellings" were excavated in the 1850s for a fascinated populace, and by 1867, de Mortillet presented French prehistory to the public at the Paris Exposition. During this formative period of archaeological science, the paradigm of the Enlightenment's logical but still conjectural history (Meek 1976) was also formed. Mankind, it was asserted, had progressed from savagery through pastoral and then agricultural barbarism to an Age of Commerce represented by the nations of western Europe; other nations had failed to so progress, or had regressed. The paradigm comfortably placed every known nation, whether ancient or contemporary, somewhere on the path of progress.

Nineteenth century historians and archaeologists (Wilson 1851:xi–xii) deferred to the novelist Walter Scott as the source of a modern sense of history. Scott filled his novels with people from all walks of life, contrasting the kings and nobles of standard histories with peasants and fisher folk and peddlers, lawyers, ministers, and Jews. Everyday objects became as much a part of the past as coins and castles. Although his empathy with all manner of men and women was great, Scott was nevertheless convinced that he lived at the acme of progress. According to Kerr (1989:21), Scott's Waverley novels contain

> a prior ideological subtext, of the unfortunate, but necessary, defeat
> and subjugation of an older and less civilized society. Representations
> of the past . . . serve at once to defer the effects of history, to suppress
> the force of the real and to perpetuate the patterns of domination the
> novel disguises.

But there is more in Walter Scott than the march of progress. Stephen Bann (1984:108) discusses the contrast between the learned antiquary, Jonathan Oldbuck, in Scott's novel of the same name (1815) and the wise old local man, Edie Ochiltree. The novelist, Bann says, pits "experience against hypothesis and, more precisely, the tradition of [localized] history against the classicising historical style." At the very inception of nineteenth-century archaeological interest, the tension between strictly factual and broadly meaningful history appears. This tension underlies many of the controversies and choices made by archaeologists and their supporters described in this book.

Science in nineteenth century America generated a contest between democratic participation and elite authority. Joseph Henry, the first director of the Smithsonian Institution and a staunch supporter of archaeological work, believed in extending the opportunity to participate in scientific investigations as widely as possible (Hinsley 1981:152–153). Historians rather glibly contrast this "democratic science" with "the German university model," which appears to neatly summarize the contest between Lewis Henry Morgan and John Wesley Powell on the one hand, and Franz Boas on the other. Real life, of course, was not that neatly dichotomized (Hinsley 1981:151). The history of science in nineteenth century America, including the history of archaeology, can be described as a process comprised of the following four phases: preemption of "democratic" participation by credentialed specialists, institutionalization, legitimation, and by the end of the century, professional autonomy (Kevles 1988:109, paraphrasing historian of science George Daniels). The outcome of the process is a professional science resting upon the claim to *expertise*, manifested through *credentials*, and the *autonomy* of the properly credentialed to demarcate and perform their expertise (Freidson 1984:10).

At the same time that Joseph Henry advocated an idealized American science carried out by collaboration among citizens of all social stations and facilitated by the few paid specialists in the Smithsonian "castle"[1] (Hinsley 1981:48), the British model of excluding "mechanics" and other non-gentlemen was instituted with the establishment of the American Association for the Advancement of Science in 1844. [The British Association for the Advancement of Science (BAAS) was founded in 1831.] As with the British model, officers formed a self-perpetuating coterie whose approval was required for the presentation of papers at the annual meetings (Kevles 1988:109), although everyone's dollar was welcomed to subscribe to the journal or register to attend the meetings. Lacking a recognized class of landed aristocrats (the governing core of both the Royal Society, founded in the seventeenth century, and the BAAS [Shapin and Schaffer 1985; Morrell and Thackray 1981]), Americans emphasized educational and vocational credentials to differentiate those whose opinions commanded respect from the common throng (Kevles 1988:110). In the nineteenth century, Americans went to Germany for graduate training, and the relatively few professional American scientists sought to legitimate their authoritative judgment by pointing to the German universities' substantial contributions to knowledge.

From 1848 to 1966,[2] the German model implicitly guided efforts to make American archaeology a scientific profession. The German model prescribed the seminar as a practicum for researchers (in contrast to English and American colleges' focus on undergraduate liberal education) and the establishment of formal structures of authoritative research. Such a structure included a research institute associated with a university to ensure a flow of specialists from student enrollments, a scholarly journal edited by professors, and a university press (Briggs 1995:253). Interlocking the training of recruits, and the dissemination of approved research methods through journals and monographs, data, and interpretations made the professors gatekeepers of their respective disciplines. In archaeology, the dissemination vehicle was introduced in 1885 with the founding of the *American Journal of Archaeology* under the editorship of Arthur L. Frothingham of the Johns Hopkins University. Johns Hopkins' first president, Daniel Coit Gilman, a geographer, received graduate training in Germany, including study in Berlin (1854–1855) with Egyptologist Karl Richard Lepsius (Briggs 1995:253). With this background, Gilman's concept of archaeology was exclusively Classical. The archaeology *of* America was subsumed into natural history, a categorization in part fostered by German romanticism about American Indian "children of nature" (Kohlstedt 1995:106).

Debate over democratic science versus professionalization ran parallel to debate over archaeological research *in* America versus collecting Classical, or even prehistoric European antiquities *for* America. Curtis Hinsley (1985:53–55) describes the second annual meeting of the Archaeological Institute of America (AIA) in 1880, presided over by Charles Eliot Norton, professor of art history at Harvard University as follows: the "Boston gentlemen" of the AIA had invited John Wesley Powell, director of the new Smithsonian Bureau of American Ethnology, to speak. Major Powell exemplified Joseph Henry's ideal of the American citizen-scientist propelled by a thirst for knowledge, gifted with a faculty for organization, indefatigably energetic and self-taught (Fowler and Fowler 1971:2). A wealthy trustee of the Boston Museum of Fine Arts rejected Powell's vision of resources devoted to the elucidation of American prehistory and ethnology, urging the Archaeological Institute's gentlemen to let those savages' relics lie while channeling funds toward furnishing American museums with the inspiring remnants of Europe's cultural roots. Mediating this continuing dispute was Harvard's Peabody Museum curator, Frederick Ward Putnam, who by the 1890s had maneuvered the factions into recognizing a professional status for archaeology. Putnam's student George Dorsey received the first Ph.D. granted in America for archaeology in 1894, a year after Putnam supervised the installation of extensive exhibits at Chicago's World Columbian Exposition, the fin-de-siècle version of the Great Exhibition held in London in 1851.

By 1900, archaeology was a professional science (Patterson 1995:51–52). Practitioners equipped with academic degrees had preempted the field, imposing upon it a model of "objective" science emphasizing the collection of concrete specimens and direct observations, with dissection of specimens and comparison of traits. Holistic context was dismissed as an amateurish inability to achieve scientific acuity (Hinsley 1983:65–68). Institutionalization had moved archaeological practice into an alliance of museums and university departments (e.g., Harvard, Pennsylvania, and soon the University of California-Berkeley with its campus museum, and Columbia and the American Museum of Natural History), plus independent research institutions (e.g., the Bureau of American Ethnology, Field Museum, and School of American Research in New Mexico). Publication of research occurred through these institutions' monograph series, subject to the editorial judgment of respective staffs. Legitimation followed the general arguments for professional science: that training in the scientific method honed intellectual powers, and that scientific knowledge could be transmuted into reliable civic guidance (Kevles 1988:111). Even archaeology was asserted to be useful in policy making, both in terms of the general argument that information on the human career from bestial savagery to European civilization illuminated the inevitable path and characteristics of progress (Hinsley 1981:138–139), and specifically, the assessment of the stage in cultural evolution reached by particular societies coming under the

jurisdiction of the United States. Once credentialed expertise was acknowledged to be the foundation of scientific practice and institutions had been
established for its creation and management, archaeology enjoyed the relative
autonomy so prized by professionals (Derber, Schwartz, and Magrass 1990:4).

There were also tacit criteria. Scientists, including archaeologists, were
modern heroes exploring the vast phenomena of the universe to capture facts
(Hinsley 1989). People hobbled by skirts could not fit the image. Nancy Parezo
(1993:5) summarizes the dissonance created by women wishing to be acknowledged as professionals as follows:

> The normative expectation . . . limited women to noncompetitive and
> nurturing kinds of behavior. At the same time, the stereotype of science
> was the opposite: tough, rigorous, impersonal, competitive, rational,
> and unemotional. . . . Women scientists were caught between two mutu-
> ally exclusive stereotypes: as scientists they were atypical and [assumed
> to be] emotional and as women they were unusual . . . cold and rational.
> . . . [Archaeologist] Marie Wormington [said] . . . "I always published my
> initials, H. M. Wormington. The director of the museum felt nobody
> would read a book written by a woman."

Women's colleges perpetuated the stereotype by orienting their students
toward careers designed to alleviate social problems, where women's nurturant
proclivities would be appropriate and "she required no specially acquired
traits or skills" (Antler 1987:66–70, quoting a letter by Wellesley professor
Vida Scudder, 1889). Settlement houses, social work agencies, and teaching,
toward which college women were directed, paid salaries lower than college
educated men would expect. Sophia Jex-Blake, who fought the British universities' ban against admitting women to medical degrees, quoted her MP's 1875
speech in Parliament on the Enabling Bill he had introduced as follows:

> You may hide it as you like, you may cover it up in fine phrases if you
> please, but at bottom the opposition to this Bill is a trades-union opposi-
> tion. It is seen by the medical profession that they will incur more com-
> petition, and that women will be their competitors (quoted in Jex-Blake
> 1970[1886]:186–187).

Men controlling professional employment seldom openly, or even con-
sciously, excluded women on the grounds of economic competition; the scientific professions claimed disinterest in economic advantage (Larson 1984:58).
Conscious or not, it is abundantly demonstrable that women have been regularly excluded from preferment in archaeology (Nelson, Nelson, and Wylie
1994; see also Claassen 1992, 1994; for comparable professions, see Scott 1988
and Moldow 1987).

The profession of archaeology was remarkably White, Anglo-Saxon, Protestant, and male until the final quarter of the twentieth century. (See, for example, Gordon Willey's selection of nearly exclusively upper-class WASP men
in his 1988 *Portraits in American Archaeology*.) Scholars descended from Afri-

cans, Asians, or American Indians have been notably marginalized throughout the history of American anthropology and archaeology. Jews achieved recognition in three of the four branches of American anthropology early in the twentieth century, but Jeremy Sabloff in 1989 was the first Jewish president of the Society for American Archaeology. (The Society's first woman president was H. Marie Wormington in 1968. After her came the upper-class Mexican Ignácio Bernal, probably the first Catholic SAA president.) Anomalously, the Society's very first president, in 1935, was Arthur C. Parker, who was one-quarter Seneca Iroquois. Parker had been New York State's first full-time archaeologist since 1906, and by 1935 was the distinguished director of the Rochester Museum. He also founded and guided the New York State Archaeological Association (Hertzberg 1971:52–55). Excepting Parker, not only leadership but also membership in the Society for American Archaeology, as in the Archaeological Institute of America, derived predominantly from Protestant Europe. Only Gero, Lacy, and Blakey's *The Socio-politics of Archaeology* (1983) has focused on the exclusion from American archaeology of persons other than descendants of Western European Protestants. Archaeology paralleled conditions in the field of history, characterized by a commentator in 1953 as rife with "discrimination . . . against Negroes, Jews, Catholics, women, and persons not 'gentlemen'" (quoted in Scott 1988:184). Race and class criteria in the recruitment and employment of professional archaeologists in America await examination (Nelson, Nelson, and Wylie 1994:xi–xii).

## Essays in the History of Archaeology

Classical, European prehistoric, and Americanist archaeologies are characterized by distinctive premises, agendas, and social conventions. Anthropologist Bronislaw Malinowski observed that "Every historical change creates its mythology . . . but indirectly related to historical fact, . . . a constant by-product . . . of sociological status, which demands precedent; of moral rule, which requires sanction" (1954[1926]:146). Archaeology has its legends and needs its history. Such history must not be merely an internal Whig history of the progress of scientific knowledge carried on by a succession of great men; social factors affecting preferment must also be addressed. R.G. Collingwood, the only professional philosopher who was also a practicing archaeologist, insisted half a century ago (1956[1946]:213) that both the "outside" and "inside" of events must be part of history.

Exemplary of social factors affecting preferment was the rejection of Franz Boas (recommended by Frederick Putnam) as curator of the Field Columbian Museum in Chicago by Marshall Field and his circle. Boas was a German Jewish immigrant to the United States. Was anti-Semitism an important factor in the rejection? In this volume, Donald McVicker explains the treatment of Boas (and Putnam) as, in part, the outcome of rivalries between the "Eastern Establishment" and the "core center capitalists of the Midwest." Don Fowler had suggested, in the AAA session, that Boas was the victim of anti-

Semitism. Commenting on McVicker's and Fowler's essays at the time of the 1989 American Anthropological Association symposium, Jonathan Reyman concluded, "The lack of documentary evidence favors McVicker's position, but the sociopolitical climate of the time (anti-Semitism was common and widely accepted, especially among the upper class) seems to me to support Fowler's argument, especially when one looks at the subsequent breakdown of votes in the later censure of Boas" at the 1919 meeting of the American Anthropological Association (Reyman 1989:6).

"Roguish practices" is Elin Danien's apt term for the antiquarian collecting condoned in the late nineteenth century. Such collecting built many major American museum holdings. White and Breitborde (1992) have published the story of how Chicago grain dealer Frank Logan bankrolled Beloit College geologist George Collie and his student Alonzo Pond to buy, beg, or permanently borrow thousands of European Paleolithic specimens. The Logan Museum of Anthropology is of course the name of the building housing the collections. If fair means or an attitude of "it's really for their own good" could move so much material from France to Wisconsin, how much more tempting must it have been to employ such stratagems in Latin America? McVicker (1992) describing "The Matter of Saville" and Givens (1992:142–143) explaining the conflicts between the Carnegie Institution's Mayan program and Mexico's Antiquities Law provide additional examples of roguish practices.

My own "Recognizing the Foundation of Prehistory" introduces the leitmotif of class interests underlying archaeology. The science of prehistory, for English-language archaeologists at least, was developed in the mid-nineteenth century by competing scholars, one a protégé of Darwin, and the other, protégé of Robert Chambers. Darwin and his wealthy, well-connected protégé John Lubbock are in all the standard histories of biology and archaeology, while Chambers and Daniel Wilson are routinely dismissed in spite of their clear precedence. Chambers' more politically liberal agenda, reflected in Wilson's works, conceived a multilinear evolution less supportive of America's Manifest Destiny ideology than Lubbock's blatantly racist unilinear evolution. The two views nevertheless continue within American archaeology to the present, as argued recently by Pinsky (1992) and myself (Kehoe 1998).

Sir William Matthew Flinders Petrie established British archaeology in the Near East, and is considered to be an early practitioner of a generally accepted scientific archaeological methodology. A bizarre legacy from Sir Flinders Petrie—his head—is Neil Asher Silberman's hook pulling us into his discussion of the racial doctrines underlying Petrie's, and by extension much turn-of-the-century, mainstream archaeology. The conviction that British civilization was the acme of human progress was—even in its heyday—so constantly threatened by historical knowledge (cf. Bernal 1987) and personal experiences with "backward races" that increasingly strenuous efforts were made to bolster the claim with "facts." One result was the creation of statistics as a recognized scientific method: as reported in *Statistics in Britain, 1865–1930* (1981), Donald MacKenzie discovered an uncomfortably close connection between the development of statistics and the advocacy of eugenics. Petrie's work, Silberman reveals, is a continuation of mid-century endeavors to demonstrate a "factual" basis to the Social Darwinist claim that the British empire represented the inevitable outcome of the "law of progress."

Petrie's head is the bizarre bequest of a pioneer archaeologist whose social class connected him early with the aristocratic mainstream of English science. In contrast, Augustus and Alice Dixon Le Plongeon's extraordinary pioneering record of Maya sites was mocked by the Harvard men dominating Mayan archaeology mainly because the two were of obscure origin. The self-made Le Plongeon entered archaeology as Ephraim Squier's photographer of Peruvian ruins. Determined to move on his own to the Maya sites hidden in the Yucatán jungle, Le Plongeon persuaded Alice Dixon, daughter and assistant to an English photographer, to accompany him as wife and colleague. The Le Plongeons made priceless plates of the untouched ruins, working under the most daunting conditions of guerrilla war and tropical climate. If they had humbly offered the photographic plates to the patrons of Mayan research, they might have earned a small notice in histories of the discipline. Instead, they published their interpretations of the stelae and hieroglyphs, and their interpretations ran counter to prevailing opinion. Although the Le Plongeons' writings do tend to run to romantic excess, their attention to themes of warfare was prescient. Ridiculing Augustus as a loony and ignoring Alice, the recently emerged university based leadership in professional archaeology purged the Le Plongeons from Mayan archaeology, and in so doing, expunged for a century their remarkable scientific recordings. Their story is yet another case illustrating the interplay between social position, ideology, and science.

In this volume, McVicker continues his exposition of the critical turn-of-the-century years when a Boasian anthropologically oriented archaeology struggled to overcome the "avid collectors" who so pleased ambitious patrons. Robert Burkitt, sketched by Danien here, was a less well-known example of the type prominently seen in Marshall Saville, described by McVicker as "the consummate turn-of-the-century museum man, avid expeditionist and collector . . . [who] clearly had an attraction to objects [but] seemed to have an aversion to reports" (1992:147–148). George Dorsey could not match Saville's panache, yet he was far from Boas's ideal of the highly intellectual visionary scientist. With an insider's feel for the chauvinism Chicago's leaders have been prone to display, McVicker balances "external" and "internal" disciplinary history, tracing the ambitions and class distinctions that hamstrung for decades the fulfillment of Chicago's hopes of ranking with Eastern institutions in archaeological and anthropological studies.

Money is always a factor in archaeology. William Dever shows us that Biblical archaeology depended upon substantial funding from patrons, primarily conservative Protestant organizations moved to document with actual sites the truth of Biblical history. These patrons typically expected their archaeologists to fit excavation data to biblical places and events. This was nothing more than antiquarianism, as Dever says, an enterprise that would have looked familiar to Walter Scott's Jonathan Oldbuck in 1815. Given such expectations, professionally trained archaeologists committed to their discipline should shun biblical archaeology. Dever identifies a fundamental shift in his field from old-style "Biblical" to "Syro-Palestinian" archaeology. He lists for his field several of the factors that Stephen Dyson (quite independently) provides to explain the change in Classical archaeology visible since the 1970s, and he also discusses the influence of William Albright whose guiding assumptions (Laudan, Laudan, and Donovan 1988) marked the mainstream in American Biblical archaeology for half a century. The death of this dominant figure left his version of archaeology to be consigned to the margin where British and European Near Eastern archaeologists had always placed it, although this disciplinary margin continues to recruit both excavators and patrons from the ranks of religious conservatives.

In Dyson's essay, we learn the central role of the "Big Dig" in Classical archaeology. An unabashed acceptance of a central tenet of the humanities, rank ordering texts within the canon, led Classical archaeologists to select the "greatest" sites from antiquity and devote lifetimes to their exacting study. Tying their projects to standards of elite classical education, American Classical archaeologists drew patrons from the country's traditional upper class. This class supported Classical archaeology to obtain moral and aesthetic models for exhibit as the highest achievements of the "cultivated races . . . where the civilization was . . . superior to our own" (Hinsley 1985:55). Even today there is a fascinating contrast between the annual business meetings of the classics-dominated Archaeological Institute of America, where wealthy sponsors sit with the Ph.D.s, and those of the Society for American Archaeology, attended only by professional archaeologists. Dyson emphasizes the heavy investment in infrastructure for the selected great sites of Classical archaeology, investments that called for directors with a corporate CEO's panoply of skills. In addition, Dyson underlines the imperialist tone of these projects run by First World professionals in less prosperous nations. As the United States gradually lost its unalloyed world dominance, and within the United States the G.I. Bill's tremendous broadening of college education (Ryan and Sackry 1984) diluted the elite class's dominance of "cultural" pursuits, Classical archaeology found itself in a new ball game. More "democratic" sources of funding, from federal endowments—the National Endowment for the Humanities (NEH) and National Science Foundation (NSF)—to Earthwatch, seem to have subtly enhanced the perceived value of surveys and excavations in the rural hinterlands and commoner precincts of the great sites. It helped that such surveys and excavations of humble buildings required smaller commitments of money and time than the old-fashioned lifetime devotion to the marble halls of a great site. What had been literally and professionally marginal in Classical archaeology before the 1970s, work outside the agora-palace precincts, has moved into the mainstream. Professional legitimation no longer rests on the display of ancient elites proffered by their modern equivalent to assert the singular virtue of the ruling class.

The next section of this collection returns to the last quarter of the nineteenth century when professionalization began to dominate archaeological research. Flinders Petrie began his career then, and among his eccentricities was his encouragement of women scholars, notably Margaret Murray (now best known, rather unfairly, for her argument that a "witch cult" was persecuted in early modern Europe). James Halporn's chapter focuses on an American contemporary of Murray's, Abby Leach, president of the American Philological Association (an affiliate of the Archaeological Institute of America) in 1899–1900. If William Albright embodied the mainstream of American archaeology in the Near East during his career, Basil L. Gildersleeve marked the mainstream in late-nineteenth-century Greek studies in America. Gildersleeve took no women pupils, nor were women admitted to the principal research libraries; ergo, there were no women scholars of Greek in early twentieth century America. Was not Leach a distinguished scholar? Yes and no: although she was recognized as able and asked to serve in the highest office in her professional organization, she was never ensconced in the inner circle—the central old boy network—of her field. Halporn found that Leach encouraged her students at the women's college where she taught to look not into philology but to archaeology as a possible field for their talents because archaeology was a new arena, and thus not yet dominated by pontifical graybeards. Abby Leach produced several eminent women scholars in what to her was a marginal field, Classical archaeology, but her own life was a continuing struggle to be seen in the mainstream of her chosen field, Greek philology.

Segregation was so taken for granted in American society a century ago that when the Anthropological Society of Washington refused membership to Bureau of American Ethnology employee Matilda Coxe Stevenson, a parallel Women's Anthropological Society of America was created. Mary Ann Levine's chapter introduces this group and profiles two noteworthy women of the period, corresponding member Zelia Nuttall and honorary member Mary Hemenway, a philanthropist, to provide some sense of the obstacles and also the opportunities, thanks to an old gals' network, realized by this generation of women. This chapter and Halporn's essay overlap in that Abby Leach and Alice Fletcher, of the Women's Anthropological Society, devoted years to organizing and strengthening the Archaeological Institute of America and its affiliate, the American Philological Association. By means of her recommendations to the Archaeological Institute of America, Fletcher advanced the career of Edgar Hewett, subject of Don Fowler's chapter.

Moving forward in time, we see in Susan Bender's examination of Marian White's career that little had changed in half a century. Segregation was less openly advocated. Women's suffrage gained in 1920 brought a sense of victory that weakened women's commitment to old gals' networks. Marian White appears isolated; she was similar to other women archaeologists in mid-century America—Dorothy Cross Jensen, Dorothy Keur, Madeline Kneberg, Frederica de Laguna, and Florence Hawley Ellis, among others—in working extraordinarily hard with little respite for socializing. Of the women of his generation, a male contemporary, Raymond Thompson, said, "they competed in a male world that expected harder work and consistently superior results from them" (Mathien 1992:119). The outstanding achievements of Marian White's career are highlighted by an analysis of proposals for archaeological support submitted to the National Science Foundation Anthropology Program 1978–1981. Only 15% of proposals came from women, and of these, only 21% were successful versus 37% of the proposals submitted by men. Furthermore, women were significantly less likely to be granted funds for fieldwork, compared to laboratory or museum collections research (Yellen 1994:53; no one has analyzed earlier NSF data). White, like the other women enumerated above, certainly merited research support and consequent notice in histories of archaeology, but as with all but de Laguna, they and their many publications are ignored by Trigger (1989), Patterson (1995), and Willey and Sabloff (1980[1993]). The latter cite a paper by a man, John Bennett, who, they note, mentioned important contributions by Kneberg and Keur. As junior author to her male partner T. M. N. Lewis, Kneberg can be found in Trigger's, Patterson's and Willey and Sabloff's bibliographies, but Keur's monograph cited by Bennett—*the inaugural volume in the Society for American Archaeology Memoirs series*—is not listed! The men who have constituted the visible majority of professional archaeologists apparently feel as did "one prominent citizen of Chicago [who] asked, 'How can the University be the dignified body of scholars that you intend if women are to be included?'" (quoted by Albisetti 1995:236).

The final section is focused on the American Southwest, the glamorous land promoted by Charles Lummis and Edgar Hewett as well as railroad tycoon Fred Harvey. In what Reyman (1989:4) called "The Battle of the Network Superstars," Don Fowler delineates the determined fight of immigrant Southwesterners to create a Mecca in Santa Fe, taking money and students but not direction from Eastern institutions. The magnitude of the Hewett group's creation can be appreciated by mentally removing all their effects from Santa Fe: no Palace of the Governors museum and Indian Market, nor decades of archaeological field schools. Thomas Patterson calls attention to a persistent contest in the United States between "the Eastern Establishment" and what he calls "the Core Culture" of the Midwest (Patterson 1995:44–45, 51), and specifically discusses Hewett as an example contestant. Beneath the overt contest, note the nexus between Boston "Brahmins" and Southwestern archaeology, a nexus that arches over and barely touches the middle continent. Rather than a struggle between classes or regions, the "Harvard-Hewett" battle can be read as internecine family wrangling over purses and power: native Southwesterners, whether Native American, Hispanic, or working class settlers, are quite absent from the story.

The last chapter incorporates one of these neglected figures from the Southwestern archaeological scene, Marietta Palmer Wetherill. Reyman lists many women who conducted professional excavation of major sites in the Southwest during the 1930s. Seldom included in the standard histories of

American or Southwestern archaeology, this group—first profiled in the 1988 exhibit and catalogue, *Daughters of the Desert*—is now chronicled in *Hidden Scholars* (1993), edited by Nancy Parezo. Reyman chooses to focus on an earlier investigator, Marietta Wetherill, because he can demonstrate the serious consequences of professional archaeologists' failure to consult her reports. Like Abby Leach, Marietta Wetherill lived during the first generation of professional archaeology when no lineage of "old boys" had yet been forged. Wetherill was as qualified as any American man of her generation to be counted as a pioneer archaeologist. Her acute observations, supported by unusual continuing firsthand experience of Southwestern Indians, constitute important primary data on her home region, Chaco Canyon. The conflict between the well-funded mainstream Chaco Project personnel and what has been dismissed as maverick, marginal research (Kelley and Hanen 1988:38) is only one example of the loss of knowledge that occurs when entrenched professionals too vigorously maintain the boundary between mainstream and marginal.

## A Binocular Vision of Archaeology

The contributions in this volume can be read as straight history; it is a rather populous history although one in which certain names, not just Hewett and Boas but also Alice Fletcher, surface again and again. These essays can also be read from a distance, as it were, wherein one views the forest instead of the trees. Women were undoubtedly marginalized. But there are also no Blacks, Asians, or Native Americans in the professional ranks of archaeologists described in these pages. Of course, few except Euro-Americans obtained university training. Of course? These social facts must not be taken for granted or overlooked. How many Euro-American men from working class families are recognized in histories of archaeology? Where is the history of farmers' and local collectors' impact upon American archaeology? Historiography becomes controversial when the tacit limitation of "history" to acclaimed public figures is challenged.

The fiftieth anniversary of the Society for American Archaeology catalyzed research on the history of the discipline (Meltzer, Fowler, and Sabloff 1986), but the breadth of concern reflected to some degree a shift away from positivist philosophies of science, opening questions about knowledge that once would have been routinely accepted. Kelley and Hanen's *Archaeology and the Methodology of Science* (1988) and Gibbon's *Explanation in Archaeology* (1989) thoroughly demolish positivism's pretensions to final truths, restoring the discipline to more realistic appraisals of its challenges and powers. Once the dominance of positivism was unseated, the history of archaeology attracted many of the discipline's more reflective practitioners: knowledge of what predated the touted New Archaeology of the 1960s might illuminate the current upheavals and transitions.

An internal audience for the history of archaeology is unquestionably growing. Another audience for the research ought to be among those interested in the history of science. Because archaeological data are less arcane than those of physics or even biology, case studies in the history of archaeology can be more accessible to non-specialists than many of the more traditional studies in the histories of the physical and natural sciences. Leaders in the history, philosophy, and sociology of science have not yet discovered the rich data in archaeology. We hope this volume may stimulate their attention.

Although none were written primarily to illustrate the sociology of a science, these essays serve to demonstrate the slow movement of mainstream thought, the masters and the challengers, and also the persons and perceptions on the margins of a discipline. Archaeology as a profession and discipline was constructed in particular times and places by particular individuals. Real people seized opportunities, or lost them; some needed to earn a living, and others were endowed with private wealth. There were—and are—crassly ambitious bastards and dedicated hardworking scholars. Most of the papers in this volume document such particularities. Together, they build a sense of the dynamism of the field and its interplay with national and class ideologies. "Interests and the growth of science," to paraphrase Barry Barnes (1977), do not refer to scholarly questions and a cumulative progress of knowledge; instead, the focus is on private and class ambitions and the gradual expansion of a scientific field as various and conflicting interests vie for funds and jobs. This perspective is termed "external," in contrast to "internal" histories of concepts in science, but the contrast is as obfuscating as most dichotomies. Concepts, even the most recondite (e.g., Forman 1971) are grounded in actual societies and inevitably reflect social as well as intellectual influences. "The very framework of [a history] has had a history," Richard Popkin reminds us (1992:7).

In the sociology of science, the Strong School (e.g., Wylie 1989:94)—derived from the "Strong Programme" advocated by Bloor (1976) and his Edinburgh colleagues—insists that any history of a science must discover whose ox will be fed, whose ox gored. The Strong School complements the Frankfurt School's Critical Theory in that the latter focuses on class interests and conflicts in the Marxist tradition, and the Edinburgh School follows a British research focus that highlights empirical cases. My own discussions with Barry Barnes and David Bloor during a 1989 sabbatical in Edinburgh strengthened my conviction that the two viewpoints should be complementary—in a binocular program, one might say—to see in depth the history of a discipline, and specifically the history of archaeology.

The history of a science cannot be restricted to activities, professionals, and institutions overtly labeled "scientific," nor to "public" events and persons. The societal context of any science enmeshes its history in class interests and conflicts, national ideologies, and contending religious and philosophical factions. A well-founded history of science must incorporate those experiences and activities that comprise the whole person of a scientist, who is a person of a particular time, place, and society. Science as a historically constituted phenomenon cannot be divorced from its political, economic, aesthetic, and adventitious entanglements. We present these essays as contributions to the history of archaeology and illustrations of the sociology of knowledge.

## Notes

1. Henry objected strongly, but without effect, to the design of America's temple of scientific research as a gothic castle. He championed simple functional architecture utilizing American materials and engineering rather than European models appealing to, as he put it, "the vulgar genteel" (Henry 1980:30–31).

2. In 1848, the Smithsonian publication of Squier and Davis's *Ancient Monuments of the Mississippi Valley* gave governmental imprimatur to American archaeology. In 1966, the National Historic Preservation Act initiated the cultural resource management business that has transformed the bulk of American archaeology from academic research to mandated inventories of heritage data.

## References Cited

Albisetti, James C. 1995. "German Influence on the Higher Education of American Women, 1865–1914." In *German Influences on Education in the United States to 1917,* edited by Henry Geitz, Jürgen Heideking, and Jurgen Herbst, 227–244. Cambridge: Cambridge University Press.

Antler, Joyce. 1987. *The Educated Woman and Professionalization.* New York: Garland.

Atkinson, R.J.C. 1975. Introduction to *From Antiquary to Archaeologist,* by Robert H. Cunnington, ix–xviii. Aylesbury: Shire Publications.

Bann, Stephen. 1984. *The Clothing of Clio.* Cambridge: Cambridge University Press.

Barnes, Barry. 1977. *Interests and the Growth of Knowledge.* London: Routledge and Kegan Paul.

Bernal, Martin. 1987. *Black Athena: the Afroasiatic Roots of Classical Civilization.* London: Free Association Press.

Bloor, David C. 1976. *Knowledge and Social Imagery.* London: Routledge and Kegan Paul.

Briggs, Ward W. 1995. "Basil L. Gildersleeve: The Formative Influence." In *German Influences on Education in the United States to 1917,* edited by Henry Geitz, Jürgen Heideking, and Jurgen Herbst, 245–256. Cambridge: Cambridge University Press.

Christianson, Andrew, ed. 1989. *Tracing Archaeology's Past: The Historiography of Archaeology.* Carbondale: Southern Illinois University Press.

Claassen, Cheryl, ed. 1992. *Exploring Gender Through Archaeology: Selected Papers of the 1991 Boone Conference.* Monographs in World Archaeology, no. 11. Madison: Prehistory Press.

———. 1994. *Women in Archaeology.* Philadelphia: University of Pennsylvania Press.

Collingwood, R. G. 1956 [1946]. *The Idea of History.* New York: Oxford University Press, Galaxy edition.

Cunnington, Robert H. 1975. *From Antiquary to Archaeologist.* Aylesbury: Shire Publications.

Daniel, Glyn. 1967. *The Origins and Growth of Archaeology.* Harmondsworth: Penguin.

Derber, Charles, William A. Schwartz, and Yale Magrass. 1990. *Power in the Highest Degree: Professionals and the Rise of a New Mandarin Order.* New York: Oxford University Press.

Forman, Paul. 1971. *Weimar Culture, Causality and Quantum Theory, 1918–1927: Adaptation by German Physicists and Mathematicians to a Hostile Cultural Environment.* Historical Studies in the Physical Sciences, no. 3. Berkeley: University of California Press.

Fowler, Don D. and Catherine S. Fowler. 1971. Introduction to *Anthropology of the Numa: John Wesley Powell's Manuscripts on the Numic Peoples of Western North America, 1868–1880,* edited by Don D. Fowler and Catherine S. Fowler, 1–34. Smithsonian Contributions to Anthropology, no. 14. Washington, D.C.: Smithsonian Institution Press.

Freidson, Eliot. 1984. "Are Professions Necessary?" In *The Authority of Experts,* edited by Thomas L. Haskell, 3–27. Bloomington: Indiana University Press.

Gero, Joan M., David M. Lacy, and Michael L. Blakey, eds. 1983. *The Sociopolitics of Archaeology.* Research Report, no. 23. Amherst: University of Massachusetts.

Gibbon, Guy. 1989. *Explanation in Archaeology.* Oxford: Blackwell.

Givens, Douglas R. 1992. "Sylvanus G. Morley and the Carnegie Institution's Program of Mayan Research." In *Rediscovering Our Past: Essays on the History of American Archaeology,* edited by Jonathan E. Reyman, 137–144. Aldershot: Avebury.

Henry, Joseph. 1980. *A Scientist in American Life: Essays and Lectures of Joseph Henry.* Edited by Arthur P. Molella, Nathan Reingold, Marc Rothenberg, Joan F. Steiner, and Kathleen Waldenfels. Washington, D.C.: Smithsonian Institution Press.

Hertzberg, Hazel W. 1971. *The Search for an American Indian Identity.* Syracuse: Syracuse University Press.

Hinsley, Curtis M. 1981. *Savages and Scientists: The Smithsonian Institution and the Development of American Anthropology, 1846–1910.* Washington, D.C.: Smithsonian Institution Press.

———. 1983. "Ethnographic Charisma and Scientific Routine: Cushing and Fewkes in the American Southwest, 1879–1893." In *Observers Observed: Essays on Ethnographic Fieldwork,* edited by George W. Stocking, Jr., 53–69. Madison: University of Wisconsin Press.

———. 1985. "From Shell-heaps to Stelae." In *Objects and Others,* edited by George W. Stocking, Jr., 49–74. Madison: University of Wisconsin Press.

———. 1989. "Zuñis and Brahmins: Cultural Ambivalence in the Gilded Age." In *Romantic Motives: Essays on Anthropological Sensibility,* edited by George W. Stocking, Jr., 169–207. Madison: University of Wisconsin Press.

Hunter, Michael. 1975. *John Aubrey and the Realm of Learning.* London: Duckworth.

Jex-Blake, Sophia. 1970 [1886]. *Medical Women*. Reprint, New York: Source Books.

Kehoe, Alice Beck. 1998. *The Land of Prehistory: A Critical History of American Archaeology*. New York: Routledge.

Kelley, Jane H. and Marsha P. Hanen. 1988. *Archaeology and the Methodology of Science*. Albuquerque: University of New Mexico Press.

Kennedy, Roger G. 1994. *Hidden Cities: The Discovery and Loss of Ancient North American Civilization*. New York: Free Press.

Kerr, James. 1989. *Fiction Against History: Scott as Storyteller*. Cambridge: Cambridge University Press.

Kevles, Daniel J. 1988. "American Science." In *The Professions in American History*, edited by Nathan O. Hatch, 107–125. Notre Dame: University of Notre Dame Press.

Kohlstedt, Sally Gregory. 1995. "German Ideas and Practice in American Natural History Museums." In *German Influences on Education in the United States to 1917*, edited by Henry Geitz, Jürgen Heideking, and Jurgen Herbst, 245–256. Cambridge: Cambridge University Press.

Kristiansen, Kristian. 1985. *Archaeological Formation Processes*. Lyngby: Nationalmuseet.

Larson, Magali Sarfatti. 1984. "The Production of Expertise and the Constitution of Expert Power." In *The Authority of Experts*, edited by Thomas L. Haskell, 28–80. Bloomington: Indiana University Press.

Laudan, Rachel, Larry Laudan, and Arthur Donovan, eds. 1988. *Scrutinizing Science*. Dordrecht: Kluwer.

MacKenzie, Donald A. 1981. *Statistics in Britain, 1865–1930*. Edinburgh: Edinburgh University Press.

Malinowski, Bronislaw 1954[1926]. "Myth in Primitive Psychology," 93–148. In *Magic, Science and Religion*. Reprint, Garden City: Doubleday.

Mathien, Frances Joan. 1992. "Women of Chaco: Then and Now." In *Rediscovering Our Past: Essays on the History of American Archaeology*, edited by Jonathan E. Reyman, 103–130. Aldershot: Avebury.

McVicker, Donald E. 1992. "The Matter of Saville: Franz Boas and the Anthropological Definition of Archaeology." In *Rediscovering Our Past: Essays on the History of American Archaeology*, edited by Jonathan E. Reyman, 145–159. Aldershot: Avebury.

Meek, Ronald L. 1976. *Social Science and the Ignoble Savage*. Cambridge: Cambridge University Press.

Meltzer, David J., Don D. Fowler, and Jeremy Sabloff, eds. 1986. *American Archaeology: Past and Future*. Washington: Smithsonian Institution Press.

Moldow, Gloria. 1987. *Women Doctors in Gilded-Age Washington*. Urbana: University of Illinois Press.

Morrell, Jack and Arnold Thackray. 1981. *Gentlemen of Science: Early Years of the British Association for the Advancement of Science*. Oxford: Clarendon Press.

Nelson, Margaret C., Sarah M. Nelson, and Alison Wylie, eds. 1994. *Equity Issues for Women in Archeology*, no. 5. Archeological Papers of the American Anthropological Association, Washington, D.C.

Parezo, Nancy J. 1993. "Anthropology: The Welcoming Science." In *Hidden Scholars: Women Anthropologists and the Native American Southwest,* edited by Nancy J. Parezo, 3–37. Albuquerque: University of New Mexico Press.

Patterson, Thomas C. 1995. *Toward a Social History of Archaeology in the United States.* Fort Worth: Harcourt Brace.

Piggott, Stuart. 1976. *Ruins in a Landscape.* Edinburgh: Edinburgh University Press.

———. 1985. *William Stukeley.* Rev., enl. ed. London: Thames and Hudson.

Pinsky, Valerie. 1992. "Archaeology, Politics, and Boundary-Formation: the Boas Censure (1919)." In *Rediscovering Our Past: Essays on the History of American Archaeology,* edited by Jonathan E. Reyman, 161–189. Aldershot: Avebury.

Popkin, Richard H. 1992. *The Third Force in Seventeenth-Century Thought.* Leiden: E. J. Brill.

Reyman, Jonathan E. 1989. "Networks: The Ties That Bind." Comments on papers presented in "Networks of the Past: The Third Annual Symposium on the History of American Archaeology." Annual meeting of the American Anthropological Association, Washington, D.C.

Ryan, Jake and Charles Sackrey. 1984. *Strangers in Paradise.* Boston: South End Press.

Schávelzon, Daniel. 1984. "La Primera Excavación Arqueológica en América Latina: Teotihuacán en 1675." *Anales de Antropología* 20 (1):21–34.

Scott, Joan Wallach. 1988. "American Women Historians, 1884–1984." In *Gender and the Politics of History, Collected Essays of Joan Wallach Scott,* 178–198. New York: Columbia University Press.

Shapin, Steven and Simon Schaffer. 1985. *Leviathan and the Air-Pump.* Princeton: Princeton University Press.

Sklenář, Karel. 1983. *Archaeology in Central Europe: the First 500 Years.* Leicester: Leicester University Press.

Trigger, Bruce G. 1989. *A History of Archaeological Thought.* Cambridge: Cambridge University Press.

White, Randall and Lawrence B. Breitborde. 1992. *French Paleolithic Collections in the Logan Museum of Anthropology.* Logan Museum Bulletin, n.s., I (2). Beloit, Wisconsin.

Willey, Gordon R. 1988. *Portraits in American Archaeology.* Albuquerque: University of New Mexico Press.

Willey, Gordon R. and Jeremy Sabloff. 1980. *A History of American Archaeology.* 2nd ed. (Third edition 1993.) San Francisco: W. H. Freeman.

Wilson, Daniel. 1851. *The Archaeology and Prehistoric Annals of Scotland.* Edinburgh: Shetland and Knox; London: Simpkin, Marshall and J. H. Parker.

Wylie, Alison. 1989. "Introduction: socio-political context." In *Critical Traditions in Contemporary Archaeology,* edited by Valerie Pinsky and Alison Wylie, 93–95. Cambridge: Cambridge University Press.

Yellen, John E. 1994. "Women, Archaeology, and the National Science Foundation: An Analysis of Fiscal Year 1989 Data." In *Equity Issues for Women in Archeology,* no. 5, edited by Margaret C. Nelson, Sarah M. Nelson, and Alison Wylie, 53–57. Archeological Papers of the American Anthropological Association. Washington, D.C.

# I

# Multiple Pasts

Alice B. Kehoe

Museums literally assemble the past. When the great museums were amassing collections for their marble halls in the later nineteenth and early twentieth centuries, competition was often keen. Reminiscing, Samuel Lothrop said,

> Most field trips used to be fishing excursions within an area. . . . [T]he major end of field work has been to collect objects. . . . Most jobs [in archaeology] at the time stemmed from Museums. . . . I felt myself lucky to find a job anywhere without salary, at first paying my own traveling and living expenses (Lothrop 1961:9).

Travel was by mule. Lothrop and W.H. Holmes, then nearly seventy, in 1916 "rode the 23 leagues from Copán to Zacapa in fourteen hours, camping for the night en route. [Sylvanus] Morley covered this distance in 13 1/2 hours in one day and killed his mule" (Lothrop 1961:1). The next year, Lothrop rode mules for thirty days to travel from Copán to Tegucigalpa. Fieldworkers always suffered from malaria and dysentery, he remembered, and one, John Owens, died of yellow fever at Copán (where he is buried in the Great Plaza) (Lothrop 1961:4, 8). George Gordon worked on the same excavation project. Robert Burkitt's forays, recounted here by Elin Danien, must be seen against that background. Burkitt and Gordon moved within a second, opposite background, the plush world of Harvard and Philadelphia. Central in this background was Frederick Ward Putnam (1839–1915), once a student of Harvard paleontologist Louis Agassiz, then curator of Harvard's Peabody Museum of Anthropology (1875–1909) and professor of American archaeology and ethnology at Harvard (1887–1909). His courses at the university, his advocacy of anthropology and archaeology, including his direction of acres of displays at the 1893 World Columbian Exposition at Chicago, and his efforts to place his graduates make him, according to Willey and Sabloff (1993:51), "the professionalizer of American archaeology."

Harvard's Peabody Professor assiduously constructed a structure for archaeology in America that subordinated museums to university graduate departments in the institutionalization of the field. Doctorates were demanded as credentials. The underbelly of professionalization is the exclusion of the uncredentialed, superficially a wise protection especially in a destructive endeavor such as archaeology. It also served to exclude women, non-Protestants, non-whites, and people from working class origins. Sam Lothrop could afford to complete years of advanced study and then pay his own expenses to gain a foothold in his chosen profession. Few were born so fortunate. By the turn of the century, Joseph Henry's ideal of democratic American science had been repudiated, the division between professional and amateur established, and "the archaeologist" defined as *Doctor*. Harvard's preeminence in archaeology, whether American or Classical, was related to its function of educating the sons of the old-money upper class. Frederick Ward Putnam assisted some exceptions, such as Franz Boas and Alice Fletcher (impeccably WASP but a woman), but his efforts did not extend beyond the educated middle class.

Alice Kehoe's "Recognizing the Foundation of Prehistory" focuses on class contests more overt in Britain than in America. Archaeology supposedly reveals segments of the past-in-itself through tangible objects-hard bits of incontrovertible reality. Archaeology is legitimated as a science; it glows in the prestige of methodological rigor dealing with objective data. This is presumed to be especially true for prehistory—Biblical and Classical archaeology, after all, began with documents and therefore were initially prone to the bias contained in those documents. Alas, it appears that nineteenth-century prehistoric archaeology also began with documents—Enlightenment conjectural universal histories—, and flourished precisely because it seemed to give witness to the bourgeois tenet of progress embodied in technology (Kehoe 1992).

The Stone Age was a wished-for past setting off the glories of European civilization against the dim recesses of bestial savagery. Sir John Lubbock best expressed the English governing class's wished-for past in his *Pre-historic Times* (1865), and the standard histories of archaeology credit him with founding prehistoric archaeology in the English-speaking world. However, in 1862 Daniel Wilson laid much the same methodological groundwork in *Prehistoric Man*, which developed from his 1851 work, *The Archaeology and Prehistoric Annals of Scotland*. The latter work represents the first use of the word "prehistory" in English. (In turn, Wilson had utilized the Danish Thomsen-Worsaae schema for prehistory.) Wilson's work reflects the lower-middle-class Scottish reformist philosophy of his mentor, Robert Chambers, and the ideas of George Combe. In Wilson's past-as-known, in contrast to Lubbock's, American Indian technology is respected. It is cited to demonstrate multicultural evolution à la Chambers' *Vestiges of the Natural History of Creation* (1844). The conservative haute bourgeoisie who professionalized science labeled Wilson a dilettante as they had labeled Chambers, and relegated both men's widely read books to oblivion, or so they hoped.

Neil Silberman suggests that William Flinders Petrie was everything Daniel Wilson dreamed of being: well connected and employed full time in research in his chosen field. The standard histories of archaeology credit Petrie with instituting sound methods in fieldwork methodology, transforming

Egyptology from undisciplined collecting to a science. Flinders Petrie's commitment to science extended beyond the grave, impelling him to order his head removed and preserved for dissection in hopes it would reveal signs of his mental superiority. Daniel Wilson's Scottish associates had advocated phrenology as a means to discover and advance intrinsic abilities among commoner children. Petrie's bequest was intended to scientifically validate the upper class's right to rule.

Next, Lawrence Desmond explores the careers of two people whose behavior clashed with their class origins. Augustus Le Plongeon was rumored to be a bastard; he was not acknowledged by any respectable family. Alice Dixon's father was admired for his professional expertise in photography, but a mere tradesman. Alice herself was, of course, a woman. The Le Plongeons worked in the Yucatán under conditions as difficult, and more dangerous, than Lothrop encountered a generation later. They could have continued as Augustus began, providing technical services in photography to gentlemen researchers; instead, the couple insisted that their opinions be respected as professional interpretations of scientific data. (Pistol-packing Alice would not defer to anyone, including her husband.)

The Le Plongeons were caught on the cusp of the shift to professionalization in archaeology. They lacked formal education credentials, money, and social status. The past-as-known they proffered from their meticulous reading of Maya monuments was no more outré than their competitors' narratives of the Maya, but their audacity in demanding public recognition on the basis of work alone imperiled the edifice of science then under construction in the elite universities. Steven Shapin notes (1994:362) that the terms *scientist* and *technician* developed conjointly in this period of the professionalization of science within the academy. The goal of professionalization was said to be science as pure objective truth, but in the event, the Le Plongeons' hubris in challenging the emerging distinction between credentialed scientist and paid technician effectively destroyed their reputations.

Anyone who thinks the history of science is an epic of disinterested virtue triumphant will be disabused by Donald McVicker's story of Chicago buying a curator. Hog butcher to the world, Chicago in the 1890s led what Patterson (1995:44–46) calls America's Core Culture, obstreperously asserting its worth against the Eastern Establishment (Rydell 1984). A small group of wealthy men had hired Frederick Putnam to create an unprecedented display of the primitive world to set off the shining White City of Civilization on Lake Michigan in 1893. They were not about to accept the insult Putnam offered by telling them to hire an obscure Jew as curator of the legacy of their World Columbian Exposition. The interesting part of the story comes when the rabidly anti-Semitic (Pinsky 1992:169),[1] properly WASP gentlemen of science Charles D. Walcott and William Holmes became as embittered as Putnam and Boas. What a nice bit of science we have here! Controlling the variable of Jewishness in this natural experiment, we see that the fundamental issue was the autonomy of professional science vis-à-vis direction from its moneyed supporters. Having preempted, institutionalized, and legitimated the collection and interpretation of data as the road to truth, the anthropological scientists, whether from Boston or Washington, could not jeopardize their professional status by yielding autonomy.

William Dever and Stephen Dyson delineate the two principal overseas research programs in which Americans participated. That there are indeed two suggests a great deal about the construction of fields in science: Biblical and Classical archaeologists work in the same geographical region and on the same time periods. The pasts-as-known they assemble are only rarely seen to overlap. Their sponsors' wished-for pasts seem to be parallel universes—the Classicists convinced that Mediterranean Europe and particularly Periclean Athens are both root and model for Western culture, while the Biblicists are sure that Judea's Patriarchal Age is the true bedrock of Christian society (and for a significant minority of Israelis, of Jewish society). These chapters that round out the first section chronicle the interplay between sponsors' visions and procedural developments in the discipline of archaeology, and professionals' demands for apparent independence of judgment. Dyson discusses at some length another feature of the professionalization of archaeology, the implicit Western business model that values efficient management of large-scale enterprises. American prehistoric archaeology has not been immune to this model, although it is seldom openly advocated (see discussion in Kelley and Hanen 1988:150).

Text authority versus accepted scientific archaeological procedures for interpretation has been an open issue for Classical and especially Biblical archaeologists. Prehistorians tended to be positivists, such as Richard Colt Hoare who shouted in 1810, "WE SPEAK FROM FACTS, NOT THEORY" (Kehoe 1992:4; Colt Hoare's capitalization). The theory they have obscured is the Enlightenment conjectural history of mankind from which the three-age system was derived. That this system constitutes a universal history of humanity has been a guiding assumption, not a scientific proof or conclusion. The chapters in this section present several grand pasts-as-known, the unilinear and multilinear cultural evolutions of Lubbock and Wilson, the Golden Ages of the Classicists, and the Godly Age of the Biblicists. Ultimately, they have been compatible under the overarching premise that the educated upper classes of modern Western societies are the best and the brightest in nature's realm.

## Notes

1. In 1921, Holmes wrote to Charles Walcott, "[A] new chairman of the [National Research] Council must be selected and it is most important that he should not be of the Hebrew kind" (Holmes 1921). The irrational extent of Holmes's prejudice can be seen in the same letter when he described Clark Wissler as "a two-faced Jew of the most cunning variety and an understudy of Boas." Wissler was a seventh-generation English Protestant American. (I thank Valerie Pinsky for sharing with me this letter she discovered.)

## References Cited

Chambers, Robert. 1994[1844]. *Vestiges of the Natural History of Creation.* Facsimile edition, edited by James A. Secord. Chicago: University of Chicago Press. (Original edition, London: Churchill.)

Holmes, William H. 1921. Letter to Charles D. Walcott, January 7. Ms. in Secretary's Correspondence, Box 62, Folder 1–2, National Anthropological Archives. Washington, D.C.: Smithsonian Institution.

Kehoe, Alice B. 1992. "The Paradigmatic Vision of Archaeology: Archaeology as a Bourgeois Science." In *Rediscovering Our Past: Essays on the History of American Archaeology,* edited by Jonathan E. Reyman, 3–14. Aldershot: Avebury.

Kelley, Jane H. and Marsha P. Hanen. 1988. *Archaeology and the Methodology of Science.* Albuquerque: University of New Mexico Press.

Lothrop, Samuel K. 1961. "Archaeology, Then and Now." In *Essays in Pre-Columbian Art and Archaeology,* edited by Doris Z. Stone, Junius B. Bird, Gordon F. Ekholm, and Gordon R. Willey, 1–13. Cambridge: Harvard University Press.

Lubbock, John. 1912[1865]. *Pre-historic Times.* 6th ed. Rev. London: Williams & Norgate.

Patterson, Thomas C. 1995. *Toward a Social History of Archaeology in the United States.* Fort Worth: Harcourt Brace.

Pinsky, Valerie. 1992. "Archaeology, Politics, and Boundary Formation: The Boas Censure (1919) and the Development of American Archaeology During the Inter-war Years." In *Rediscovering Our Past: Essays on the History of American Archaeology,* edited by Jonathan E. Reyman, 161–189. Aldershot: Avebury.

Rydell, Robert W. 1984. *All the World's a Fair.* Chicago: University of Chicago Press.

Shapin, Steven. 1994. *A Social History of Truth.* Chicago: University of Chicago Press.

Willey, Gordon R. and Jeremy Sabloff. 1993. *A History of American Archaeology.* San Francisco: W. H. Freeman.

Wilson, Daniel. 1851. *The Archaeology and Prehistoric Annals of Scotland.* Edinburgh: Shetland and Knox; London: Simpkin, Marshall and J. H. Parker.

———. 1862. *Prehistoric Man.* Cambridge and London: Macmillan.

# 1

## Robert James Burkitt and George Byron Gordon

## An End and a Beginning[1]

Elin C. Danien

Modern Mesoamerican archaeology is said to have begun with John Stephenson and Frederick Catherwood in the 1840s, but as an academic discipline it invented itself during the last years of the nineteenth century (Willey 1968:36; Sabloff 1990:30–36). The hardy individuals who followed the pioneering footsteps of Stephens and Catherwood (Stephens 1841, 1843) were more accurately described as "antiquarians" (Bernal 1977:19; Fagan 1977:266, 343) who delighted in the collection of ancient relics; they were frequently adventurers, seeking freedom from society's restrictions. The museums of the period were display galleries and repositories for collections rather than the research centers they are today (Fagan 1977:276, 343; Osgood 1979). Attitudes toward excavation and collection changed slowly as the century drew to a close; its final years and the early years of the twentieth century were a time of transition. As with all such major shifts, the upheaval damaged some participants while carrying others into a new era.

This episode in the professionalization of archaeology focuses on two men, Robert James Burkitt and George Byron Gordon. One remained rooted in the nineteenth century; the other was clearly able to adapt to the changing world of the twentieth. Their experiences, reputations, and contributions to the discipline reflect the revolutionary changes that took place in the conduct of archaeology, changes that would value the efforts of some and marginalize the endeavors of others. Their different personalities affected the growth and development of the Mesoamerican collections at the University of Pennsylvania Museum of Archaeology and Anthropology[2] in ways that still resonate.

The museum was launched by a group of philanthropists in 1887 with a proposal to send an exploring expedition to Babylon. In the nurturing climate of Philadelphia's post-Civil War affluence, Victorian philanthropy, and American expansionism, the museum prospered. It organized expeditions, and by 1899 had moved into its own quarters on the university campus, complete with curators and collections. A department of archaeology and paleontology was created within the university, with financial support from the University

Archaeological Association, a citizens' organization devoted to raising funds for and promoting interest in exploration (Madeira 1964:15–29; Winegrad 1993:3–4).

During its first few years, the new museum directed its attention primarily to the ancient Near East. Its interest in Mesoamerica came later, and was perhaps indirectly influenced by the excavations of Harvard's Peabody Museum at the great Maya site of Copán in Honduras. George Byron Gordon—who later became the first director of the University of Pennsylvania Museum—served, while an engineering student at Harvard, as the surveyor for the Peabody's Second Copán Expedition in 1892–1893. When the expedition's director died of fever in the middle of the season, Gordon, the only person on the scene with any authority, had to close down the camp. Despite some problems created by his arrogance, he was able to bring the season to an orderly, if somewhat abrupt, conclusion. Albeit difficult, the field experience had a positive impact, for it changed the direction of his career (PA).

Upon returning to Harvard in 1893, Gordon left the engineering department and began the study of archaeology. He maintained his friendship with a former fellow student, Robert James Burkitt, who had received a degree in engineering in 1891. When Gordon was charged with leading the Peabody Museum's Fourth Copán Expedition, he invited his friend Burkitt to join him as second-in-command (Gordon 1896:1). After the season ended, Gordon returned to Harvard, took his graduate degree, and in 1903 joined the staff of the University of Pennsylvania Museum as assistant curator (UMA).

Burkitt, however, found Central America much more to his taste than life in Boston. The third son of an impoverished Irish cleric, he had been sent for his education to relatives in Canada. Poverty and a lack of social skills undoubtedly contributed to his early reputation for eccentricity, established in Canada and burnished at Cambridge. The young man was a square peg in Victorian society's round hole, one of those misfits who sometimes found themselves by becoming expatriates, recluses, curmudgeons, or archaeologists. Burkitt became all of these. At the close of the Copán season, he remained in Guatemala, where his idiosyncratic behavior seems to have been accepted within the small foreign community. Burkitt turned to ranching and mining to support himself, but spent much of his time pursuing a burgeoning interest in linguistics.

In 1901, Burkitt wrote to Charles Bowditch of Harvard regarding the possible publication of some Kekchi manuscripts he had discovered in Guatemala. Bowditch sent the manuscript on to Franz Boas, who, although lamenting its unorthodox orthography, commented favorably on the precision and accuracy of the linguistic material and published it in the *American Anthropologist* (Burkitt 1902). At the same time, Bowditch and Peabody director Frederick W. Putnam were casting about for someone to serve as their explorer in Central America. Burkitt seemed a likely candidate, and Gordon's advice was solicited regarding the qualifications of his former assistant. Gordon replied that Burkitt "would not make a success as an explorer and excavator" (PA).

Gordon's comment is interesting in that less than two years later this role was the precise one he would ask Burkitt to fill for the University of Pennsylvania Museum.

Burkitt and Gordon maintained a sporadic correspondence and, once he was appointed assistant curator in 1903, Gordon began to urge Burkitt to collect for the University Museum. Gordon joined a museum that was parochial in outlook; he envisioned it transformed by his efforts into an institution that might challenge the British Museum. His personality was said to be "as sharp as the long needles of his waxed mustache" (Madeira 1964:30). Through the years as assistant curator, then as curator, and later as director, Gordon sought to create both a comprehensive archaeological collection and a representative assemblage of ethnographic material from extant traditional societies. As director, his tenacity, sound scientific and artistic judgment, and superb political sense enabled him to enlarge the museum's collections, improve its storage, and attempt to incorporate it more fully into the academic life of the university. He believed strongly in the museum as an educational institution (King and Little 1986:41). In those areas where the museum's collections were scanty, Gordon followed then-current general museum practice and engaged "acquisitioners" to purchase objects or entire collections.

Burkitt's presence in Guatemala presented an ideal solution for the museum's lack of Maya artifacts. His knowledge of the land and the people, his field experience, the fact of his and Gordon's long friendship, and his personal loyalty, made him the perfect surrogate. When Gordon first approached Burkitt with the idea of working for the museum, he was reluctant to commit himself to any long-term project because archaeology would take him away from his great passion of compiling grammars and dictionaries of the Indian languages. It was not until the end of 1912, some two years after Gordon became director of the museum, that Burkitt finally agreed to an arrangement whereby he would collect for several months, and then be free to follow his other interests. During the time he was employed on museum business, his salary was to be $100 a month, plus expenses.

Burkitt may have believed that his involvement would be minimal, but Gordon's grand concepts were never tightly contained. In a letter to Burkitt dated March 13, 1913, Gordon hints at a greater undertaking: "I am glad that we have at last come to some arrangement and that you are to take part in the good work of our Museum. I believe that you will get good results and that these small beginnings will develop into a large piece of Central American work which we ought to be doing" (UMA, Gordon letters, 1913). In subsequent years, Burkitt would periodically terminate his relationship with the museum in favor of devoting more time to his other interests, only to be wooed back by Gordon. Each time Gordon would convince him to stay on, and ply him with promises that the major excavation he had spoken of would be forthcoming, and that Burkitt would be its director. Gordon wrote of his dream, rather reminiscent of the days of Stephens and Catherwood, of "buying up all of the land around Copán," as well as the site itself, to engage in what would have been a truly monumental excavation. Burkitt had but to bide his time until Gordon could arrange the necessary funding (UMA, Gordon letters, 1915).

Gordon tried to arouse enthusiasm among the Penn Museum Board of Managers for his long-hoped-for expedition to the Maya area. Despite his excellent relations with the Board, and his extraordinary ability to elicit financial support, agreement for an "acquisitioner" was all he could muster. In that role, Burkitt would have to seek out, assess, bargain for, purchase, or excavate based on nothing but his own opinions and information, without recourse to the judgment or involvement of others. Along with these responsibilities, the acquisitioner's function carried with it certain problems, both real and imaginary. Gordon's sense of his own importance, and the swashbuckling opportunism of his colleagues convinced the Director that all eyes would be on any potential museum activity. From the beginning of their business relationship, he cautioned Burkitt on the importance of discretion. Other institutions were organizing expeditions; the Carnegie Institution had begun to express interest in undertaking a major project at Chichén Itzá; and the Peabody Museum continued to be a presence in Maya archaeology. These institutions had men in the field, agents who might outmaneuver him if they suspected the University of Pennsylvania was after an object or knew of a previously untouched site.

Burkitt delighted in the request for secrecy, for it merely reinforced his own quirky inclinations. Over the years, Burkitt's frequent disappearances on museum business were accepted by those who knew him as additional evidence of his peculiarity, in the same vein as his linguistic quests and his solitary nature. He had cards printed in the name of Roberto Brown, and as Mr. Brown he conducted negotiations, ostensibly for his own purposes. In my interviews with old Guatemala hands, I found that this subterfuge worked not at all: everyone knew that Burkitt was Brown, and Brown, Burkitt, and that whether as Brown or Burkitt, he collected for the University of Pennsylvania.[3]

In the early years of this century, Guatemala was home to an odd assortment of foreigners—American, English and German—who had come to make their fortunes as ranchers, miners, and traders (de la Cruz Torres 1978:65–68; King 1974:42, 208). It was a small group, and Burkitt knew them all; indeed, he occupied permanent "guest quarters" on plantations both in the Alta Verapáz and Pacific highlands. He thus was able to begin his work for Gordon by photographing a collection of artifacts acquired by one of his acquaintances, a German planter named Kanter, a collection later scattered by marauding soldiers during a rebellion. The photographic record in the University Museum is all that survives, and it has served on at least one occasion to identify some of the objects when they turned up in another context (UMA).

His correspondence reveals that from the very beginning, Burkitt believed that exploration should follow a regional approach. "The Alta Vera Paz is sprinkled with Indian ruins and remains," he wrote in 1905, "but in my opinion they should be explored not as individuals but as a whole, or at least in groups." And then he added, "In a business way I suppose what you would like perhaps at once would be portable finds of some sort to make a showing with" (UMA, Burkitt 1905). And again in 1916, as the museum's acquisitioner, Burkitt wrote:

> The notion often crosses my mind; instead of groping about for places to dig, what a thing it would be for museums if they could begin by having a general antiquarian survey of the country. Have a force of young chaps go about and see all the ruins they could hear of; and note their situation and character, and make drawings of the more striking. I suppose it's too big a scheme. I've never been quite clear in my mind whether you attach more importance to the study of ruins or to getting things that you can carry away (UMA 1916).

At that time Gordon was indeed anxious to acquire "things that you can carry away" as beautiful objects for display in the galleries of the museum's new and imposing quarters. He and Burkitt agreed that before attempting any excavation, Burkitt should first purchase likely objects from private collections. In addition to his friendships among the Guatemalan planters, Burkitt was trusted by the Kekchi Maya, in part because of his command of their language. They took him to burial caves known only to the Maya, and helped him acquire some outstanding objects for the museum.

After exhausting the possibilities of acquisition and isolated finds, Burkitt went on to dig at Chama, a site first excavated by the German trader and Mayanist Erwin Dieseldorff. He mapped and excavated Xultun, Chipal, Chocola, Koopom, Chiwatal, and other sites along the Chixoy River. An examination of his field notes reveals that they are extensive and precise; his information on purchased material includes detailed provenience for each piece. His field technique, so primitive by today's standards, was on a par with that of many of his contemporaries in the Maya area, and reflected the training he had received from Gordon (UMA).

With the onset of the World War, the shipment of any material was all but impossible. Burkitt packed and stored the results of his labors until 1920 when, through circuitous routes, he was able to ship 30 cases to the museum. Gathered within those crates were artifacts of stone, bone and clay (polychrome vessels, figurines, jades, metates, carved bones), as well as ethnographic materials (the model of a Maya house, a loom, textiles, along with instructions on their construction and use); indeed, a surfeit of material for Gordon's Mesoamerican gallery. Gordon's delight was apparent in his letter to Burkitt. He assured Burkitt that these were among the most important and the most beautiful collections obtained for the institution. Burkitt's continued purchases and excavations through the 1920s and into the 1930s gave the museum a wide range of carefully documented Maya material from the Alta Verapáz and the neighboring Guatemalan highlands, an area all but unknown archaeologically then, and relatively little known even today.

Burkitt and Gordon were part of an era in Mesoamerican archaeology when anything was possible. Central American governments were less than stable, and laws regarding the exportation of artifacts were largely ignored by museums in Europe and the United States (Schavelzón 1988). When Burkitt and Gordon began, others were as cavalier in their quests for archaeological treasure, but as the century matured and museums filled their galleries, a more responsible approach developed.

Gordon, whose political acumen had enabled him to survive academic skirmishes and serious monetary problems, still hoped for major additions to the museum's collections. Perhaps as archaeological ethics shifted, he would have moved the museum toward more accountability. Certainly he was the one person who might have helped Burkitt move from isolated independence into the newer, more structured approach to archaeology, but tragically, Gordon died suddenly at the beginning of 1927. The museum secretary, Jane McHugh, sent the news to Burkitt. "He had a deep affection for you and there were no letters or reports that came to the Museum that gave him more pleasure than those which came from you." Burkitt's acknowledgment came, in his typically understated way, at the end of a long letter on his current archaeological work for the museum. "I needn't speak of Mr. Gordon's death. It was a shock to me. We had been friends from old times. And he was the only old time friend in North America with whom I still corresponded" (UMA, Burkitt 1927).

The material he had sent and continued to send to Philadelphia was magnificent, but its method of acquisition was a growing source of embarrassment to the new museum administration. Some of the objects were exhibited, and some were used to illustrate articles in the museum's journal (Mason 1927a, b, c). The labeling was without attribution or discussion of the means by which the museum had acquired this collection. Several of Burkitt's polychrome vessels were illustrated in a magnificent three-volume book of paintings of Maya pottery (Gordon and Mason, 1927—1933), again without attribution or provenience.

J. Alden Mason, new curator in the American Section, in a 1928 memorandum on proposed publications, was clear about both the value of Burkitt's collections, and the problems they created for the Museum:

> Mr. Burkitt's specimens are, as far as I know, the only carefully documented material secured from the Guatemalan highlands. His notes are . . . full and detailed . . . his plans and drawings are admirable. The material is . . . of the greatest scientific importance and his notes in perfect shape for a thoroughly scientific work which will be the fundamental authority in this field . . . The publication of the Burkitt collection, however, must be done with great tact, inasmuch as it is essential that information of his activities in Guatemala be kept from the official attention of the authorities of that country. In view of this, and also of the fact that Mr. Burkitt is still continuing to excavate and ship specimens to us, it is probably better that publication of this monograph be suspended until the close of Mr. Burkitt's work . . . " (UMA)

Perhaps nothing so epitomizes the change in the archaeological climate as the strategies, craft, and diplomacy required to obtain permission for the museum to excavate the site of Piedras Negras. In 1927, the year Gordon died, Herbert Spinden of Harvard spent time in Guatemala to negotiate a contract that would allow the Peabody Museum to excavate Piedras Negras. Before arrangements had been completed, the outline of this proposal reached the public (some said it was because Spinden was too confident, and too vocal) (UMA). The implication that important artifacts might be removed from the country was seen as arrogant flouting of Guatemalan sovereignty; public discussions resulted in a major outcry by the press, denial by the politicians, and a halt to all negotiations.

In 1930 the University Museum opened quiet talks with the Guatemalan government regarding the feasibility of mounting an expedition to the Maya lowlands. Because of the political firestorm the name might revive, the site of Piedras Negras was not mentioned at first, although it was always the objective. The new director, Horace Jayne, sent J. Alden Mason, curator of the museum's American Section, to investigate the possibility of excavation and the removal from Piedras Negras of some of its more spectacular monuments. Mason's letters reveal a relatively inexperienced and idealistic young man confronted by the ambiguity of a different cultural milieu. Fortunately, he and Burkitt got on well together. Although in Philadelphia he had frowned on Burkitt's methods, once in Guatemala he found the older man's knowledge of Latin American politics and procedures invaluable, and his methods much more acceptable than he had thought. Burkitt's ability to smooth the way enabled Mason to avoid some of the more obvious pitfalls in maneuvering through the intricacies of Latin American bureaucracy (UMA). There were months of frustrating negotiation, during which Mason frequently despaired of the proposal ever coming to a successful conclusion. It was only after Burkitt's personal intervention to convince one important individual of the worth of such an undertaking that Mason finally had his contract. The two-page document was signed on May 15, 1930. It included a clause that divided all finds equally between the University Museum and the Guatemalan Museum. It also permitted the museum to remove large monuments for a ten-year loan to Philadelphia, provided an equal number were sent to the new museum in Guatemala City. Both Mason and Jayne were delighted with this outcome, because it would place the museum in the unique position of being able to display original Maya stelae in its galleries, something no other institution had been able to boast since the Stephens and Catherwood New York exhibition of the 1840s (Danien 1991).

Piedras Negras was the major excavation Gordon had hoped for, the one that would establish the museum as an important institutional presence in Maya archaeology. Its new relationship with the Guatemalan government meant that Burkitt's unorthodox methods of collection were even more embarrassing to the museum. The consequences were not unexpected. The signing of the contract meant the end of the museum's unofficial "acquisitions." Any involvement by Burkitt/Brown would have had a disastrous effect on the Piedras Negras project. Ironically, after years of promises regarding his central role in such an excavation, he was to have no connection, central or peripheral, with the museum's work there. He agreed that it would be best for him not to engage in any excavations, and to hold any shipments of artifacts until the Piedras Negras excavation was complete, to avoid any possibility of institutional embarrassment.

This was not quite the end of Burkitt's relationship with the museum. In 1930 *The Museum Journal* published two articles based on Burkitt's letters of over a decade earlier (1930a, b). He was angry at the way they omitted and rearranged information, changed his maps, confused the photographs, and, in his view, made a mess of things (UMA, Burkitt 1930). His 1930 manuscript recording his discovery of the site of Monte Alto was placed in a drawer at the Museum and ignored; the site was later published by others (Parsons and Jenson 1965). There were two small shipments of previously excavated material. His pottery vessels and figurines were the basis of two important articles on typology (Butler 1935, 1940), but the definitive Burkitt monographs remained—and still remain—unwritten. The Guatemalan government was becoming more sensitive about the cultural treasures that had been taken from the country in earlier years; archaeologists and museums had become more conscious of the rights of host countries, and more aware of the sensitive nature of many of their collections. The tenuous web of relationship that had begun to unravel with Gordon's death finally came undone in 1937. When Mason visited Guatemala in 1938 to negotiate further excavations, he appears to have avoided all contact with Burkitt.

The once tolerated—even encouraged—idea of individual exploration and exploitation became anathema as archaeology moved closer to the academic center. After Piedras Negras, the museum went on to major excavations of other Maya sites, and is well-known for its fifteen-year interdisciplinary excavation of Tikal. Noted Mesoamerican scholars Wendy Ashmore, William R. Coe, Jill L. McKeever-Furst, Peter Furst, Christopher Jones, and Robert J. Sharer are among its curators and research associates; Jeremy A. Sabloff is the museum director. Its publications are frequently cited in academic circles, and Gordon's dream of the museum as educational center has long since been fulfilled.

Clearly, the era of the individual explorer had given way before the impact of the larger, more impersonal institution. Continuing philosophical and ethical debate eventually resulted in the UNESCO convention of November, 1970, which was preceded by the University Museum statement of April 1, 1970. With an announcement that came to be known as the Pennsylvania Declaration, the University Museum became the first American institution to refuse from that day forward to purchase antiquities not accompanied by full and publishable provenience (Rainey 1970; Meyer 1973:75). The statement marked an emphatic close to the museum's role in an earlier, less disciplined time in archaeology.

Today, Burkitt is all but forgotten. He worked in isolation, had few friends, and limited most of his professional correspondence to only one destination. He published only nine articles during his lifetime (1902, 1905, 1906, 1918, 1924, 1930a, 1930b, 1930/31, 1933), and much of his archaeological and linguistic material has never been analyzed. His anthropological legacy is less recognized than his celebrity among old Guatemala hands as "the man who came to tea and stayed for thirty years" (Danien 1985). And yet, if one considers the past with "some real understanding of context, some real respect for the potentials and possibilities that were available, and a decent humility about our ancestors' accomplishments . . . " (Chippendale 1989:33), Burkitt's contribution looms larger. He provided the University Museum with an important collection of provenienced Maya artifacts from a region little known archaeologically, and played an important if unpublicized role in the negotiations leading to its institutional entrance into Maya archaeology (UMA, J. Alden Mason letters).

Burkitt's tragedy is that his view of archaeology, formed during the days of such singular men as the suspicious Teobert Maler and the intuitive Edward Thompson, was never able to move to the more structured and disciplined approach of people like Sylvanus Morley, J. Eric Thompson, or even the somewhat looser and politically astute ethic of his old friend Gordon. As archaeology moved further away from those tumultuous early years, Burkitt was marginalized to no more than a footnote in the history of Maya exploration.

Burkitt's last years were spent perfecting his Maya dictionaries, linguistic efforts that did not survive their author. When he died in 1945, his world had already disappeared. He himself had become a relic . . . an archaeologist in amber.

## Notes

1. An earlier version of this chapter was presented in "Networks of the Past," the Third Annual Symposium of the History of Archaeology at the annual meeting of the American Association of Anthropology, November 16, 1989, Washington, D.C.

2. This institution was originally named the Free Museum of Science and Art. By 1913 it had become known as The University Museum. In the 1980s, the name was changed to The University Museum of Archaeology and Anthropology of the University of Pennsylvania. Since 1994, its official title has been The University of Pennsylvania Museum of Archaeology and Anthropology.

3. Personal communications from Ed Shook, Dennis Koester, Robert Smith, and Barbara Kidder de Aldana (1980).

## References Cited

UMA: University of Pennsylvania Museum of Archaeology and Anthropology, American Section Boxes, Central America Boxes 1–4, Director's Letterboxes 1910–1937.

PA: Peabody Museum Archives.

Bernal, Ignácio. 1977. "Maya Antiquaries." In *Social Process in Maya Prehistory: Studies in Honor of Sir Eric Thompson,* edited by Norman Hammond, 19–43. New York: Academic Press.

Burkitt, Robert J. 1902. "Notes on the Kekchi Language." *American Anthropologist* n.s. 4: 441–463.

———. 1905. "A Kekchi Will of the Sixteenth Century." *American Anthropologist* 7: 271–294.

———. 1906. "A Stone Ruin at Se-Tsak, Guatemala." *American Anthropologist* 8: 13–14.

———. 1918. "The Hills and the Corn." *The Museum Journal* 9: 273–289. [Reprinted 1920 as "The Hills and the Corn." *Anthropological Publications* (University Museum), 8 (2): 181–227.]

———. 1924. "A Journey in Northern Guatemala." *The Museum Journal* 15: 115–137.

———. 1930a. "Excavations at Chocola." *The Museum Journal* 21: 5–40.

———. 1930b. "Explorations in the Highlands of Western Guatemala." *The Museum Journal* 21: 41–72.

———. 1930–31. "The Calendar of Soloma and of Other Indian Towns." *Man* 30: 103–107; 31: 146–150.

———. 1933. "Two Stones from Guatemala." *Anthropos* 28: 9–26, 781–782.

Butler, Mary. 1935. "A Study of Maya Mouldmade Figurines." *American Anthropologist* 37: 636–672.

———. 1940. "A Pottery Sequence from the Alta Verapáz." In *The Maya and Their Neighbors,* edited by Clarence L. Hay, Ralph L. Linton, Samuel K. Lothrop, Harry L. Shapiro and George C. Vaillant, 250–267. New York: D. Appleton-Century. Reprint. New York: Dover, 1977.

Chippendale, Christopher. 1989. " 'Social Archaeology' in the Nineteenth Century: Is It Right to Look for Modern Ideas in Old Places?" In *Tracing Archaeology's Past: The Historiography of Archaeology,* edited by Andrew L. Christenson, 21–33. Carbondale: Southern Illinois University Press.

de la Cruz Torres, Mario Enrique. 1978. *Monografía del município de Senahu del departamento de Alta Verapáz.* Guatemala: José de Piñeda Ibarra.

Danien, Elin. 1985. "Send Me Mr. Burkitt, Some Whisky and Wine." *Expedition* 27: 26–33.

———. 1991. "The University Museum at Piedras Negras: Rehearsal for the Future." Paper presented at the Fourth Symposium on the History of American Archaeology, "Continuity and Diversity: The Development of Regional Traditions in Americanist Archaeology," Annual Meeting of the Society for American Archaeology, New Orleans, Louisiana, April 27.

Fagan, Brian. 1977. *Elusive Treasure: The Story of Early Archaeology in the Americas.* New York: Charles Scribner's Sons.

Gordon, George Byron. 1896. *Prehistoric Ruins of Copán, Honduras.* Peabody Museum Memoirs vol. I, no. I. Cambridge: Harvard University Press.

Gordon, George Byron and J. Alden Mason. 1927–1933. *Examples of Maya Pottery in the Museum and Other Collections.* 3 parts. Philadelphia: The University Museum.

King, Arden R. 1974. *Copán and the Verapáz: History and Social Process in Northern Guatemala*. New Orleans: Middle American Research Institute.

King, Eleanor M. and Bryce P. Little. 1986. "George Byron Gordon and the Early Development of the University Museum." In *Raven's Journey: The World of Alaska's Native People*, edited by Susan A. Kaplan and Kristin J. Barsness, 16–53. Philadelphia: University Museum.

Madeira, Percy C. Jr. 1964. *Men in Search of Man: The First Seventy-Five Years of the University Museum of the University of Pennsylvania*. Philadelphia: University of Pennsylvania Press.

Mason, J. Alden. 1927a. "Native American Jades." *The Museum Journal* XVIII (1): 47–73.

———. 1927b. "Mirrors of Ancient America." *The Museum Journal* XVIII (2): 201–209.

———. 1927c. "What We Know About the Maya." *The Museum Journal* XVIII (4): 351–380.

Meyer, Karl E. 1973. *The Plundered Past: The story of the illegal international traffic in works of art*. New York: Atheneum.

Osgood, Cornelius. 1979. *Anthropology in Museums of Canada and the United States*. Milwaukee: Milwaukee Public Museum.

Parsons, Lee A. and Peter S. Jenson. 1965. "Boulder Sculpture on the Pacific Coast of Guatemala." *Archaeology* 18: 132–144.

Rainey, Froelich. 1970. "The Pennsylvania Declaration" *Expedition* 22 (2): 1.

Sabloff, Jeremy A. 1990. *The New Archaeology and the Ancient Maya*. New York: W. H. Freeman.

Schavelzón, Daniel. 1988. "Las Excavaciones en Zaculeu (1946–1950): Una Aproximación al Análisis de la Relación entre Arqueología y *Política* en América Latina." In *Recent Studies in Pre-Columbian Archaeology*, edited by Nicholas J. Saunders and Olivier de Montmollion, 167–190. BAR International Series 421. Oxford: Clarendon Press.

Stephens, John L. 1841. *Incidents of Travel in Central America, Chiapas and Yucatán*, 2 vols. New York: Harper & Bros.

———. 1843. *Incidents of Travel in Yucatán*, 2 vols. New York: Harper & Bros.

Willey, Gordon R. 1968. "One Hundred Years of American Archaeology." In *One Hundred Years of Anthropology*, edited by John O. Brew, 27–53. Cambridge: Harvard University Press.

Willey, Gordon R. and Jeremy A. Sabloff. 1974. *A History of American Archaeology*. New York: W. H. Freeman.

Winegrad, Dilys P. 1993. *Through Time, Across Continents: A Hundred Years of Archaeology and Anthropology at the University Museum*. Philadelphia: The University Museum.

# 2

## Buying a Curator

## Establishing Anthropology at Field Columbian Museum

Donald McVicker

### Introduction

At the time of Chicago's World Columbian Exposition (1893) two anthropological centers existed in the United States, both on the Eastern seaboard. In Washington, D.C., government anthropology at the Smithsonian Institution brought together the resources of the U.S. Geological Survey, its offspring the Bureau of American Ethnology, and the U.S. National Museum. Major John Wesley Powell was at the center of the Washington network.

In Cambridge, Massachusetts, archaeology at the Peabody Museum combined Harvard University's prestige with its access to wealthy patrons and created a private center for anthropological expansion. Frederick Ward Putnam was at the center of the Cambridge network.

These two centers balanced and complemented each other, one public institution and one private university, each having attached museums. While maintaining their autonomy, the Smithsonian combined archaeology with ethnography and linguistics, and the Cambridge center emphasized archaeology.

In 1904, when the Louisiana Purchase Exposition was held in St. Louis, anthropology had passed through an explosive growth phase. New centers were established from coast to coast. These new centers in New York, Chicago, the Southwest, and California were the sites of bitter rivalries and fierce competitions for research territories, museum artifacts, wealthy patrons, and human resources. During the same decade, universities emerged as competitors for many of the same resources.

As new networks developed around museums and universities, members of the established networks attempted to manipulate them and maintain control of the field. The most successful was Putnam, who through Franz Boas and Alfred Kroeber managed to tie museums in New York and California to Cambridge. However, Putnam's and Boas's attempt to dominate the field in

Chicago through the newly established Field Columbian Museum was doomed, just as the next attempt by William H. Holmes and T. C. Chamberlin failed.

To some extent their failure to maintain control over key positions at the museum was based on personalities and particular historical circumstances. However, it was also indicative of an impending struggle between museums and universities to dominate a professionalizing archaeology, and was an expression of regional rivalries pitting the "core center capitalists" of the Midwest against those of the "Eastern Establishment" (Patterson 1995:49).

Regardless of the cause, the bitter legacy of Putnam's and Boas's and (later) Holmes's Chicago experience led to the exclusion of Chicago's museum people from the East Coast networks of power. Despite the millions of Marshall Field and John D. Rockefeller, archaeology in both Chicago's museum and university would fail to fulfill its national potential until well into the 1920s.

## The Founding of Field Columbian Museum

In 1890 Putnam envisioned a great future for anthropology in Chicago. He accepted the position of chief of anthropology for the Chicago World's Columbian Exposition and hired Franz Boas as his chief assistant. Before the fair opened Putnam (1891) proposed that a permanent museum should be established after it closed. Although great efforts were expended by Putnam and the dedicated citizens of Chicago, the plans for the museum almost foundered. Financing for the proposed museum was not secured until the late fall of 1893, only weeks before the fair closed.

In one of the more famous incidents in the cultural history of Chicago, Edward E. Ayer, a wealthy Chicago businessman and world-class collector, convinced Marshall Field that he should be shown through the fair by Ayer. So impressed was Field that on October 16, 1893, he pledged one million dollars toward the Chicago Columbian Museum (Bay 1929, Ch. IV:4–5; Webber 1984).

Putnam of course was delighted, and he immediately proposed that Boas take charge of the moving and ordering of the anthropological collections. Their temporary home was to be in the soon-to-be-vacated Fine Arts Building. In the confusion of the close of the fair and the transfers of massive collections to the Fine Arts Building, the officers of the museum scarcely seemed aware of whom Putnam was placing where. In his December 25, 1893 letter to Ayer, Putnam felt called upon to remind Ayer that "Dr. Franz Boas is my man and he is the man whom you have appointed in temporary charge of the anthropology department" (FMA).

It is quite possible that Putnam's noble labors in the interest of establishing a great city museum and preserving the integrity of his anthropological collections from the fair were not entirely altruistic. Putnam may have seen himself as the scientific director of the new museum and Boas as the curator of anthropology (cf. Dexter 1970:21).

When John D. Rockefeller funded the University of Chicago, Putnam recognized a unique opportunity and almost immediately went to work to develop a positive relationship between the new university and the independent museum. Unfortunately for Putnam's plans, University of Chicago president William Rainey Harper had chosen Frederick Starr to initiate academic anthropology in Chicago; Starr personally disliked Putnam. When Putnam first came to town, Starr had complained to Harper in a June 29, 1892 letter as follows:

> Please do not call the Harvard archaeologist [Putnam] an anthropologist. There is a difference. He has been growing huffy ever since I went to the [Peabody] Museum. He lately wrote me a letter which was not polite. . . . Possibly he feels there is not room for two in Chicago (WRHP).

Despite Starr's somewhat "quirky" personality and personal dislikes, he correctly called president Harper's attention to the difference between an archaeologist and an anthropologist. Starr was as committed as Boas to incorporating archaeology within the four fields of anthropology; he was rightly suspicious of archaeologists taking over anthropology in the museum. In spite of several parallels in their early careers, Starr's relationship with Boas was quite complex and less than cordial (McVicker 1989).

Between Starr's hostility and the university's desire to extend its control over the Field Columbian Museum, Putnam's plans to develop Chicago anthropology in the context of a positive relationship between university and museum foundered.

As the fair neared its end, Thomas C. Chamberlin, head professor of geology, was appointed by president Harper to represent the interests of the University of Chicago in the negotiations for collections. However, Chamberlin had more in mind than collections. After numerous meetings, Chamberlin wrote to Putnam on September 4, 1893, a "memorandum expressive of the attitude of the University," which Chamberlin hoped was not only "fair but magnanimous" (FMA). Essentially, under certain conditions the university offered to release all claims to collections at the fair providing that an appropriate museum could be established to house and maintain the collections.

Curiously, over a month later the university had not heard from Putnam or the officers of the proposed museum, and Chamberlin again wrote to Putnam on October 13, 1893 as follows:

> We desire to continue to aid the Columbian Museum as much as we consistently can, but are unwilling, in the absence of any action on the University's proposition, to compromise our own freedom of action (FMA).

Putnam was rightly suspicious that Chamberlin's "fair and magnanimous" offer disguised a plan for the University to control the Museum once it was established. Chamberlin had already included on his departmental roster, as nonresident geologists, Charles D. Walcott and William H. Holmes, both of the Smithsonian's Geological Survey and Bureau of Ethnology. As indicated in a January 24, 1894 letter to Ayer, Chamberlin's plan was to bring these men to

Chicago as head curators of geology and anthropology at the museum (FMA). This would establish a new network in Chicago that would be tied directly to Washington and dominated by geologists in Chicago's museum and university. The Chicago-Washington axis would then be considerably stronger than Putnam's Cambridge based network.

Although Chamberlin's plan was only partially successful, it contributed to Putnam's fall from grace in Chicago, and led to Boas being ousted. Boas summed up his view of the history of these events in a letter (February 18, 1894) to Putnam:

> You will remember that when you inaugurated the caucus for a museum, you were met with Harper's opposition in so far as he wanted the Museum for the University of Chicago. He left the management of the campaign for the University in the hands of Professor Chamberlin who has proved to be a most shrewd politician. . . .
>
> Chamberlin has two ends in view, one to make the Museum subservient to the University, second to strengthen the Geological Survey. In order to accomplish this he cast around, after gaining the desired influence with the Trustees, for the man he could influence the most. First Walcott was his candidate, then Holmes (FBP).

And Putnam later responded (May 14, 1894) as follows:

> So I have wiped my hands of the whole Columbian Museum business, which has been a dirty piece of work on the part of many, and I am glad that I got out of it before Chamberlin began his intriguing and Skiff began playing his double game (FBP).

## Putnam's Fall from Grace

Toward the end of the fair, rumors about Putnam began to circulate in Chicago. First it was said that the reason for the delays in the completion of the anthropological building was Putnam's lack of administrative ability (FBP, Boas to Putnam letter, February 18, 1894). Then it was rumored that exhibits planned for the Fair had never arrived and were in Cambridge. Finally, it was whispered that Putnam was shipping collections that belonged to the new museum back to the Peabody.

Putting their faith in these rumors, the "Chicago gang" was prepared to put Putnam in his place. First, the trustees chose Frederick J.V. Skiff as director. Skiff was not an illogical choice because he had served as a deputy director of the fair under Harlow N. Higginbotham, president of the World's Columbian Exposition. Skiff had also served as chief of the Department of Mines and Minerals.

The trustees then elected Higginbotham president of the board, a position he held for many years. The longstanding and bitter conflict dating back to 1891 between Putnam and Higginbotham (Collier 1972:8) would be played out by their respective protégés Boas and Skiff.

The board's directors, a circle of Chicago's top captains of industry, controlled the purse strings and the museum director. They were not about to consider Putnam, an outsider with his own ideas, for the position of director. Putnam was correct when he later wrote to Boas (July 24, 1894[?]) that Skiff was a "factotum of the [Board of Trustees] directors" (FBP/WCE).

Douglas Cole (1985:134) sums up Putnam's position in Chicago quite well:

> Putnam, never popular with the dominant forces of the exposition's administration and no more so with their successors in the Columbian Museum, found his influence thin and his advice ignored.

Putnam, having been passed over for all significant positions at the new museum, returned to the Peabody in early 1894 extremely bitter. His reaction to the events in Chicago seemed to have released a certain amount of bottled-up hostility toward the upstarts on the shores of Lake Michigan. Putnam wrote to Samuel A. Crawford on March 7, 1894, as follows:

> [A]fter squeezing all the juice out of me they threw me aside as a used up orange. . . . In fact I never before have experienced so much ingratitude as in connection with this Columbian Museum to which I gave so much time and energy (FBP/WCE [copy to Boas]).

Putnam further vented his spleen in a personal letter to Boas (March 7, 1894).

> I am very much disgusted at the turn things have taken at the Columbian Museum, and I feel that I have been very shabbily treated by Mr. Skiff and the Trustees, after the protestations which were made to me and all the work I did for the Museum, the conception of which was mine and which would never have been accomplished had I not worked for it as I did. Such ingratitude I have never heard of before and I am very much disappointed (FBP/WCE).

In his anger, Putnam even discouraged archaeologist Edward Thompson in a letter (May 19, 1894) from having anything to do with Chicago, and informed him what to expect if he did.

> In Chicago all would be drive and rush and largely sensational effects. That is what they are now after, and it is natural in a place which has started out with great hopes and plenty of money and a feeling that money will do anything. By and by they will realize that while money is an important factor in the work, it alone will not make a scientific institution. . . .

In the same letter to Thompson, Putnam then went on to deny that politics had any place among men of science:

> All political methods I sincerely detest and one side seems to be just as bad as the other in such affairs; and when these methods come into

science they are so thoroughly disgusting and contemptible as to make one wish for a radical change in things. One thing is evident that no purely scientific men will ever condescend to them. . . . (FWP/WCE).

The twin themes in Putnam's letter, science over money and science over politics, are repeated over and over again during this era of professionalization. Self-effacing science must triumph over the big show and personal power. In this respect Putnam's eastern sensibilities stood in stark contrast to the midwesterners of Chicago. Putnam and the Chicagoans were of different cultural worlds, and these worlds did not intersect.

Holmes in Washington viewed the future of the profession in the same way. In 1893 he had "ventured to express the hope that a new era was dawning in American archaeologic science" and had stated how strongly he "deprecate[d] personalities in scientific discussion" (Holmes 1893:135).

Despite Putnam's declared dislike of Chicago-style ostentation and politics, there can be little doubt that he was ambitious; he too sought the power of position to promote his vision of professional anthropology. Although he lost Chicago, as soon as he returned to Cambridge he negotiated for the position of head curator of anthropology at the American Museum in New York.

When the American Museum accepted his terms (he would retain his position at the Peabody, and spend one week a month in New York), and offered him the position, he prepared to "reorganize the department on a broad basis, to plan for its future development and for exploration, and to direct its work" (Harvard University 1894:7).

Although Putnam's feelings toward Chicago and the Museum were to moderate in years to come, he never regained his enthusiasm for anthropology in Chicago. As Cole (1985:143) suggests:

> Much of his [Putnam's] work at the American Museum would be done with an eye back to the shores of Lake Michigan and with a bitterness, both on his own account and on behalf of Boas, toward the Chicago trustees. "I'll show Chicago I can go them one better," he wrote with obvious relish.

### Buying a Curator

Shortly before he left Chicago Putnam counseled Edward Ayer in a December 21, 1893 letter as follows:

> I therefore most earnestly advise that Dr. Boas be requested to take charge of all the anthropological collections until a permanent organization is perfected and by that time I am confident the Trustees will find out that he is the man for the permanent Curator of the Department of Anthropology (FMA/BP).

If Putnam assumed that the powers in Chicago were going to be content hiring as their curator of anthropology a young, not yet well-known, German-

Jewish immigrant who had never held a major museum position, he clearly did not understand Chicago's money and its second city boosterism. In 1895, as head curator of botany, Charles Frederick Millspaugh asserted that

> We have here in Chicago, the center of the most populous portion of this great country, a Museum, whose influence is already being felt throughout America. It has been founded on truly American lines, and upon the greatest of America's events. It is distinctively an American Institution, and its collections in American Science and History should afford every opportunity of study and exploitation (FMA Millspaugh, #31, 1893–1907).

Nor did Putnam understand Chicago's determination to buy itself instant cultural and scientific prestige equal to New York's. The University of Chicago had turned the trick with Rockefeller's money, and the Field Columbian Museum would do the same. Reflecting on this period, J. Christian Bay (1929, Ch.VI:3), museum chronicler, could write that the founding of the museum was " . . . a typical American endeavor: to organize in a few months what older institutions had developed gradually during centuries."

From the trustees' perspective, Boas was never hired as nor considered to be a permanent curator of anthropology for the Field Columbian Museum. At the close of 1893 all appointments were temporary, and individuals were hired, as was Boas, to accomplish the herculean task of receiving, arranging, and installing collections. Even Boas described his position as having "temporary charge of the Anthropological Department of the Museum" until a director of anthropology was appointed (FMA/BP, Boas to Skiff letter, February 16, 1894).

However, whether from his mentor Putnam or on his own, Boas clearly had the expectation that he would be hired permanently. Unfortunately for Boas, Putnam left before Boas could consolidate his position. Shortly after Putnam's departure, the museum was offered the opportunity to buy a government anthropologist of national renown for his archaeological investigations. Boas reacted violently when he heard of this "conspiracy" to bring William H. Holmes from the Smithsonian to replace him.

By 1893 Holmes (1846–1933) had earned a solid reputation in his chosen field. As a young man he had trained as an artist and had joined the U.S. Geological Survey. Major Powell became his mentor, and Holmes's career aspirations shifted from art to archaeology. He became the leader in classification and distribution studies of Prehispanic ceramics and stone technology (Willey and Sabloff 1993:87). As a younger scholar he had even entered into the scientific dispute over the antiquity of man in the New World; he had opposed Putnam and others who claimed Pleistocene roots for Western Hemisphere populations (Patterson 1995:55; Meltzer 1983). When he accepted the offer from Field Columbian Museum (over one from New York), Holmes was both the head of archaeological research at the Bureau of American Ethnology and curator of American Antiquities in the U.S. National Museum. From the perspective of Skiff and Higginbotham, he was also well connected with the Eastern Establishment and appropriately "WASPish" in background.

Very much a museum man of his time, Holmes tended to narrow his focus to archaeological and material culture studies (Pinsky 1992:171). This focus and his artistic background led to a fascination with "industrial arts," the amassing of collections of ceramics and casts of ancient sculptures (McVicker 1993). Although tied to anthropology, Holmes's archaeology also led to a distrust of evolutionary thinking and a tendency toward marked historical particularism. According to Willey and Sabloff (1993:90), these were the preconditions for the subsequent marginalization of archaeology within Boasian anthropology.

## Boas Gets the Boot

Because Boas was already in place temporarily, confidential negotiations were carried out with Holmes in early 1894. In a personal letter to Holmes dated January 27, 1894 (RRL vol. 7, sect. I:8–9), Chamberlin wrote that

> . . . owing to the delicate relations of the Museum to professor Putnam and Dr. Boas, the proposed arrangement with you will be best kept confidential for a time. . . .

All went smoothly until the next month when Boas heard of the "plot." As Putnam had done before him, Boas reacted strongly. On February 16, 1894, Boas wrote to Skiff (FMA/BP) requesting that his relationship to the museum be formalized. By February 18, Boas had determined that

> Mr. Holmes has been practically appointed director of the anthropological department and the Museum authorities are willing to let me step down and take the ethnology under him which he does not want. This information comes from Harper (FBP, Boas to Putnam letter, February 18, 1894).

The next day (February 19, 1894) Boas addressed an arrogant letter to Skiff which stated the following:

> As you can not give me the assurance that since I have had temporary charge of the Anthropological Department nobody besides myself has been or is being considered in connection with the position of Director of the Department of Anthropology, I decline to work for the Museum any longer under the present terms (FMA/BP).

Most remarkably, Boas wrote to Holmes on February 17, 1894, stating that he was in charge of the anthropological department, and that this position apparently had been offered to a "Washington Ethnologist," although he did not know whom. Boas then snapped, "If this were true, I would consider it, of course, *an unsurpassed insult* . . . " (FMA, Letter enclosed with Holmes to Skiff, February 21, 1894).

In a February 21, 1894 letter to Boas, Holmes replied somewhat coolly that "The proposition made to me by the Directors of the Field Columbian Museum was confidential," and that "the proposition contemplated no interference with anyone, but concerned the establishment of a new position." Holmes went on to deny knowing anything of Boas's official relations with the Field Columbian Museum except that he was "installing the anthropologic collections brought together by your department at the Fair . . . " (FMA, enclosed with Holmes to Skiff letter, February 21, 1894). Skiff replied to Holmes (RRL vol. 7, sect. 1:27–28) that his "treatment of the case [of Boas] was judicious and dignified. . . . " In the same letter he also comments on Boas's contributions to setting up the new anthropology section:

> Dr. Boas is handling the installation of the material intrusted in his care superbly. His methods are economical, intelligent, and to an extent artistic . . .

Although a month later (March 30, 1894) Holmes could still complain to Skiff that Boas's "antagonistic position with respect to my coming has given me a good deal of discomfort" (FMA), he was obviously giving the situation considerable thought. The next day he addressed a letter to Skiff that contained a remarkable proposition regarding the future of anthropology at Field Columbian Museum (FMA). Holmes stated that he considered it "of the utmost importance that he [Boas] be kept on the Museum force," that under the assistant director he (Boas) be given charge of physical anthropology and "made the agent of the Museum for all the great northern regions of the globe," and that his time be divided somewhat equally between the field and the museum (McVicker 1990).

Thus it would appear that the primary cause of Boas getting the boot was not Holmes's animosity toward Boas but the decisions of Skiff and Higginbotham strongly influenced by Chamberlin. There is no evidence that Boas ever knew of Holmes's letter to Skiff or the professional respect that Holmes held for him. Instead, after having received his "unsurpassed insult," Boas only agreed to stay until May of 1894. (He demanded $1,100.00 for his services during that period.) As he wrote Putnam on February 18, 1894, "I may be willing to make a new bargain with them to finish the installation for a decent pay and this I should do only because I must try to make money" (FBP).

The fact that Boas considered the actions of Field Columbian Museum an "unsurpassed insult" can be understood in terms of his expectations, his personal and financial situation, and his somewhat arrogant professional and scientific reaction to the chicanery of the Midwest merchant aristocracy.

It is evident that Putnam had raised Boas's expectations that he would obtain a permanent curatorial position in Chicago. However, when Putnam was effectively pushed to the side, Boas was in a particularly vulnerable position. As Putnam's protégé, he too could be suspected of mishandling anthropology at the fair.

Boas had given up his professorship at Clark University when Putnam called him to Chicago. He was married with young children to support, and outside of Chicago he had no secure job prospects. In fact, despite Putnam's claim in a December 21, 1894 communique to Ayer that "the Doctor has two calls to positions in the East" (FMA/BP), Boas would not find regular employment for two years after he left the museum. Only after Putnam was in charge at the American Museum was Boas placed at both the American Museum of Natural History and at Columbia University (Dexter 1976:306).

For Eurocentric Boas with his ties to the east coast, Chicago must have been insupportable. He had been put down by people for whom, as a scientist, he had little respect, in a city famous for its nouveau riche upstarts. Boas was never to forget the "unsurpassed insults" he had received in Chicago.

Putnam's bitterness on behalf of Boas is well expressed in a May 19, 1894 letter to Edward Thompson:

> You know how they treated poor Boas there [Chicago] . . . After getting all this hard labor out of him they have simply kicked him out and put in Holmes of Washington in his place to take charge of the department (FWP/WCE).

It has sometimes been assumed that Boas got the anti-Semitic boot (this volume p. 22 n-1). However, there is no direct evidence available that Boas was replaced by Holmes specifically because of anti-Semitism on the part of Marshall Field (who had little to do with the operation of the museum) or on the part of any other officers of the museum. Although it is true that "gentlemanly" anti-Semitism was common among Chicago's elite, the fact that Boas was a non-WASP immigrant probably counted as much against him as his Jewishness in the jingoistic world of 1890s Chicago.

In fact, Boas's Jewishness was probably irrelevant to the board and officers of the museum. From their perspective he was neither a significant person nor issue. They recognized him only as Putnam's former chief assistant who had been hustled into a temporary job to help install exhibits.

It is interesting to note that when, many years later, Boas related to Alfred Kroeber his own recall of the fateful events in Chicago, Boas blamed Museum director Skiff for his departure rather than Holmes. According to Kroeber (1943:13), Boas told him as a "personal confidence" that the scientific staff at the museum had been revolting against Skiff in 1894, but that when it came to the firing line he alone went forward, and fell!

### Aftermath

Several years after the departure of Boas, Putnam made his peace with the museum. The events following Putnam's departure from Chicago were to be considered a "series of complications and misunderstandings." Putnam also suggested to Higginbotham that "malicious statements" had been made about him in Chicago by a man whom he was obliged to dismiss from his department at the Fair. After suggesting that the "unfortunate past is to bury its dead," Putnam proposed the following in a letter to Skiff (February 15, 1896):

> Your Museum and mine will pull together for the great object for which they were founded. Let us work in harmony and without jealousy. Each taking pride and satisfaction in what the other accomplishes and work for a common end (FMA).

However noble Putnam's sentiments might have been, museums cannot pull together, only people can. Although Putnam proposed rising above the complications of the past, Boas remained unforgiving.

## Holmes in Chicago

In Holmes's unpublished "Random Records of a Lifetime," several sections are devoted to his "Chicago Venture." Money was a major factor in his decision to accept the position of curator of anthropology.

> A salary of $5,000 was in sight, along with free and untrammeled control of the Department to carry out my ideals of what such a Department should be (RRL, vol. 7, sect. 1[A]).

Although Holmes did not quite reach the $5,000 he had in sight, the Museum agreed to a salary of $333.33 a month, a salary which was second only to Skiff's salary as director.

It should come as no surprise that Chicago was professionally attractive to Holmes. Anthropology in Washington during the last decade of Powell's rule was marking time (Hinsley 1981). At the Bureau of American Ethnology there were few routes of mobility open to Holmes. In fact, with Powell under pressure at the U.S. Geological Survey, it was quite possible that Powell would lose his directorship and be forced to return for his salary to the Bureau. If such were to be the case, Holmes's own position would be threatened.

Powell did lose his position at the Survey and return to the Bureau payroll but this is hardly sufficient explanation of why Holmes went to Chicago. However, Chicago with its money, driving ambitions, and new museum would have proved an attractive pull regardless of any push out of Washington. In addition, Holmes's friend Chamberlin was an effective salesperson, and in a communique dated January 27, 1894, he tempted Holmes with opportunities to lecture at the University and even to continue with some artistic work at the Bureau (RRL, vol. 7, sect. I:8–9).

Indeed Holmes's first year in Chicago seemed like a honeymoon. His early letters to Skiff were warm, and he seemed to have been well supported by the board of trustees. No sooner had Holmes settled in at the museum than Allison Armour invited Holmes and the head of botany, C. F. Millspaugh, to accompany him on his yacht for a four-month expedition to Mexico. Out of this expedition came Holmes's still valuable *Archaeological Studies Among the Ancient Cities of Mexico* (Holmes 1895–1897), illustrated in part by impressionistic, but highly accurate sketches by the author (cf. Willey and Sabloff 1993:69).

When and why things went sour for Holmes in Chicago is difficult to say. In "Random Records of a Lifetime," written many decades after the events in Chicago, Holmes recounts experiences as bitter as those recalled by Boas and Putnam. Once again Chicago politics and money take the blame. Holmes described his view of the situation at the museum in a letter (January 28, 1897) to Walcott:

> The trouble developed out of the Chicago idea that only a business
> man, and a business man only, can conduct the business of an institu-
> tion—museum or otherwise.

Although the field in Chicago was a great one and promised much for the future, Holmes feared "that years of crudeness, struggle and uncertainty must follow . . . " (RRL, Vol. 8 [draft]).

Holmes was somewhat prescient in regard to all museums, not just Chicago's. Businessmen dominated the boards and patrons the funding of scientific research. Patrons wanted collections and business men exhibitions. Even Boas, when he achieved prominence at the American Museum in New York, ultimately left for the university, frustrated by the emphasis placed on exhibits of material culture and patron-funded expeditions (McVicker 1992).

Skiff was viewed by Holmes as a hatchet man for the board of trustees and as a protégé of board president Higginbotham. Holmes refers to Skiff's "innate cunning" as the "outstanding feature of his character" and felt that "At the bottom of it all was Mr. Skiff's fear that my position and popularity might lead to his own discomfiture" (RRL, vol. 7, sect. I [A]).

During Holmes's tenure the face-off between the administration and the scientific staff intensified. Holmes, like Boas before him, placed the blame on Skiff.

> The scientific staff of the Museum was gradually getting into a state of
> rebellion against Director Skiff as a result of his unappreciative and ty-
> rannical attitude. . . . (RRL, vol. 8, sect. IV [A]).

Under these circumstances Holmes's thoughts turned back toward Washington. Fortunately he had not lost touch with his Washington network. His old friend Walcott was now acting assistant secretary of the Smithsonian, and Secretary Samuel P. Langley was well disposed toward Holmes. When a suitable job as head curator of anthropology at the U.S. National Museum opened up, notwithstanding a cut in salary, Holmes resigned and returned to government anthropology in June of 1897.

Like his predecessors Boas and Putnam, Holmes was to leave Chicago with a lifelong negative feeling, if not animosity, toward the Field Columbian Museum. He had been bought as a curator, and his expectations had not been met. He probably regretted not heeding the words of John Coulter, president of Lake Forest College, who had warned him before coming to Chicago that

> [t]he danger has been the common danger of Chicago, namely, to make the Columbian Museum a big show instead of a center for scientific collections for study and work (RRL, vol. 7, sect. XXX, Coulter to Holmes letter, April 23, 1894).

Coulter's advice was prophetic, for under Holmes' successor George A. Dorsey, the Field Columbian Museum was indeed a big show. Dorsey's showmanship and highly personal style failed to excite admiration on the east coast, and neither Boas nor Holmes would recognize him as an equal in their respective scientific circles. Further, since Dorsey had been Putnam's student, and had written his dissertation in archaeology, Frederick Starr successfully blocked his full participation in anthropology at the University of Chicago. From the eastern point of view the big show at the Chicago Museum remained academically and institutionally marginal.

## Epilogue

Boas's suspicion of Holmes and his bitterness toward Chicago endured for decades and continued to affect the establishment of cooperative arrangements between New York, Washington, Cambridge, and Chicago. For example, in 1902 following Major Powell's death, Holmes was proposed as the head of the Bureau of American Ethnography. His appointment was to be at the expense of William J. McGee, Powell's chosen successor and a favorite of the anthropological establishment. Boas took the position that he was "fully prepared to befriend McGee against the man who had taken his place in Chicago" (Hinsley 1981:251). McGee in turn would write Boas reminding him that "you saw Holmes's cloven foot in Chicago, but I see both of them and the forked tail as well" (McGee to Boas, quoted in Hinsley 1981:253).

Boas's animosity toward the appointment of Holmes as Bureau Chief was not based on personal reasons alone. Pinsky (1992:172) notes that there were professional reasons as well. Boas was committed to the independence of the Bureau from the Museum, which he felt was essential to the future growth of anthropology. Boas was rightly concerned that under Holmes the Bureau would become the "collecting arm" of the National Museum.

Regardless of his motivations, Boas's opposition to Holmes did little to improve relations between the two men and undoubtedly contributed to the professional censure of Boas by the American Anthropological Association in 1919 (Pinsky 1992). When the censure vote was taken, it was members of Holmes's network of museum men and government anthropologists committed to material culture studies who lined up against Boas and his university based supporters.

Despite their antipathy Boas and Holmes shared one thing in common: a distrust, if not dislike, of Chicago. Because of this these powerful men of science excluded Dorsey and the Chicago Museum from full participation in the profession until the 1920s.

After Dorsey's resignation it appeared that the Boasian agenda would finally occupy a prominent position in Chicago anthropology. Berthold Laufer, a close friend and colleague of Boas who had worked with him on the American Museum's Jesup North Pacific expedition, was appointed head curator of anthropology. Unfortunately for the Field Museum, Laufer's concentration on the Asian Rim and his brand of Teutonic scholarship may have appealed to the profession but failed to capture the imagination of Chicago's supporters and donors.

The reverse was true at the University of Chicago when Starr finally retired and Fay-Cooper Cole took over as head of the department (Stocking 1979). Cole saw archaeology as the means of moving the department out of its doldrums and embarked on a series of excavations that captured the imagination of the public. Ironically, archaeology in the university's anthropology department became dominant, while archaeology in the museum remained marginalized. The situation then reversed itself in the 1930s when Paul S. Martin, one of Fay-Cooper Cole's students, took over the curatorial reins at Field Museum, while at the University, British social anthropology became dominant.

Clearly, despite the importance of personalities and antipathies, the history of anthropology curatorships at Field Museum is a product of the relationships between museums and universities as well as the rivalries between Chicago and New York. The university has always resisted domination by New York based Boasian anthropology. The museum, recognizing the position of archaeology within Boasian anthropology, has similarly resisted its hegemony. Today, although the "big show" has passed from the scene and Chicago boosterism has become less strident, Chicago institutions consider themselves as central to their profession as any other institutions, east or west. Mainstreams and margins are always a matter of perspective. One person's periphery is always another's center.

## Acknowledgments

This paper was made possible by a Summer Research Fellowship granted by the Smithsonian Institution. Various archival sources were made available to the author during his research. Permission to use archival materials was granted by the American Philosophical Society, the University of Chicago Regenstein Library Special Collections, the Field Museum of Natural History, Harvard University Peabody Museum, and the National Anthropology Archives. All support is gratefully acknowledged.

## References Cited

FBP: American Philosophical Society, Franz Boas Papers.
FBP/WCE: American Philosophical Society, Franz Boas Papers, World's Columbian Exposition.

FMA: Field Museum of Natural History Archives, Director's General Correspondence.

FMA/BP: Field Museum of Natural History Archives, Franz Boas Papers.

FWP/WCE. Peabody Museum, Frederick Ward Putnam Papers, World's Columbian Exposition.

RRL: National Anthropology Archives, William H. Holmes, Random Records of a Lifetime.

WRHP: University of Chicago Regenstein Library Special Collections, William Rainey Harper Papers, Correspondence.

Bay, J. Christian. 1929. "History [of the Field Museum]." In *MS*. Chicago: University of Chicago, John Crerar Library.

Cole, Douglas. 1985. *Captured Heritage: The Scramble for Northwest Coast Artifacts*. Seattle: University of Washington.

Collier, Donald. 1972. "Men and their work." *Field Museum Bulletin* 43 (8): 7–9.

Dexter, Ralph W. 1970. "The Role of F. W. Putnam in Founding the Field Museum." *Curator* 13 (1): 21–26.

———. 1976. "The Role of F. W. Putnam in Developing Anthropology at the American Museum of Natural History." *Curator* 19 (4): 303–310.

Harvard University. 1894. *Report of the President of Harvard University for 1893–94*. Cambridge: Harvard University.

Hinsley, Curtis M., Jr. 1981. *Savages and Scientists: The Smithsonian Institution and the Development of American Anthropology 1846–1910*. Washington, D.C.: Smithsonian Institution.

Holmes, William H. 1893. "A Question of Evidence." *Science* 21 (527): 135–136.

———. 1895–1897. *Archaeological Studies Among the Ancient Cities of Mexico: Part I. Monuments of Yucatán; Part II. Monuments of Chiapas, Oaxaca and the Valley of Mexico*. Field Columbian Museum Anthropological Series, vol. 1, no. 1, pub. 16. Chicago.

Kroeber, Alfred L. 1943. "Franz Boas the Man." In *Franz Boas, 1858–1942*. American Anthropological Association Memoir 61.

McVicker, Donald. 1989. "Parallels and Rivalries: Encounters Between Boas and Starr." *Curator* 32 (3): 212–228.

———. 1990. "Footnotes for the History of Anthropology: Putnam, Boas, and Holmes—Establishing Anthropology at the Field Columbian Museum." *History of Anthropology Newsletter* XVII (2): 3–8.

———. 1992. "The Matter of Saville: Franz Boas and the Anthropological Definition of Archaeology." In *Rediscovering Our Past: Essays on the History of American Archaeology*, edited by Jonathan E. Reyman, 145–159. Hampshire: Avebury.

———. 1993. "Museums, Collections and World's Fairs: The NMNH at the LPX." Paper presented at symposium, "Archaeology in Museums: Dynamic Interactions and Mutual Constraints." Society for American Archaeology, St. Louis, Missouri.

Meltzer, David J. 1983. "The Antiquity of Man and the Development of American Archaeology." In *Advances in Archaeological Method and Theory*, edited by Michael B. Schiffer, no. 6, 1–51. New York: Academic Press.

Patterson, Thomas C. 1995. *Toward a Social History of Archaeology in the United States*. Fort Worth, Texas: Harcourt Brace College Publishers.

Pinsky, Valerie. 1992. "Archaeology, Politics, and Boundary-Formation: The Boas Censure (1919) and the Development of American Archaeology During the Inter-War Years." In *Rediscovering Our Past: Essays on the History of American Archaeology*, edited by Jonathan E. Reyman, 161–189. Hampshire: Avebury.

Putnam, Frederick W. 1891. "The Columbian Memorial Museum." Paper presented at the meeting of the Commercial Club of Chicago, November 28. Chicago: Field Museum of Natural History archives.

Stocking, George W. 1979. *Anthropology at Chicago: Tradition, Discipline, Department*. The University of Chicago Library, Chicago.

Webber, E. Leland. 1984. "Books, Business, and Buckskin." *Field Museum Bulletin*.

Willey, Gordon R. and Jeremy A. Sabloff. 1993. *A History of American Archaeology*. 3rd ed. New York: W. H. Freeman.

# 3

## Recognizing the Foundation of Prehistory

## Daniel Wilson, Robert Chambers, and John Lubbock

Alice B. Kehoe

### Evolution and Prehistory

Factual knowledge claims come to individuals and centers of assessment through *systems of recognition* (Shapin 1994:304; Shapin's italics).

The sociology of science elucidates the processes and factors through which some individuals are lauded and others elided. Data are cited to support a thesis proffered to an audience constituting a body of assessors reached through systematized means such as scientific journals and lectures. Editors and the organizations providing venues for research have the power, indeed the obligation, to exclude knowledge claims deemed unworthy. Ethnographic and historical sociological studies have demonstrated the falsity of conventional assertions that truth, or validity, guarantee acceptance of knowledge claims. Instead, the sciences are political arenas echoing ideological struggles in the wider society. The beginnings of the British version of prehistoric archaeology reflect conflicts between Scottish nationalism and English imperialism, and between the tradesmen class and the gentry.

The word "prehistory" was first used in 1851 by a young Scots antiquarian, Daniel Wilson, in *The Archaeology and Prehistoric Annals of Scotland*. In the Preface, Wilson asserted,

> Archaeology . . . not only furnishes valuable auxiliary truth in aid of physiological and philological comparisons, . . . it adds distinct psychological indices by no other means attainable, and yields the most trustworthy, if not the sole evidence in relation to extinct branches of the human family, the history of which possesses a peculiar national and personal interest for us. . . . The following work . . . has been undertaken under the conviction that this science [archaeology] is the key to great truths which have yet to be reached, and that its importance will

hereafter be recognized in a way little dreamt of by those students of
kindred sciences (Wilson 1851:xiii, xvi).

Charles Lyell's *Principles of Geology* (1830–1833) introduced into the British scientific universe an essentially limitless time (in contrast to the notion
of a Biblical history) and a geological record of slow but relentless change.
Lyell's principles easily fit the gradualistic unilinear evolution of humankind conjectured by eighteenth-century Enlightenment philosophes and embedded in John Lubbock's *Pre-historic Times* (1865). Lubbock's work is well
known; its model, Daniel Wilson's *Prehistoric Man* (1862) is virtually ignored.
*Prehistoric Man,* Wilson's ambitious construction of a science of prehistory,
was equally founded on geologic method but reflected a saltational multilinear evolution argued since 1844 by Wilson's mentor, Robert Chambers of
Edinburgh (see Kehoe 1998 for extended discussion).

The first editions of Wilson's *Prehistoric Man* sold out. The work was
widely disseminated in America particularly through its third edition (1876).
It has clear priority over Lubbock's cobbled together imitation; the quality and
contemporary significance of Wilson's work are evidenced by Robertson Smith
selecting Wilson to prepare the magisterial article "Archaeology" for the ninth
*Encyclopedia Britannica* (1878). (Edward B. Tylor wrote the parallel article on
"Anthropology.") Yet Wilson is given a scant page in Bruce Trigger's *A History
of Archaeological Thought* (1989), while Lubbock is granted an entire section
and gets his photograph included as well. Trigger claims that Lubbock's *Prehistoric Times* "was almost certainly the most influential work dealing with
archaeology published during the nineteenth century" (Trigger 1989:114).[1]
Two factors militated against Wilson receiving the historical recognition
he deserved. First, he resisted the hard-core racism espoused by leading ide-
ologues, such as Lubbock. Second, Wilson's class origins were petit bourgeois
(cf. Desmond 1989:23–24). Lubbock represented the aristocratic establishment centered in London around the Royal Society. In contrast, Wilson was
a product of the reform-minded petit bourgeoisie of Scotland molded by the
Scottish Enlightenment.

Daniel Wilson was part of an Edinburgh circle of politically liberal bourgeois men with literary and scientific interests, a group that included George
Combe and Robert Chambers. As a young man Chambers had used an interest
in antiquarian research to break into Edinburgh salon society centered on Sir
Walter Scott (Scott's favorite of all his novels was *The Antiquary,* published in
1815 [Stephen 1897:92]). Daniel Wilson, working in the 1840s under the aegis
of the still aristocratic Society of Antiquaries of Scotland, invoked the name of
the revered Sir Walter Scott and yoked it to the growing prestige of science.
Using Scott's style of enlivening history with vivid portrayals, Wilson capti-
vated contemporaries with his delightful *Memorials of Edinburgh in the Olden
Time,* published serially in 1846–1847 and as bound volumes in 1848. The *Memorials* also contained the underlying engagement with the dynamics of class
relationships that made Scott a favorite of Georg Lukács and before him, Karl

Marx (Brown 1979:195–197). In Scott's work, this feature was sufficiently muted that the ordinary reader perceived Scott to be a Tory (Secord 1989:169).

In winning recognition through engravings of landmarks and lively historical text, Wilson followed Chambers' route, and won his support. Wholly untainted by the suspicions of radical opinions that denied Chambers the honor of being named Lord Provost of Edinburgh in 1848 (Watt 1887:24), Wilson could incorporate his mentor's now-seasoned ideas without prejudicing their general reception. The Society of Antiquaries collections Wilson organized under Chambers' initiative served as Wilson's *bona fides* displayed for all to see in the Society's museum. Reworking his catalogue for the collections into *The Archaeology and Prehistoric Annals of Scotland,* Wilson created a new context for antiquities, no longer primarily relics of Roman power valued by wealthy dilettantes such as Jonathan Oldbuck, Scott's fictional antiquary. At this time, the artifacts arranged in a series from primitive hunters' stone choppers to medieval monuments, gave Scottish history a depth that, like Jens Worsaae's *Danmarks Oltid* (1849[1842]), asserted the solid strength of these peripheral North Sea nations (Wilson 1851:18).

John Lubbock, born into wealth, a bank presidency, and a baronetcy, a Member of Parliament, raised to the peerage in 1900 as Lord Avebury, did almost no original research in archaeology, although he did make significant primary contributions to entomology (Somkin 1981:528–529). In archaeology, Lubbock was a synthesizer whose claim to a place in the canon should be his coinage of the terms "Paleolithic" and "Neolithic" (Lubbock 1912[1865]:2, 3). Sir John's position in the standard history of archaeology is the outcome of the fact that he was, quite literally, a member of the right clubs—the Royal Society, the Geological Society of London, the Linnean Society, and above all, the highly select X-Club[2] (Russell 1983:258; Hull 1985:811, n. 7; Barton 1990). Lubbock lived in London and nearby Kent, and met daily with leading scientists, politicians, and writers.[3] In 1884, Lubbock consolidated his influence in archaeology by marrying (as his second wife) Alice, daughter of General Pitt-Rivers, an earl's grandson who had inherited an immense estate where he conducted archaeological excavations. Lubbock was Charles Darwin's fellow squire (Down House adjoins the Lubbock estates) (Moore 1985), and as a youth became Darwin's protégé and later a member of his primary research team (see Secord 1985:528). When Darwin used material from archaeology, he cited Lubbock, as he cited Joseph Hooker, another of his stalwart confréres, on botany. Sir John Lubbock was a man of privilege sought as a patron, who could confer privilege on others; with his neighbor Charles Darwin, the relationship was reciprocal.[4]

Lubbock's *Pre-historic Times* introduced neither the concept of cultural evolution (the standard framework of eighteenth-century conjectural histories) nor the science of prehistory. The sales of Wilson's 1862 *Prehistoric Man* had prompted its publisher, Macmillan, to commission a second edition, and rival publishers Williams and Norgate to take advantage of popular interest by reprinting Lubbock's periodical articles on archaeology in book form. When

Lubbock stated in his Preface, "My object has been to elucidate, as far as possible, the principles of pre-historic archaeology; laying special stress upon the indications which it affords of the condition of man in primeval times" (Lubbock 1912[1865]:vi), he did not pretend to have originated his subject. His principal "elucidation" was the distinction (p. 2) between Paleolithic and Neolithic.

As we would expect from Darwin's close friend, on Lubbock's last page we read, "Thus, then, the great principle of Natural Selection, which is to biology what the law of gravitation is for astronomy, not only throws an unexpected light on the past, but illuminates the future with hope" (Lubbock 1912[1865]:481). John Lubbock had little need to argue for evolution in 1865. Two generations of scientists and popularizers had been wrangling over it (Lovejoy 1959; Ruse 1979 esp. p. 128; Bowler 1985:655). Far from inaugurating the concept of organic evolution, Darwin had asserted natural selection to be its mechanism (e.g., Sober 1985). Lubbock overstated Darwin's thesis by declaring "Natural Selection . . . is to biology what the law of gravitation is for astronomy" (1912[1865]:481). Lubbock's statement was a direct challenge to Robert Chambers' *Vestiges of the Natural History of Creation* (1844), which Darwin wished to be seen as no more than "preparing the ground" (Secord 1994:xlv) for his own *Origins.* In *Vestiges,* the Scottish popularist declared that "The inorganic has one final comprehensive law, GRAVITATION. The organic, the other great department of mundane things, rests in like manner on one law, and that is—DEVELOPMENT" (Chambers 1994[1844]:360).

A radical book anonymously published, *Vestiges of the Natural History of Creation* was ascribed to Prince Albert; Ada, Lady Lovelace (Lord Byron's rakish daughter); Harriet Martineau; Charles Lyell (Millhauser 1959:6); Thackeray; and Charles Darwin (Brent 1981:399; Cohen 1985:545). Any perspicacious reader (and there were many, including Darwin) guessed "Mr. Vestiges" should be Robert Chambers (Brent 399; Cohen 545). There are extensive and detailed similarities between *Vestiges* and essays of the previous few years printed in the mass market weekly, *Chambers' Edinburgh Journal.* Published in separate essays in the Saturday tabloid, Robert Chambers' ideas were stimulating, liberal, and served as provocative material for Sunday afternoon discussion. Strung together in argument, they had the rebel smell of George Combe's *The Constitution of Man*—as Robert Chambers wanted them to.

Robert Chambers and George Combe shared the vision of a grand science of man, in which political economy is based on the natural constitutions of human beings. George Combe, now remembered as a phrenologist, sought association with the recently formed British Association for the Advancement of Science in 1834, but as Morrell and Thackray explain (1981:278; see also Desmond 1989:174, 176), phrenology was not just craniscopy: it was a reformist movement which

> presented an alternative view of social change and self-help. As such it
> presented a challenge to the Gentlemen of Science [of the BAAS] and

their articulations of science as social anodyne and agent of social ac-
commodation.

Combe's *The Constitution of Man* (first ed., 1828) argued that human nature could be studied like any other natural phenomenon, its design and laws
discerned. Not only did this position attack the androcentric universe as
Kepler and Copernicus had attacked the geocentric universe, Combe claimed
that *only* by attention to human physiognomy could a rational society be established. The Enlightenment's deification of rationality was made the foundation of reform. Thus far, Combe's position may not appear radical, but his
definition of a rational society came with corollaries. Combe believed that the
phrenological research of Franz Gall and J. C. Spurzheim had mapped physical signs of intellectual and emotional capabilities that ought to be routinely
used to identify individuals' potentials, that education should be provided for
children thus identified as suitable, and careers opened on that basis. On the
Continent, the Catholic Church banned Gall's publications (Wolf 1994:4).
In America, the immensely popular minister Henry Ward Beecher favored
phrenology to provide pastors with clues to parishioners' characters (Haskell
1977:83 n. 48). In Britain, the aristocratic gentlemen of science in the BAAS
noticed that Combe and most of his followers were men, and women, of the
middle class. Middle class enthusiasts bought over 100,000 copies of *The Constitution of Man* in Britain and 200,000 in America by 1860 (Cooter 1984:120).
If these literate thousands were swayed toward implementing a meritocracy, it
would be no minor threat.

Combe's best-seller status had been facilitated by the 1832 bequest of an
Edinburgh youth who left 5,000 pounds, when he died at the age of 22, for
the promotion of phrenology. Such promotion was to include publication of
Combe's *Constitution* "in a cheap form, so as to be easily purchased by the
more intelligent individuals of the poorer classes and Mechanics' Institutions,
&c." (Henderson will quoted in Combe 1860:v). The job of publishing a cheap
edition was awarded to the Edinburgh firm of William and Robert Chambers,
the obvious choice because the brothers had built their firm's success on state-
of-the-art mass publishing, a series of educational books and tracts written
expressly for the workingman. Robert Chambers was a close friend and supporter of George Combe. Like Combe and Daniel Wilson (who in the 1840s
earned cash by writing several "potboilers," as he called them, for the Edinburgh publishers), the Chambers brothers were ambitious sons of the Scottish middle class. They too were advocates of social reform, using innovative
achievements in mass printing and distribution as instruments for change
(W. Chambers 1883:231–233, 240–241). William Chambers, the elder brother,
was the astute businessman. Robert was the principal writer, held in check by
the calculating William.[5]

More bluntly than Combe (e.g., 1860:403–405), who ten years before had
tried, and failed, to incorporate phrenology and its associated reform platform
into the BAAS, Chambers espoused a deistic but not Christian position:

It may be that, while we are committed to take our chance in a natural system of undeviating operation, and are left with apparent ruthlessness to endure the consequences of every collision into which we knowingly or unknowingly come with each law of the system, there is a system of Mercy and Grace behind the screen of nature, which is to make up for all casualties endured here, and the very largeness of which is what makes these casualties a matter of indifference to God (Chambers 1994[1844]:384–385).

In place of the historicism of a Biblical universe, Chambers introduced, "as far as I am aware, . . . the first attempt to connect the natural sciences into a history of creation" (Chambers 1994[1844]:388), and ingenuously asked (pp. 389–390), "What is there in the laws of organic creation more startling to the candid theologian than in the Copernican system or the natural formation of strata?" Where Combe had humbly presented his ideas as following "Dr. [Francis] Hutcheson, Dr. Adam Smith, Dr. [Thomas] Reid, Mr. [Dugald] Steward, and Dr. Thomas Brown" (Combe 1851:viii), Chambers boldly elevated his to the revolutionary status of Copernicus and Lyell (Cohen 1985:545).

Interestingly, *Vestiges* appeared four months after[6] Darwin's first fully written, but not published, version of his own argument, on which he instructed his wife on July 5, 1844 as follows: "[I]n case of my sudden death, . . . you will devote 400 pounds to its publication, and further, will yourself, or through Hensleigh [Wedgwood], take trouble in promoting it" (Darwin 1958[1892]:180). *Vestiges* was radical not so much for its espousal of evolution as for its challenge to the landed aristocracy's domination of science and government.

## The Struggle to Establish Prehistoric Archaeology

Daniel Wilson's family were small tradesmen; he had no money and little overt influence outside, eventually, Canada's University College in Toronto. After 1853, Wilson described himself as "a Scottish exile" (Wilson 1863) in an "out of the way corner" (Wilson 1863, 1865). Considering that the Atlantic did not remove him from fellow Scotsman Robertson Smith's purview, it is reasonable to hypothesize that the canonical neglect, in histories of archaeology, of Wilson's two pioneering works in prehistoric studies parallels the neglect, in histories of biology, of his mentor's *Vestiges*. James Secord, defending the continuing importance of *Vestiges* to the history of science, says (1994:xlv) that it "defied the structure of authority which was being created for the sciences in the nineteenth century." Merely by advertising his work as a major contribution, Chambers' protégé Daniel Wilson similarly defied that same structure of authority, one that had not changed from the late seventeenth-century institution of the Royal Society. Primarily a face-to-face community of men of the governing class, any effort by men of a lower class to break into the circle of acknowledged scientific leaders was *ipso facto* an assault upon the power of the aristocracy (Shapin 1994:305).

In his Preface to *Archaeology and Prehistoric Annals of Scotland*, Wilson contended that "a small company of Englishmen," far from giving "[m]an a new history of himself and his civilization" as Arthur Keith would eulogize Lord Avebury (quoted by Daniel 1967:113), actively smothered attempts to achieve such knowledge:

> The British Association [for the Advancement of Science] . . . embraced within its original scheme no provision for the encouragement of those investigations which most directly tend to throw light on the origin and progress of the human race. . . . During several annual meetings, elaborate and valuable memoirs, prepared on various questions relating to this important branch of knowledge, and to the primeval population of the British Isles, were returned to their authors without being read. This pregnant fact has excited little notice hitherto (Wilson 1851:xii).

Morrell and Thackray (1981:276 n. 185, 284–286, 344) confirm Wilson's observation. We might add that the Association's actions noted by Wilson continued in subsequent years. It has taken a century and a half for the conclusion of the paragraph to be realized:

> [W]hen the scientific history of the first half of the nineteenth century shall come to be reviewed by those who succeed us, and reap the fruits of such advancement as we now aim at, it [the BAAS rejection] will not be overlooked as an evidence of the esoteric character of much of the overestimated science of the age (Wilson 1851:xii).

What lay behind this rejection of papers on prehistory? The BAAS was founded in 1831, the year the successful Reform Bill was introduced into Parliament. Like the Royal Society a century and a half earlier, the BAAS aimed to provide a place where gentlemen could "assemble about some *calm,* and *indifferent* things, especially experiments" (Thomas Sprat, 1667, quoted in Morrell and Thackray 1981:246; Sprat's italics). It should be apolitical, above politics; this stance nearly guaranteed unquestioned allegiance to conservative politics. The great debates on human nature were given to theologians, represented in the BAAS by latitudinarian Anglicans including authors of the *Bridgewater Treatises* (Morrell and Thackray 1981:224–229). Natural history would confine its study to the Book of Nature, given to humankind by the Deity as a text for discerning His design and laws. Man, God's steward on earth, is the reader, not the subject, of the Book of Nature.

Contrary to this approved English position, Robert Chambers subsumed humans under a natural (if Deity-instituted) process exemplified in *Vestiges* as a continuum from the formation of stars and planets by gravitational attraction toward nuclei within nebulae, through the formation of rocks and of organic life in geologic time, all "to be regarded as a series of *advances of the principle of development,* which have depended upon external physical circumstances, to which the resulting animals are appropriate" (Chambers 1994[1844]:203).

> The probability may now be assumed that the human race sprung from one stock, which was at first in a state of simplicity, if not barbarism. . . . *The leading characters . . . of the various races of mankind are simply representations of particular stages in the development of the highest or Caucasian type* (Chambers 1994[1844]:305, 307; Chambers' italics).[7]

Chambers' final chapters on human development are not particularly original, as they utilize without citation the conjectural history of the eighteenth century philosophes (v. Meek 1976; cf. Piggott 1976:151) and cite James Prichard's *Researches in the Physical History of Man* (1841, 4th ed.) as a primary source (Chambers 1994[1844]:255, 278). Chambers may have believed that another book could elaborate on the development of man, a strategy that Darwin followed.

Is it a coincidence that Chambers began zealously to reorganize the Society of Antiquaries when he returned to Edinburgh after writing *Vestiges?* Or that he supported young, energetic, ambitious[8] Daniel Wilson for membership early in 1846, only months after *Explanations* (1845) appeared, the first effort at a rebuttal to *Vestiges* critics? (Wilson soon became an officer in the Society with Chambers' assistance.) Without Chambers' patronage, Wilson could not have accomplished his revolutionary transformation of Scottish antiquarianism into archaeology. Was Wilson the instrument of Chambers' desire to substantiate the development of civilization in the manner that geologists had substantiated the development of organisms? Correspondence attests to Chambers' continuing directives and advice to Wilson as he organized the Society's collection and wrote the guide to it published by the Society in 1849 (Ash n.d.:77, 81).

In light of Wilson's close relationship to "Mr. Vestiges," his reference in *The Archaeology and Prehistoric Annals of Scotland* to "psychological indices" is particularly telling because by the late 1840s, Robert Chambers, like other serious supporters of phrenology, was moving beyond its pioneering scheme (Secord 1989:174; Cooter 1984:256–259). In *Vestiges,* Chambers suggested (1994[1844]:342) that psychological faculties are activated by "a process which seems to be intimately allied with some of the phenomena of the new science of photography, when images impressed by reflection of the sun's rays upon sensitive paper are, after a temporary obliteration, resuscitated on the sheet being exposed to the fumes of mercury." Thus boldly Robert Chambers demolished Cartesian duality of mind and framed a new guiding assumption (Laudan, Laudan, and Donovan 1988:9–10): human thinking is a faculty that reflects material conditions. Although Chambers deplored atheistic, vulgar "materialism" (Chambers 1994[1845]:169), he demarcated a scientific approach that sought evidence of general processes in sets of material phenomena.

Daniel Wilson pursued the materialist approach in *Prehistoric Man*, pooling material evidence from ethnographic and archaeological observations to explore the working of the "Laws of Development" and variety-production (Chambers 1994[1844]:283) in the many realms of human habitation. In Chapter 1, Wilson firmly stated, "[M]an's physical nature is modified by the same laws as that of animals" (Wilson 1862:I:8). His own observations of Great Lakes Indians and Midwest archaeological sites, and the information recorded by other Europeans throughout the Americas, were to be "as it were, a parallax of man, already viewed in Europe's prehistoric dawn" (i.e., Prehistoric) (Wilson 1862:I:xii). The scientific archaeologist should first stand investigating the mute sites and relics of prehistoric strata, and then take a parallel position viewing sites, relics, and living individuals of a distant land such as America, presumed isolated from any pre-Columbian transoceanic contacts (Wilson 1862:I:x). "[A] long obliterated past of Britain's and Europe's infancy . . . was here reproduced in living reality," Wilson postulated (1862:I:xiii). Like Chambers, Wilson devoted pages to comparative linguistics, but the bulk of the book concerns artifacts—boats, tools, mounds, pots, visual art, and recording systems. He concluded with a manifesto for prehistoric archaeology:

> So much that is natural to the habits and simple arts of savage life, as seen among the Indians of the New World, has presented itself to my eye and mind as the realization in a living present of what I had already conceived of amid the relics of Britain's allophylian [non-Anglo-Saxon] tribes, that I am led to believe such archaeological researches may be found to have constituted a useful preparative for the study of American ethnology, and the solution of some of the deeply interesting problems which are suggested by the phenomena it discloses; nor can I now doubt that the observation of man in such primitive stages of social development furnishes important aid towards the true interpretation of some of the first traces of human history which so curiously underlie the later records of his presence in Europe (Wilson 1862:II:455).

The conflation of prehistoric with American Indian societies goes back to the seventeenth century, such as in Locke's famous dictum, "In the beginning, all the World was *America*" (Meek 1976:3). Yet, it was Daniel Wilson in 1862 who *demonstrated the method* of (1) conducting archaeological investigations, and then (2) carrying out double "parallax," on the one side comparing archaeological data to ethnographic observations of societies premised to be in habitats similar to those of the archaeological strata. This *model* of prehistoric archaeological method appeared three years later in Lubbock's *Pre-historic Times*, first in a set of reviews of archaeological data, and then in chapters on "Modern Savages." To give Lubbock credit for instituting this basic method is not only to ignore Wilson's priority, but also the fact that Lubbock's book consists of reviews, of tours to sites and collections already excavated, and citations of travelers' narratives of contemporary peoples. Not all of Wilson's *Prehistoric Man* derived from firsthand field observations, and his ethnography was colored, as he admits, by his prior efforts to interpret Scottish antiquities, but the significant core of Wilson's book is his own innovative research—initially stimulated by Robert Chambers (Wilson 1878:140–147).

Secord (1994:xliv) characterizes Chamber's *Vestiges* as "a skilled intervention in some of the great public debates of the nineteenth century." Chambers unequivocally championed what we would now term human rights and rejected English superiority as a manifest destiny:

> [T]he production of original, inventive, and aspiring minds . . . when circumstances are not decidedly unfavourable . . . is the process which seems to form the destined means for bringing mankind from the darkness of barbarism to the day of knowledge and mechanical and social improvement (Chambers 1994[1845]:321–322).

In Canada, Daniel Wilson collected evidence of both aboriginal manifestations of civilization and of race mixture, and published on its beneficial effects (McCardle 1980:97–98, 126–129). This was a decidedly less popular view in the colony, and certainly not one useful to Kiplingesque jingoistic imperialism in the heyday of English expansion. Multilinear cultural evolution, in one sense an Enlightenment question, sank in the nineteenth century under the weight of Manifest Destiny (Kennedy 1994:222), not to reappear until after World War II (Steward 1955).

## Conclusion

Archaeology is not an innocent science. A generation after Wilson's *Prehistoric Annals,* an editor of the periodical *Antiquarian* insisted that

> without a knowledge of the Past, most of the facts of present life are incomprehensible. Nay, all power of regulating the future comes from a knowledge of the present state of things, gained by a knowledge of the past. . . . [T]he antiquarian is able to arrive at general ideas which explain present matters and which may be used by the philosopher for the regulation of the future. . . . The archaeologist . . . is not, therefore, the useless person that is sometimes thoughtlessly portraited, but a valuable contributor to the world's progress (quoted by Hudson 1981:100).

Hobsbawm (1962:261) points out that "With the American and French Revolutions major political and social transformations were secularized," and no longer "fought out in the traditional language of Christianity, orthodox, schismatic, or heretical." There were new premises, terms, and structuring concepts used—in brief, a new paradigm (Foucault 1973:238–239) or "Second Reformation" (Moore 1986:69). The secularization of salvation is expressed in Lubbock's closing line in *Pre-historic Times* (1912[1865]:490), "[T]he most sanguine hopes for the future are justified by the whole experience of the past." This is an unsurprising comment coming from a gentleman enjoying the perquisites of high social position "seek[ing] to induce contentment with the status quo" (Frank Govett, a contemporary of Lubbock's, quoted in Rivière 1978:xxiv).

In 1851, the year Wilson's *Archaeology and Prehistoric Annals* introduced "prehistory" to the English-speaking world, Britain hosted the stupendously successful grand exhibition of its coveted *status quo* in the sparkling Crystal Palace. George Stocking (1987:1–6) spotlights the Crystal Palace as icon and symbol of the Victorian quasi-Reformation. Its breathtaking combination of hard steel and fine glass vaulted over extraordinary displays of artifacts wonderfully illustrated the "Law of Development"—*Prehistoric Annals* brought up to the cutting edge of technological invention. Albert, the Prince consort, had guided the creation of the Palace. Albert shared with Robert Chambers an admiration for Adolphe Quetelet (Bennett 1977:22, 215), whose discoveries of regularities in what had seemed random social behavior were taken to demonstrate the hidden reality of natural law. *Vestiges* had been attributed to His Royal Highness; he openly defended it (Bennett 1977:236). Albert's speech launching the Great Exhibition echoed a Chambers principle: "the realisation of the unity of mankind . . . the Exhibition of 1851 is to give us a true test and a living picture of the point of development at which the whole of mankind has arrived" (Albert, 21 March 1850 quoted in Bennett 1977:200).

Wilson realized that nationalist ideologies can be expressed through artifacts, and therefore through archaeology (1851:18; cf. Fowler 1987). Both *The Archaeology and Prehistoric Annals of Scotland* and *Prehistoric Man* were published before the first incorporation of prehistoric archaeology in 1867 at a nationalistic public exhibition in Paris (Daniel 1950:103). Scottish nationalism is muted in Wilson's books, but it is there as it is in Chambers' writings (cf. Davie 1964; Noble 1982; Shapin 1981:320–322). His statements of the Laws of Development and "variety-production" support diversity, not unilinear evolution. Wilson's respect in *Prehistoric Man* for American Indian civilizations echoes his mentor's conviction that inventive minds are characteristic of the primates, particularly humans—that "even the noble art of letters is . . . original alike amongst the ancient Egyptians and the dimly monumented Toltecans of Yucatán" (Chambers 1944[1844]:320–322). Bruce Trigger notes (1992:71) that Wilson, and we may add Chambers, seem ahead of their time in repudiating the arrant racism of John Lubbock. Yet, because both Wilson and Chambers perpetuated Scottish Enlightenment principles, they were more truly behind their time. As Scotsmen, Wilson and Chambers could not comfortably support the glorification of the English haute bourgeoisie and its imperialism promoted by Lubbock. Conversely, the English elite led by Lubbock's X-Club could not endorse the works of the petit bourgeois Scottish reformers.

Standard histories elevate only men of the right citizenship and class to the status of founding figures. Shapin (1994:305) points out that English gentlemen of science simply did not recognize "a woman, a servant, a Jew." Sir John Lubbock of London and Kent, fourth baronet, was worthy of recognition by his peers. A faraway college teacher in Canada, son of a poor Scots trades-man, could not be recognized by the gentlemen of the X-Club, nor could his works be adduced by researchers hoping for their valuable recognition (cf. Shapin 1994:299–302).

A history of archaeology seeking seminal work even if by a woman, a ser-vant, a Jew, or a Scottish exile in raw Toronto must acknowledge the clear precedence of Daniel Wilson's *The Archaeology and Prehistoric Annals of Scot-land* and *Prehistoric Man,* and their wide readership (especially of the 1876 edi-tion of the latter). The standard neglect of Daniel Wilson, as of his mentor Chambers, is a telling sign of the continuing power of social class over histori-cal narratives.

## Notes

1. A good case could be made for Jens Worsaae's 1842 *Danmarks Oltid (The Primeval Antiquities of Denmark,* Eng. trans. 1849), which laid out the principles of prehistoric archaeology and the manner in which antiquities could serve in nation building. Wilson and Lubbock, as well as Continental prehistorians, all acknowledged Worsaae's influence.

The influence of Wilson's *Prehistoric Man* is indicated by his 1864 election to the Société d'Anthropologie de Paris, his 1877 election to the chairmanship of Section H (Anthropology) of the American Association for the Advance-ment of Science, and Horatio Hale's 1893 remark that Wilson's book enjoyed "special success" in Germany (McCardle 1980:144–148).

2. Besides Lubbock, members included Thomas Huxley, Joseph Hooker, Herbert Spencer, George Busk, John Tyndall, Thomas Hirst, William Spottis-woode, and Edward Frankland.

3. Cribb (1980:353) points out the insidious effect of "quoting circles or citation cliques."

4. For discussion of "interest groups" in science, see for example, Barnes and MacKenzie (1979), and Collins (1985:129ff) for a constructive critique.

5. "Dr. Robert Chambers presented a curious admixture of antiquarian and conservative instincts, and old nonjuring [refers to the oath of allegiance to the Church of Scotland] sympathies, with an extreme liberalism in thought on all educational or scientific questions of his own day, which often gave occasion for friendly banter in the lighter moods of social intercourse. But he was himself very tender in regard to the feelings of others; and had all the sensitiveness of a singularly gentle and loving nature, which made his friends careful not to push their banter to an extreme. With his keen Jacobite senti-ment, and his no less ardent sympathy with all modern progress; his archaic veneration, and the bold scientific radicalism which won for him, rightly or not, the repute of author of the *Vestiges of Creation:* there was a rare compass in the genial sympathy of the man. . . . one who amid all the prosperity of maturer years, never forgot his early struggles, or allowed himself to grow cal-lous to early strugglers" (Wilson 1878:II, 150).

6. I thank James Secord for clarifying the chronology on this for me (personal communication, August 3, 1990).

7. Chambers, like Spencer after him, used Karl von Baer's embryology as described in English by William Carpenter, who wrote for W. and R. Chambers (Secord 1989:180–181, Gould 1977:109).

8. In December, 1848, Wilson applied for the position of Keeper of the Library of the Faculty of Advocates, Edinburgh (the forerunner of Edinburgh University Library), and solicited letters of support from his friends. Robert Chambers replied as follows: "Your age, your active habits, your obliging and courteous manners, and your general taste and talents in literature. . . . [Y]ou would conduct the business of the establishment vigorously and with great attention to details. You would maintain order, punctuality, and dispatch. You would be accessible and serviceable on all occasions" (R. Chambers 1848).

## References Cited

Ash, Marinell. n.d. "Life of Daniel Wilson." Ms. in possession of Ash's Margaret Mackay, School of Scottish Studies, Edinburgh University. Following Ash's death, a revised version was published with Elizabeth Hulse's editing: *Thinking with Both Hands: Sir Daniel Wilson in the Old World and the New.* Toronto: University of Toronto Press, 1999. Pp. 3–80.

Barnes, Barry and Donald MacKenzie. 1979. "On the role of interests in scientific change." In *On the Margins of Science: The Social Construction of Rejected Knowledge,* edited by Roy Wallis, 49–66. Sociological Review Monograph, no. 27. Keele: University of Keele.

Barton, Ruth. 1990. "An Influential Set of Chaps: The X-Club and Royal Society Politics 1864–65." *British Journal of the History of Science* 23: 53–81.

Bennett, Daphne. 1977. *King Without a Crown.* London: Heinemann.

Bowler, Peter. 1985. "Scientific Attitudes to Darwinism in Britain and America." In *The Darwinian Heritage,* edited by David Kohn. Princeton: Princeton University Press.

Brent, Peter. 1981. *Charles Darwin.* New York: Harper and Row.

Brown, David. 1979. *Walter Scott and the Historical Imagination.* London: Routledge and Kegan Paul.

Chambers, Robert. 1994[1844]. *Vestiges of the Natural History of Creation.* Facsimile edition, edited by James A. Secord. Chicago: University of Chicago Press. (Original edition, London: Churchill.)

———. 1994[1845]. *Explanations: A Sequel.* Facsimile edition, edited by James A. Secord. Chicago: University of Chicago Press. (Bound with *Vestiges of the Natural History of Creation.*) (Original edition, London: Churchill.)

———. 1848. Letter of 18 XII 1848, in "Testimonials in favor of Mr. D. W." Edinburgh University Library.

Chambers, William. 1883. *Memoir of William and Robert Chambers.* Edinburgh: W. & R. Chambers.

Cohen, I. Bernard. 1985. *Revolution in Science.* Cambridge: Belknap Press of Harvard University Press.

Collins, Harry M. 1985. *Changing Order.* London: Sage.

Combe, George. 1851. *The Constitution of Man Considered in Relation to External Objects.* 6th ed. Edinburgh: Machlachlan and Stewart; London: Longman and Simpkin, Marshall; Glasgow: Griffin; Dublin: James M'Glashan.

———. 1860. *The Constitution of Man Considered in Relation to External Objects.* 9th ed. Edinburgh: Machlachlan and Stewart; London: Longman and Simpkin, Marshall. (First edition 1828.)

Cooter, Roger. 1984. *The Cultural Meaning of Popular Science.* Cambridge: Cambridge University Press.

Cribb, Roger L. D. 1980. "A comment on Eugene L. Sterud's 'Changing aims in Americanist archaeology: a citation analysis of *American Antiquity.*'" *American Antiquity* 45 (2): 352–354.

Daniel, Glyn. 1950. *A Hundred Years of Archaeology.* London: Duckworth.

———. 1967. *The Origins and Growth of Archaeology.* Harmondsworth: Penguin.

Darwin, Francis, ed. 1958[1892]. *The Autobiography of Charles Darwin and Selected Letters.* Reprint. New York: Dover.

Davie, George Elder. 1964. *The Democratic Intellect.* 2nd ed. Edinburgh: Edinburgh University Press.

Desmond, Adrian. 1989. *The Politics of Evolution.* Chicago: University of Chicago Press.

Foucault, Michel. 1973. *The Order of Things.* New York: Vintage.

Fowler, Don D. 1987. "Uses of the past: archaeology in the service of the state." *American Antiquity* 52 (2): 229–248.

Gould, Stephen Jay. 1977. *Ontogeny and Phylogeny.* Cambridge: Belknap Press of Harvard University.

Haskell, Thomas L. 1977. *The Emergence of Professional Social Science.* Urbana: University of Illinois Press.

Hobsbawm, E. J. 1962. *The Age of Revolution, 1789–1848.* New York: New American Library.

Hudson, Kenneth. 1981. *A Social History of Archaeology.* London: Macmillan.

Hull, David L. 1985. "Darwinism as a historical entity: a historiographic proposal." In *The Darwinian Heritage,* edited by David Kohn, 773–812. Princeton: Princeton University Press.

Kehoe, Alice Beck. 1998. *The Land of Prehistory: A Critical History of American Archaeology.* New York: Routledge.

Kennedy, Roger G. 1994. *Hidden Cities: The Discovery and Loss of Ancient North American Civilization.* New York: Free Press.

Laudan, Rachel, Larry Laudan, and Arthur Donovan. 1988. *Scrutinizing Science.* Dordrecht: Kluwer.

Lovejoy, Arthur O. 1959. "The argument for organic evolution before the *Origin of Species,* 1830–1858." In *Forerunners of Darwin: 1745–1859,* edited by B. Glass, O. Temkin, and W. L. Straus, Jr., 356–414. Baltimore: Johns Hopkins University Press.

Lubbock, John. 1912[1865]. *Pre-historic Times.* 6th ed. Rev. London: Williams & Norgate.

McCardle, Bennett. 1980. "The Life and Anthropological Works of Daniel Wilson (1816–1892)." Master's thesis, University of Toronto.

Meek, Ronald L. 1976. *Social Science and the Ignoble Savage.* Cambridge: Cambridge University Press.

Millhauser, Milton. 1959. *Just Before Darwin.* Middletown: Wesleyan University Press.

Moore, James R. 1985. "Darwin of Down: the evolutionist as squarson-naturalist." In *The Darwinian Heritage,* edited by David Kohn, 435–481. Princeton: Princeton University Press.

———. 1986. "Crisis without revolution: the ideological watershed in Victorian England." *Revue de Synthèse* IV (1–2): 53–78.

Morrell, Jack and Arnold Thackray. 1981. *Gentlemen of Science.* Oxford: Clarendon Press.

Noble, Andrew. 1982. "Versions of the Scottish Pastoral: the Literati and the Tradition, 1780–1830." In *Order in Space and Society,* edited by Thomas A. Markus, 263–310. Edinburgh: Mainstream.

Piggott, Stuart. 1976. *Ruins in a Landscape.* Edinburgh: Edinburgh University Press.

Prichard, James C. 1841[1813]. *Researches into the Physical History of Man.* 4th ed., vol. I. London: John and Arthur Arch.

Rivière, Peter, ed. 1978. *The Origin of Civilization and the Primitive Condition of Man,* by John Lubbock, Baron Avebury. Classics in Anthropology. Chicago: University of Chicago Press.

Ruse, Michael. 1979. *The Darwinian Revolution.* Chicago: University of Chicago Press.

Russell, Colin. 1983. *Science and Social Change, 1700–1900.* London: Macmillan.

Secord, James A. 1985. "Darwin and the breeders: a social history." In *The Darwinian Heritage,* edited by David Kohn, 435–481. Princeton: Princeton University Press.

———. 1989. "Behind the veil: Robert Chambers and Vestiges." In *History, Humanity and Evolution,* edited by James R. Moore, 165–194. Cambridge: Cambridge University Press.

———. 1994. Introduction to *Vestiges of the Natural History of Creation and Other Evolutionary Writings,* by Robert Chambers. Edited by James A. Secord, vii–xlv. Chicago: University of Chicago Press.

Shapin, Stephen. 1981. "Science." In *A Companion to Scottish Culture,* edited by David Daiches, 318–322. London: Edward Arnold.

———. 1994. *A Social History of Truth: Civility and Science in Seventeenth-Century England.* Chicago: University of Chicago Press.

Sober, Elliott. 1985. "Darwin on natural selection: a philosophical perspective." In *The Darwinian Heritage,* edited by David Kohn, 867–899. Princeton: Princeton University Press.

Somkin, Fred. 1981. "Lubbock, Sir John (Lord Avebury)." In *Dictionary of Scientific Biography,* edited by C. C. Gillispie, 527–529. New York: Charles Scribner's Sons.

Stephen, Leslie. 1897. "Scott." In *Dictionary of National Biography,* edited by Sidney Lee, 80–105. London: Smith, Elder.

Steward, Julian. 1955. *Theory of Culture Change: The Methodology of Multilinear Evolution.* Urbana: University of Illinois Press.

Stocking, George W., Jr. 1987. *Victorian Anthropology.* New York: Free Press.

Trigger, Bruce G. 1989. *A History of Archaeological Thought.* Cambridge: Cambridge University Press.

——. 1992. "Daniel Wilson and the Scottish Enlightenment." *Proceedings of the Society of Antiquaries of Scotland* 122: 55–75.

Watt, Francis. 1887. "Chambers, Robert." In *Dictionary of National Biography,* edited by Leslie Stephen, 23–25. London: Smith, Elder.

Wilson, Daniel. 1848. *Memorials of Edinburgh in the Olden Time.* 2 vols. Edinburgh: Hugh Paton.

——. 1851. *The Archaeology and Prehistoric Annals of Scotland.* Edinburgh: Shetland and Knox; London: Simpkin, Marshall and J. H. Parker.

——. 1862. *Prehistoric Man.* Cambridge and London: Macmillan. (2nd ed., Macmillan, 1865; 3rd ed., Macmillan, 1876.)

——. 1863. Letter of April 2 to John Stuart Blackie. National Library of Scotland.

——. 1865. Letter of December 13 to Charles Lyell. Ms. Lyell 1, Edinburgh University Library.

——. 1878. *Reminiscences of Old Edinburgh.* Edinburgh: David Douglas.

Wolf, Eric R. 1994. "Perilous Ideas: Race, Culture, People." *Current Anthropology* 35 (1): 1–7, 10–11.

Worsaae, Jens J. 1849. *The Primeval Antiquities of Denmark.* Trans. by W. J. Thoms. London: Parker.

# 4

## Petrie's Head

## Eugenics and Near Eastern Archaeology

Neil Asher Silberman

In the annals of Near Eastern archaeological history and folklore, the life and achievements of William Matthew Flinders Petrie, even today, loom large. Petrie, whose gaunt, bearded image has been a familiar icon in archaeological textbooks for decades, is widely recognized by scholars as one of the founding fathers of the discipline. In that sense, he can be said to have helped establish the mainstream of a major branch of world archaeology. Petrie's 1890 excavation at Tell el-Hesy in southern Judea is almost universally celebrated as the official date of the beginning of "modern" archaeological research in the Holy Land (e.g., Albright 1957:49–52; Wright 1957:23–25; Schoville 1978:87–89; Mazar 1990:11; Biran and Aviram 1993). Indeed, conventional wisdom credits Petrie with being the first to demonstrate the importance of stratigraphy and artifact typology in Near Eastern excavation methodology, thereby laying the groundwork for all subsequent mainstream Near Eastern archaeological research (e.g., Callaway 1980, Fargo 1984, Drower 1985).

There is no question that Petrie's achievements within the discipline he helped create were impressive. From the time of his arrival in Egypt in 1880 at the age of 27 to his death in Jerusalem in 1942 at age 89, he excavated more than sixty of the most historically important—and richest—sites in Egypt and Palestine, published well over 100 excavation reports, general works, and monographs, and wrote almost 450 articles and about 400 reviews (Uphill 1972). His importance to Near Eastern archaeology, however, goes far beyond mere numbers. Dr. Valerie Fargo, project director of the renewed excavations at Tell el-Hesy (1970–1983), went so far as to assert that Petrie's methodological innovations "formed the very foundation of the work of all who followed him" (Fargo 1984:222).

Yet like so many other founding fathers, Petrie has also become the subject of colorful legends, whose folkloristic exaggerations often obscure a realistic view of his intellectual contribution to Near Eastern archaeology. Generations of archaeology students have been treated to tales of his uncanny instinct for choosing rich sites that other scholars had rejected; of his some-

69

times tyrannical control of staff and workers; and his outlandishly spartan lifestyle in the field (Drower 1985). Perhaps the most famous of the Petrie legends is, at least at first hearing, unconnected with digging or discovery. For it has become an oft-told anecdote among students of Near Eastern archaeology and visitors to Jerusalem that beneath the headstone marked with an ankh-sign and simply inscribed "Flinders Petrie" in the Protestant cemetery on Mount Zion lies a body . . . without a head.

This is not just an archaeological ghost story. Although several bizarre and unreliable versions of the story of Petrie's decapitation are familiar to scholars who have lived or worked in Jerusalem,[1] the story does have a basis in historical fact. According to Petrie's student and biographer, Margaret Drower, when the elderly and ailing Flinders Petrie was admitted to the government hospital in Jerusalem in the autumn of 1940, he requested that—should he not recover—his head be donated to the Royal College of Surgeons in London (Drower 1985: 424). And so it was done less than two years later—at the time of his death. Petrie's head was surgically removed by the Jerusalem hospital director, placed in a jar, and preserved with formaldehyde. Because of the wartime restrictions on merchant shipping in the Mediterranean, it was not possible to send the jar to England immediately, but in the autumn of 1944, it finally reached its destination in London, exported from Palestine with the cooperation of the director of Palestine Department of Antiquities, Robert Hamilton—in a box labeled as an antiquity.[2]

Why *did* Petrie donate his head to science? Drower mentions two reasons (1985:424). First, she suggests, Petrie was anxious that his head be studied as a specimen of a "typical" British skull. For the second reason, she quotes one of the attending physicians as expressing the hope that a physical examination of the great archaeologist's brain tissue might be able to "reveal some of the reasons for the remarkable capacity and retentive memory" Petrie had, even up to the day he died. Petrie's decision to donate his head to science is today often dismissed as an old man's eccentric whim, but I hope to demonstrate in this paper that Petrie's deathbed wish was entirely consistent with his lifelong belief in the power of race and heredity. I will further argue that some of Petrie's most important archaeological interpretations and methodological advances were profoundly shaped by this belief. Moreover, I will suggest that the story of Petrie's head can today serve as a cautionary tale for how intellectual—or in this case, archaeological—mainstreams may conceal within them philosophies or ideologies that have, over the course of time, become discredited or marginalized.

The particular philosophy so important in understanding Petrie's career is a late-nineteenth century racialist doctrine known as "eugenics"—a field of study, speculation, and biological engineering that was both popular and influential in England, Germany, and the United States until the Second World War (Higham 1965:150–153; Gould 1981; Kevles 1985; Proctor 1988). The term "eugenics" was coined in 1883 by Sir Francis Galton, a respected gentleman scholar in late Victorian England, world traveler and first cousin of

Charles Darwin, who sought to apply the principles of "natural selection" to the improvement of the human race (Cowan 1972; Forrest 1974; Fancher 1983; Stocking 1987:92–96). Although eugenics did not arise within an established disciplinary framework, its influence was enormous, due both to the author's powerful social connections and the ideological implications of his work (Cowan 1985).

According to the genetic theory first detailed in Galton's most famous book, *Hereditary Genius: An Inquiry into its Laws and Consequences,* various racial groups possess varying levels of inborn intelligence and other mental abilities—linked to their varying physical characteristics (Galton 1869:336–362). The ability of each race, so the theory went, could be measured to provide a clear hierarchy of racial groups, ranked by such criteria as intelligence, moral character, ambition, and creativity. Like the phrenologists before him, Galton had no doubt that these qualities were manifested in physical characteristics, and could thus be documented and measured precisely. The significance of racial differences was, in the minds of Galton and his followers, enormous. The movement of history, they contended, was propelled primarily by hereditary inequality—with "superior" races naturally dominating the "inferior" ones.

Galton, however, did not envision this scheme of inequality and domination as static. He believed that uncontrolled interbreeding between "superior" and "inferior" races led inevitably to the degeneration of the former, and to their eventual conquest by yet purer and superior racial groups. The thrust of eugenics was therefore not strictly historical; its main field of interest was the future. Galton and his followers actively opposed trade unionism and social welfare legislation for the British working class and the "inferior" immigrant races (primarily Irish, Jews, and Italians) then streaming into the country. They believed that England could stave off impending, disastrous racial degeneration only by careful "weeding" of the national "germ plasm," as the nation's genetic pool was then commonly called (Kevles 1985). This weeding was to be effected through strict supervision of marriage and reproduction within the native British population and tight restriction of immigration from abroad. In arguments that would reappear repeatedly at times of economic stress, the eugenicists argued that the abolition of most social welfare legislation would not only reduce an unfair burden borne by productive taxpayers but also allow the supposed "laws" of competition and natural selection to work freely in British society.

William Matthew Flinders Petrie came to the eugenics movement through a circuitous intellectual course. A sickly child, Petrie was educated at home by his middle class parents. His father, a freelance surveyor, inventor, and active member of a nonconformist Protestant sect, imbued Petrie with a fascination for ancient history and a particular obsession with Piazzi Smyth's quasi-religious doctrine of pyramidology (Petrie 1874; Tompkins 1978; Drower 1985:27–30). Growing up as a largely self-educated polymath, Petrie was quite clearly out of the intellectual mainstream of Victorian England, where university degrees had already been recognized as a primary criterion of academic respectability. Petrie had none. In fact, his decision in 1880 at age 27 to travel to Egypt at his own expense is ample evidence of his unconventional archaeological agenda. Deeply influenced by both biblical and historical determinism, Petrie was determined to undertake a detailed survey of the pyramids to assess their true symbolic or prophetic significance.

As it happened, Petrie's first project in Egypt completely undermined his faith in the theories of Piazzi Smyth, for Petrie's meticulous survey of the pyramids ultimately proved that many of Smyth's most important measurements were wrong (Petrie 1883). Yet while Petrie lost his faith in pyramidology, eugenics proved to be an attractive alternative with its own sweeping, deterministic theory of history. In fact, in 1880, shortly before leaving for Egypt, in response to Galton's public request for information on the hereditary gifts of native Britons, the 27-year-old Petrie had written a letter to Galton detailing his own quite impressive mathematical ability (Drower 1985:68, 476–477). Galton, always on the lookout for examples of unusual intelligence, was duly impressed by the self-educated young man and subsequently described Petrie as a mathematical genius (Galton 1883:95).

For Petrie, eugenics offered a way to reconceptualize himself as an insider, not an outsider. And in the colonial atmosphere of Egypt in the 1880s, it was a powerful ideological tool. Just two years after Petrie's arrival in Egypt, in 1882, the British invaded. The ease with which the British forces overran the country was widely seen (at least in England) as a substantiation of British racial vigor, a source of pride to all Englishmen, everywhere. Petrie, already a strong supporter of the idea of eugenics in the present, soon became one of its most eloquent advocates for the remote past. In 1883, after completing his Pyramid Survey, he was appointed an explorer for the British-funded Egyptian Exploration Society and in his early excavations at the Delta sites of Tanis, Naucratis, Nebesha, and Daphnae, he interpreted the great quantities of imported Greek pottery as evidence of earlier episodes of European and Middle Eastern racial contact, and conquest (Petrie 1890a:271–273, 276–277; Drower 1985:65–104).

In the meantime back in England, Francis Galton recognized the need for more extensive detailed statistics in order to substantiate his far-reaching genetic theories, and in 1884 opened what he called an "anthropometric laboratory" in London at the South Kensington Science Museum (Kevles 1985:14). In subsequent years, the skulls, height, weight, arm span, and even breathing power of thousands of visitors—schoolchildren, workmen on holiday, and vacationing families—were measured to provide a more accurate reading of the national "germ plasm." Because Galton was convinced that racial types remained stable over millennia, he needed anthropometric data on ancient populations as well. He therefore obtained the services of the temporarily unemployed Flinders Petrie to collect accurate measurements and photographs of the ancient Egyptians, Libyans, Hittites, Syrians, Nubians, and Bedouin, as they were depicted in relief on the various temple walls throughout Upper Egypt (Drower 1985:106).

The result of this eugenical expedition was Petrie's book *Racial Types from Egypt,* published in 1887, in which he began to apply Galton's modern ideas about racial mixture and the stability of types to archaeological material (Petrie 1887; see also Petrie 1888). Even after Petrie resumed his career of excavation—indeed for the rest of his life—the racial element remained central to his interpretation of ancient history and material culture remains. In 1887, he discovered a vast cemetery of Roman-period mummies with painted portraits at Hawara in the Fayyum and reported on what seemed to him to be the obvious mixture of native Egyptian and western anatomical types (Petrie 1888:130; Petrie 1889). And in 1888 in the Middle Kingdom levels at Illahun and the New Kingdom tombs at nearby Gurob, Petrie perceptively recognized the presence of Bronze Age Aegean pottery (Petrie 1890a:273–277; Petrie 1890b; Petrie 1891a). This was a truly impressive archaeological deduction, for Mycenaean pottery was still virtually unknown in Egypt and the Minoan culture of Crete would not be discovered for another twelve years. Yet for Petrie the principal significance of these pottery finds was racial: he termed the Aegean pottery "one of the great prizes we have been waiting for, the contemporary remains of the western races in their earliest contact with Egypt" (quoted in Drower 1985:149).

Petrie's initial historical theories in Egypt were based on a collation of finds from widely scattered sites. But his employment by the Palestine Exploration Fund in 1890 and his subsequent work at Tell el-Hesy in southern Judea confronted him with the challenge—and opportunity—of testing and ultimately illustrating Galton's theories of racial conquest and conflict at a site that had been continuously occupied for thousands of years. Methodologically, this *was* a challenge, for stratigraphical excavations—of the type pioneered in England by Augustus Pitt-Rivers (Thompson 1977) and by Heinrich Schliemann and Wilhelm Dörpfeld at the mound of Hissarlik (Döhl 1986)— were still within the realm of experimental archaeology. Petrie's achievement was not only to introduce these principles into Near Eastern archaeology, but to utilize them to bolster his racialist ideology (Silberman 1993).

Petrie, already becoming recognized as one of his generation's leading archaeologists, found Tell el-Hesy a perfect medium to illustrate his eugenical theories. By dividing the mound's deposits into discrete levels based on their characteristic pottery, he was able to outline several successive episodes of racial domination. And he saw in each of these episodes the eugenically predicted stages of conquest, *floruit,* and eventual decline. Because the site had been identified (mistakenly, as it turned out) with Lachish, one of the cities conquered by Joshua, Petrie not only associated a thick level of ash with that conquest, but added a eugenical commentary. "The invasion of the nomad horde of the Israelites on the high civilization of the Amorite kings," he wrote, "must have seemed a crushing blow to all culture and advance in the arts; it was much like the terrible breaking up of the Roman empire by the northern races; it swept away all good with the evil; centuries were needed to regain what was lost . . . " (Petrie 1891b:17).

The evidence of pottery was, of course, central to this interpretation. In his unhesitating identification of pottery styles with racial or ethnic groups, and in tracing each type through a regular pattern of initial appearance, growing popularity, and eventual degeneration, Petrie provided another clear illustration of the ideology of eugenics and the mechanics of racially based history. His description of the various pottery types at Tell el-Hesy sound uncannily similar to Galton's racial description of the unwitting immigrant and working class visitors to the Anthropometric Laboratory. Petrie spoke, for instance, of "Jewish" pottery as the result of "a mixture of characters," noting that some of the earlier Phoenician forms had "deteriorated, or passed into a mongrel type. . . . " The Amorite bowls, after the Israelite conquest, were represented by poorly made vessels, with "coarse, rough faces." And the earlier upright vessels with combed faces "survived only in a coarse type . . . " (Petrie 1891b:47–48).

While it is ultimately impossible to prove conclusively that Petrie's choice of these adjectives was directly influenced by his deep racial obsessions, it is unquestionable that race and racial conflict remained the primary emphasis of his career. Following his excavations in Palestine, Petrie returned to Egypt, and during the next twenty years, he refined his reading of the progress of ancient Near Eastern culture as a melodramatic Gilbert and Sullivan opera of racial destiny played out again and again throughout human history. He was by this time a thoroughly mainstream figure, acknowledged as a legitimate archaeological authority. In 1906, when Petrie was honored with the privilege of presenting the annual Huxley lecture to the Royal Anthropological Institute in London, he expounded on an unmistakably eugenical theme (Petrie 1906a). His lecture, entitled "Migrations," dealt with a subject crucial to his reading of history. Tracing the full range of Egyptian history that he had uncovered at sites like Meydum, Tell el-Amarna, Koptos, Naqada, Ballas, and Abydos, he saw an unending series of racial conquests, with the abler races in any given period, conquering and colonizing the exhausted ones.

Indeed, Petrie's parade of excavated physical types strangely mimicked the contemporary eugenical hierarchy of modern races, with the "hairy bushmen" of the Paleolithic period being ousted by the Berbers of the predynastic period. The Berbers were in turn conquered by a "dynastic race" from the Red Sea region, who were themselves displaced by the Sudanese at the end of the Old Kingdom. The Sudanese were followed by Caucasoid Hyksos, Nubians, Libyans, Greeks, Romans, and finally Arabs in the medieval period. Tracing the same sort of racial mixture and conquest in the formation of medieval Europe, Petrie argued that the contact and inevitable conflict of races, always described in purely anatomical terms, was the motive factor in all of human history.

By the time of his lecture to the Royal Anthropological Institute, Petrie had begun to utilize his intellectual authority to become active in a wide variety of modern political causes, including the British Constitution Association and the Anti-Socialist Society (Drower 1985:342–343). He also took time from his purely archaeological work to contribute a volume to a popular sociological series called "Questions of the Day," in which he made his eugenical faith explicit (Petrie 1906b). Confidently equating mental and physical variations in various modern races, he ascribed the present social problems of England to racial degeneration brought on by communism, trade unionism, and misguided government assistance to inferior human types. He concluded the book with a utopian vision of a future, eugenically improved world in which "the equatorial races, tending to have less initiative and vigor than those of colder climates . . . will tend to be each attached to a temperate land which will supply more energy to their development" (Petrie 1906b:103).

These ideas were further expanded in his book *The Revolutions of Civilisation,* published in 1911, which Petrie considered his most important work (Drower 1985:303–304, 428). "If the view really becomes grasped," he wrote, "that the source of every civilization has lain in race mixture, it may be that eugenics will, in some future civilization, carefully segregate fine races, until they have a distinct type" (Petrie 1911:131). This dogma of progress through the triumph of "fine" races was to guide his work for the rest of his life. All of Near Eastern history, he believed, was a function of interaction between biologically distinct races. In fact, near the end of his active field career, while digging at Tell el-Ajjul near Gaza, Petrie formulated and privately published a plan for the "revival of Palestine" in which he expressed the hope that "the various elements in this country will form a united whole" (Petrie 1937:6).[3]

Of course Petrie, like other supporters of eugenics, naturally believed that he himself was born of a "fine" race. Having proved to his own satisfaction throughout his archaeological career that the hereditary inequality of races was a key to understanding political and cultural history, Petrie hoped posthumously to serve the cause of racial science by allowing researchers of future generations to study his own quite exceptional head. Thus, he gave the deathbed order to his physicians at the Government Hospital in Jerusalem. This useless act of decapitation might be no more than a curious footnote to a brilliant archaeological career, were it not for the fact that Petrie's broader historical philosophy and archaeological interpretations were also permeated by dangerous racist assumptions. The practical consequences of such a doctrine, in theory and in practice, must be recognized by Petrie's scholarly successors today.

For by the time of Petrie's death in 1942, eugenics was no longer a harmless philosophy of progress; its racialist pseudo-science had become a warrant for racial discrimination and, ultimately, genocide. In England, the Eugenics Education Society sponsored the 1913 Mental Deficiency Act, with its sweeping classification of the "feebleminded" (Kevles 1985:99). In the United States, the Galton Society and the Eugenics Record Office at Cold Spring Harbor, Long Island were instrumental in the passage of the restrictive 1924 Immigration Act (Higham 1965:312–316). In 1933, racial legislation reached its ultimate and most horrible form in Nazi Germany's Eugenic Sterilization Law and aggressive policy of *Rassenhygiene* (Kevles 1985, Proctor 1988).

Revulsion at that final solution to "racial degeneration," however, ultimately paved the way for the final fall of eugenics, both as a respectable social program and a mainstream scientific theory (Kevles 1985; Barkan 1988, 1992). In the 1940s, a reexamination of Galton's statistics showed only a spurious correlation between intelligence and physical types (Kevles 1985:129–147). At the same time, the concept of "races" as distinct or even measurable entities was shown to be a dangerous oversimplification. In the 1950s, with the discovery of DNA and the beginning of research into population biology and the complexity of genetic inheritance (Haraway 1988), it became clear that the theory of eugenics had no basis in physical reality. Except for the continued loyalty of a small, fanatical following, eugenics was no longer considered mainstream science and was tossed on the trash heap of obsolete ideas.

Petrie's head, floating in formaldehyde at the Royal College of Surgeons, could therefore offer only a cautionary lesson. No medical student or scholar, so far as is known, ever gained any scientific insights from it. Although Lady Petrie was assured in 1948 that "the brain has been the subject of concentrated study" (Drower 1985:424), the scientific basis for such an examination had been completely undermined. For while Petrie's ability, intellect, commitment, and energy were undoubtedly great, those qualities were now seen as the product of family, environment, and opportunity, rather than membership in a phantom "British" race whose physical hallmarks could be recognized and measured in the folds of his cerebellum or in the size and shape of his skull.

That is certainly not to say that Petrie's severed head is today without interest to archaeologists concerned with the ideological development of their discipline. For while few contemporary scholars would openly subscribe to the racially based view of history and natural ability that so deeply influenced Petrie, the indirect impact of his eugenical thinking on Near Eastern archaeology endures. Even if no modern archaeologist would today speak of national "germ plasm" or favor laws to encourage racial improvement by sterilization or selective breeding, those ideas are still deeply (if unconsciously) embedded in the categories of significance of modern Near Eastern archaeology. Through the continuing use of Petrie's basic methodology of distinguishing discrete strata often uncritically linked to invasions of historically mentioned ethnic groups, race remains a prominent (though scientifically unverified) element in reconstructions of ancient Near Eastern history (Silberman 1991, 1995). The impact of theories of timeless conflict between "East" and "West," between "Desert" and "Sown," between "sedentary" and "nomadic" populations, between "Semites" and "Indo-Europeans" still offer intuitive (i.e., non-empirical) and deterministic models of cultural change. In the continuing recognition of rise-*floruit*-fall cycles in pottery types, scholars still implicitly illustrate the "rise" and (presumably inevitable?) "fall" of ancient ethnic groups.

This type of racialist thinking would be considered laughably outdated and marginal were it to be utilized in modern political science or sociology. Yet, strangely, it survives as an unspoken subtext of many mainstream Near Eastern archaeological narratives. Petrie's pioneering utilization of stratigraphy and pottery typology can not be easily separated from the larger ideology they served. Petrie's archaeological successors, who fondly claim him as a founding father, rarely recognize how much ideological baggage they have inherited from him. In their uncritical acceptance of Petrie's methodological innovations without due regard for his underlying ideological assumptions, modern Near Eastern archaeologists may be in danger of perpetuating the very same pseudo-scientific ideas about racial conflict and racial inequality that once filled Petrie's head.

## Notes

1. I have been able to isolate two main variants of the story. The first ascribes Petrie's posthumous decapitation to extreme, eccentric egotism, suggesting that since he was convinced of his own genius, he made the bizarre deathbed request that his brain be preserved for future generations so that the physical hallmarks of superior intelligence might be studied and understood. Unfortunately, because of wartime conditions prevailing at the time of Petrie's death in 1942, it was temporarily impossible to ship the severed head in its container to England. According to the story, it was subsequently kept at the American School of Oriental Research in Jerusalem (now the Albright Institute of Archaeological Research), where Petrie had lived in his last years. Here enters a macabre, comic element: the container was supposedly kept in the school's refrigerator, or, alternatively, was stored among the artifacts of its study collection—becoming a prop for grotesque practical jokes and a source of horrified reactions over the years until it was finally shipped to England after World War II.

The second main version of the "Petrie's Head" story ascribes the decapitation to the devotion of his wife, Lady Hilda Petrie, who, according to the stories lovingly kept her late husband's head in its container under her bed at the American School.

Both versions are equally preposterous, yet they are, even today, half facetiously retold by scholars who readily admit that they cannot vouch for their historical reliability. For this information, I am indebted to Mr. Joseph Zias and Dr. Benjamin Sass of the Israel Antiquities Authority.

2. Verification of this unusual export permit has been located in the administrative records of the Palestine Department of Antiquities preserved in the Palestine Archaeological (Rockefeller) Museum in Jerusalem. However, the relevant file, ATQ/979, opened sometime between October 12 and November 20, 1944, and marked "Confidential" (according to the file list) has itself disappeared. I obtained this information in a personal communication from Dr. Benjamin Sass of the Israel Antiquities Authority on January 15, 1988.

3. It should be noted, however, that in this last attempt at social philosophizing, Petrie made no specific mention of selective breeding or immutable

genetic characteristics. In his appeal for Jews and Arabs to establish cooperative settlements and share in the appreciation of public parks and historical
monuments as a means of establishing channels of communication, he provided a potentially non-racialist, if quixotic, vision of inter-ethnic harmony
in Palestine.

## References Cited

Albright, William F. 1957. *From the Stone Age to Christianity*. Garden City: Doubleday.
Barkan, Eleazar. 1988. "Mobilizing Scientists Against Nazi Racism, 1933–
1939." In *Bones, Bodies, Behavior: Essays on Biological Anthropology*, edited
by George W. Stocking, 180–205. Madison: University of Wisconsin Press.
———. 1992. *The Retreat of Scientific Racism: Changing Concepts of Race in Britain and the United States Between the World Wars*. Cambridge: Cambridge
University Press.
Biran, Avraham and Joseph Aviram, eds. 1993. *Biblical Archaeology Today 1990*.
Jerusalem: Israel Exploration Society.
Callaway, Joseph A. 1980. "Sir Flinders Petrie: Father of Palestinian Archaeol-
ogy." *Biblical Archaeology Review* 6: 44.
Cowan, Ruth Schwartz. 1972. "Francis Galton's Statistical Ideas: The Influence
of Eugenics." *Isis* 63: 509–528.
———. 1985. *Sir Francis Galton and the Study of Heredity in the 19th Century*.
New York: Garland.
Döhl, Hartmut. 1986. "Schliemann the Archaeologist." In *Myth, Scandal, and
History*, edited by William M. Calder and David A. Traill, 95–109. Detroit:
Wayne State University Press.
Drower, Margaret S. 1985. *Flinders Petrie: A Life in Archaeology*. London: Victor
Gollancz.
Fancher, Raymond E. 1983. "Biographical Origins of Francis Galton's Psychol-
ogy." *Isis* 74: 227–233.
Fargo, Valerie M. 1984. "A Portrait: Sir Flinders Petrie." *Biblical Archaeologist*
47: 220–223.
Forrest, D. W. 1974. *Francis Galton: The Life and Work of a Victorian Genius*.
London: Taplinger.
Galton, Francis. 1869. *Hereditary Genius: An Inquiry into its Laws and Conse-
quences*. London: Macmillan.
———. 1883. *Inquiries into the Human Faculty*. London: Macmillan.
Gould, Stephen Jay. 1981. *The Mismeasure of Man*. New York: W. W. Norton.
Haraway, Donna J. 1988. "Remodeling the Human Way of Life: Sherwood
Washburn and the New Physical Anthropology, 1950–1980." In *Bones,
Bodies, Behavior: Essays on Biological Anthropology*, edited by George W.
Stocking, 206–259. Madison: University of Wisconsin Press.
Higham, John. 1965. *Strangers in the Land: Patterns of American Nativism,
1860–1925*. New York: Atheneum.
Kevles, Daniel J. 1985. *In the Name of Eugenics: Genetics and the Uses of Human
Heredity*. Berkeley: University of California Press.

Mazar, Amihai. 1990. *Archaeology of the Land of the Bible*. New York: Double-day.

Petrie, William M. F. 1874. *Researches on the Great Pyramid*. London: W. H. Dalton.

———. 1883. *The Pyramids and Temples of Gizeh*. London: Field and Tuer.

———. 1887. *Racial Types from Egypt*. London: privately printed.

———. 1888. "The Earliest Racial Portraits." *Nature* 39: 128–130.

———. 1889. *Hawara, Biahmu, and Arsinoe*. London: Field and Tuer.

———. 1890a. "The Egyptian Bases of Greek History." *Journal of Hellenic Studies* 11: 271–277.

———. 1890b. *Kahun, Gurob, and Hawara*. London: Kegan, Paul, Trench, Krübner.

———. 1891a. *Illahun, Gurob, and Hawara, 1889–90*. London: Nutt.

———. 1891b. *Tell el-Hesy (Lachish)*. London: Palestine Exploration Fund.

———. 1906a. "Migrations." *Journal of the Royal Anthropological Institute* 36: 189–232.

———. 1906b. *Janus in Modern Life*. London: Constable.

———. 1911. *The Revolutions of Civilisation*. London: Harper.

———. 1937. *The Revival of Palestine*. Jerusalem: The Commercial Press.

Proctor, Robert. 1988. "From *Anthropologie* to *Rassenkunde* in the German Anthropological Tradition." In *Bones, Bodies, Behavior: Essays on Biological Anthropology*, edited by George W. Stocking, 138–179. Madison: University of Wisconsin Press.

Schoville, Keith N. 1978. *Biblical Archaeology in Focus*. Grand Rapids: Baker Book House.

Silberman, Neil Asher. 1991. "Desolation and Restoration: The Impact of a Biblical Concept on Near Eastern Archaeology." *Biblical Archaeologist* 54: 76–87.

———. 1993. "Petrie and the Founding Fathers." In *Biblical Archaeology Today 1990*, edited by Avraham Biran and Joseph Aviram, 545–554. Jerusalem: Israel Exploration Society.

———. 1995. "Promised Lands and Chosen Peoples: The Politics and Poetics of Archaeological Narrative." In *Nationalism, Politics, and the Practice of Archaeology*, edited by Philip Kohl and Clare Fawcett, 249–262. Cambridge: Cambridge University Press.

Stocking, George W. 1987. *Victorian Anthropology*. New York: The Free Press.

Thompson, Michael W. 1977. *General Pitt-Rivers: Evolution and Archaeology in the Nineteenth Century*. Bradford-On-Avon: Moonraker Press.

Tompkins, Peter. 1978. *The Secrets of the Great Pyramid*. London: Penguin.

Uphill, Eric P. 1972. "A Bibliography of Sir William Matthew Flinders Petrie (1853–1942)." *Journal of Near Eastern Studies* 31: 356–379.

Wright, G. Ernest. 1957. *Biblical Archaeology*. Philadelphia: Westminster Press.

# 5

## Augustus Le Plongeon

## A Fall from Archaeological Grace

Lawrence Desmond

> Poor Man [Augustus Le Plongeon]! [W]hy are some people accepted & not others? Dr. Seler often makes mistakes, & changes his opinions, but he founds a school & is thought a shining light.
> *(Adela Breton, February 15, 1909. In Giles and Stewart 1989:18)*

Why was Augustus Le Plongeon, a pioneering Mayanist, renowned for having made the earliest thorough and systematic photographic documentation of archaeological sites in Yucatán, later regarded by archaeologists as no more than a troublesome eccentric who proposed preposterous theories about the Maya?

To understand the process of Augustus Le Plongeon's rejection by mainstream archaeology, we will first look at his development as a Mayanist and how he came to his conclusions about the Maya and Egypt, and then review the many professional conflicts which developed between Le Plongeon and other Americanists.

Le Plongeon's initial contact with archaeology came in the 1860s while he was working in Peru as a photographer. The use of photography for documentation and research was obvious to Le Plongeon who was familiar with the pioneering photographic work of Maxime du Camp and Francis Frith in Egypt.

He had departed in 1862 for Lima after ten years in San Francisco as a photographer, and spent eight years in the Andean region working as a commercial and archaeological photographer. His travels were extensive. He photographed all the important archaeological sites in the region and took photos of artifacts in his studio. He was hired as a photographer by diplomat-archaeologist Ephraim G. Squier to make illustrations for his book, *Peru: Incidents of Travel and Explorations in the Land of the Incas* (1877).

It was while Le Plongeon was in Peru that he became intrigued with the civilizations of the New World, and sought to understand their origins and development. He found photography to be an excellent tool to record archaeological subjects, but soon realized there were no easy answers to questions of civilization and origins.

In search of ideas, he read the works of important Americanists of the time such as the French scholar Abbé Charles Etienne Brasseur de Bourbourg. Brasseur, writing on the civilizations of the Americas in the 1850s, provided the foundation for Le Plongeon's developing theory that the New World was the place of origin of world civilization. By the 1870s he had concluded the Maya had founded ancient Egyptian civilization, but within twenty years his conclusions were found unacceptable.

Leaving Peru in 1870, Le Plongeon returned to San Francisco and lectured on his Peruvian finds at the California Academy of Sciences, and then traveled to London for research at the British Museum. While at the museum he met the photographer Alice Dixon. Alice Dixon had learned photography from her father Henry Dixon who was known in London for his photographs of important buildings and monuments, art objects, and as one of the inventors of panchromatic film.

Intrigued with both modern and ancient Maya civilization after her long talks with Le Plongeon, Alice Dixon concurred with him that an accurate and systematic photographic record should be made of the Maya ruins for later analysis and to illustrate their writings. The living Maya of the nineteenth century also captured her imagination, and she began a lifelong study of their language and culture.

Before leaving for Mexico, Augustus Le Plongeon stated he was going there "with the fixed intention of finding either proof or the denial of an opinion formed during my ramblings among the ruins of Tiahuanuco, that the cradle of the world's civilization is this continent on which we live" (1879:69).

Thus, his first step into the world of Mesoamerican studies was controversial. Brantz Mayer, writing for the Smithsonian Institution in 1857, had admonished scholars to be strictly inductive: "The American antiquarian should, as yet, avoid the peril of starting in his investigations with an hypothesis. . . . " (Mayer 1857:2). Mayer was expressing the view of most scholars of the time including Samuel Haven, librarian for the American Antiquarian Society and manuscript reviewer for its *Proceedings*. Le Plongeon knew he was on a collision course with the scholar Haven, but seems to have disregarded the potential consequences.

As expected, Haven rejected one of Le Plongeon's first articles for the *Proceedings*, "Archaeological communication on Yucatán," submitted in 1879, but Stephen Salisbury, Jr., son of the founder of the American Antiquarian Society and influential in Latin American studies, disregarded Haven's rejection and approved publication.

Salisbury had a great interest in the Maya which had been developed through his friendship with David Casares, a Yucatecan, during their days at Harvard College. After college Casares invited Salisbury to visit his family and the Maya ruins, and he spent considerable time traveling in the Yucatán.

After Salisbury became president of the American Antiquarian Society, he continued for many years to support archaeology in Yucatán and backed the appointment of Edward H. Thompson, known for his archaeological work at Chichén Itzá, to replace Louis Aymé as American Consul in Mérida in the mid-1880s. The position of consul provided Aymé, and then Thompson, with financial support while they carried out their archaeological investigations.

In 1873, the recently married Le Plongeons left New York for Mérida, capital of the state of Yucatán. Warned by authorities against landing at the port of Progreso because of yellow fever, the Le Plongeons recklessly disembarked and soon were on their way to Mérida. Shortly after their arrival Alice Le Plongeon contracted the fever, but luckily survived. Their first two years were spent near Mérida learning local customs and the Maya language, writing about life in the capital, working in the archives, and visiting the ruins at Uxmal.

At Uxmal, determined to adhere to their plan of systematic and thorough recording, the Le Plongeons photographed, surveyed and drew plans of all important architecture including the Adivino Pyramid, Nunnery Quadrangle, and Governor's Palace, and made molds of and photographed the most important motifs and iconography. In a *tour de force* of early wet plate photography, the Le Plongeons photographed the intricate stone motifs of the entire length of the Governor's Palace east facade in overlapping stereo photos using a twenty foot tall tripod to raise the large view camera high enough to make distortion-free photos.

Uxmal provided Le Plongeon with his first evidence that the New World was the source of world civilization. A Freemason, Le Plongeon noted a number of motifs on Temple IV of the Adivino Pyramid which he related to Masonic iconography. These included crossed bones and skeletons with hands raised, and a carved hand on an apron on the lower half of a sculptured bust.

But for Le Plongeon, the most important evidence of cultural diffusion was the Mayas' corbelled arch. The arches of Temple V atop the Adivino Pyramid, he believed, had proportions that related to the "mystic numbers 3.5.7" which he stated were used by ancient Masonic master builders (Le Plongeon 1886:37). Those same proportions, he also noted, were found in tombs in Chaldea and Etruria, in ancient Greek structures, and as part of the Great Pyramid in Egypt, and were due, he said, to Maya influence. While some scholars already had reservations about Maya influence in ancient Egypt, there was little serious opposition to his views until the chronology of Egypt was fully developed.

Inspired by their exciting finds at Uxmal, the Le Plongeons traveled to Chichén Itzá in 1875 with a small force of armed soldiers to begin their work. There had been considerable danger from the Chan Santa Cruz Maya who controlled large areas of the Yucatán peninsula east of Mérida, so the Le Plongeons had waited two years until they could muster armed protection for their work. As at Uxmal, they began with documentation of all standing architecture, motifs, and iconography, by photography and molds, and surveyed and drew plans of the most important structures.

While Uxmal provided a link to the Old World through Masonry, it was at Chichén Itzá that the Le Plongeons thought they had found the Mayas' own account of their history, including an exodus to Egypt by a Maya queen. The key pieces of evidence were murals in the Upper Temple of the Jaguars, and a statue they called Chaacmol or "Thunder Paw" (now called Chacmool) which they had excavated from the Platform of the Eagles and Jaguars.

In his book *Sacred Mysteries Among The Mayas and the Quiches* Le Plongeon wrote, "There [at Chichén Itzá], we not only see their portraits carried in bas-relief, on stone or wood, or their marble statues in the round, or represented in the mural paintings that adorn the walls of the funeral chamber [Upper Temple of the Jaguars] built to the memory of the victim, but we discover [in the Platform of the Eagles and Jaguars] the ornaments they wore, the weapons they used, nay, more, their mortal remains" (1886:84).

In short, his interpretation of the murals and iconography at Chichén Itzá and Uxmal allowed him to develop a single generation account of the Maya elite at those sites. He also concluded that the Platform of the Eagles and Jaguars was the burial place of Chaacmol, prince consort to a dethroned Maya queen who had escaped to Egypt. He excavated the mound, and to his delight the statue of Chaacmol was recovered. The find was fortunate because it brought to light an outstanding example of Maya sculpture, but unfortunate because it convinced Le Plongeon that his iconographic interpretation, and therefore, diffusionist theories were correct. He would defend those ideas to the day he died.

After several months at Chichén Itzá, the Le Plongeons returned to Uxmal, and work there provided Le Plongeon with additional support of his regional history of the Maya.

Uxmal, according to Le Plongeon, was a rival to Chichén Itzá under the control of a Maya prince he called Aac who occupied Chichén Itzá after he defeated his brother and sister, Chaacmol and Móo. The evidence Le Plongeon found to bolster his history of two cities was a carved stone profile near the north end of the east facade of the Governor's Palace which he identified as the Maya Queen Móo, the sculpture of another brother he called Prince Cay, and a sculpture of Aac over the center door of the Governor's Palace.

In Le Plongeon's words, "Aac caused his statue—the feet resting on the flayed bodies of his kind [members of the defeated royal family], their heads being suspended from his belt—to be placed over the main entrance of the royal palace at Uxmal" (1886:82).

Augustus Le Plongeon felt that the extensive time he and Alice Le Plongeon had spent in the ruins and among the living Maya allowed him to disregard the prevailing moratorium on interpretation. In 1857, Brantz Mayer issued a second admonition that Le Plongeon chose to ignore:

"In the present state of archaeology, all labors should be contributions
to that store of facts, which, in time, may form a mass of testimony
whence future historians shall either draw a rational picture of ante-
Columbian civilization, or be justified in declaring that there is nothing
more to be disclosed" (1857:2).

Had Le Plongeon done no more than document Uxmal and Chichén Itzá, avoiding all but the most minor of interpretations, he might be regarded today as one of the fathers of American archaeology. Unfortunately, he considered his interpretations as important as his documentation.

When he began his writings on the Maya and Egypt he found few who would oppose his conclusions. He could juggle the origins of the two civilizations with little worry of contradiction. But, within a few years of his first pronouncements, he was faced with new data that placed the Maya much later than ancient Egypt. And even before 1896 when he published what he considered his most important work, serious doubts were being raised about his theories. But, it seems there was more to the dispute than a rarefied theoretical argument about the merits of cultural diffusion. The feuds with colleagues that began in the 1880s may have also contributed to his downfall.

In 1881 Le Plongeon began writing to his patron Stephen Salisbury, Jr. about the incompetence of Louis Aymé, American Consul in Mérida, as a photographer and archaeologist, but the complaints fell on what, he felt, were deaf ears. Thus, in 1882 Le Plongeon resigned from the Society with an angry letter filled with accusations against Aymé.

Two years later as part of their documentation at Chichén Itzá, the Le Plongeons made tracings of the murals in the Upper Temple of the Jaguars. The murals were already in a bad state of decay due to the tropical heat and humidity, but Alice Le Plongeon reported in an article published by *Scientific American* in August, 1884, that she and Augustus Le Plongeon had been told by soldiers in their escort that the American Consul in Mérida, Louis Aymé, had defaced the murals, attempting to clean them by "scratching" the dirt off with a machete.

Possibly having heard of the impending *Scientific American* article through connections in the very close Mérida community, Aymé wrote to Stephen Salisbury, Jr. in June 1884, "I have decided that I will not return to Mérida as U.S. Consul," and petitioned his friends in high places for a position in Peru. "I shall invoke your aid and the powerful influence of Senator Hoar on my behalf" (Aymé 1884). Augustus Le Plongeon's victory over Aymé in 1884 solved nothing, and turmoil continued in his professional life.

Within a few months of Le Plongeon's resignation from the American Antiquarian Society in 1882, Phillip J. J. Valentini published his article, "The Olmecas and the Tultecas," in the *Proceedings of the American Antiquarian Society,* and in it, two of Le Plongeon's photographs of bearded figures in bas-relief taken at Chichén Itzá.

The photos were published without the permission of Le Plongeon. To make matters worse, Valentini's photo captions stated that the beards on the photographed bas-relief figures had been retouched into the photos by Le Plongeon in order to bolster his diffusionist theories. It is interesting that the photos and captions have no association with his article! They appear to have been inserted to discredit Le Plongeon. The original negatives and prints are not retouched.

On a personal level, Valentini may have been stirred to action by Le Plongeon's letter to Salisbury in 1880 in which he states that Valentini had failed to cite the contribution of Mexican scholar Alfredo Chavero in an 1878 article focused on the "Mexican calendar stone." It is also possible that Valentini believed the photos to be faked and saw this as an opportunity to not only discredit Le Plongeon the diffusionist, but to bolster the strong anti-diffusionist paradigm then developing in American archaeology.

Valentini knew of the 1877 article published by the American Antiquarian Society where Le Plongeon used a description of the bearded figures to bolster his own diffusionist views. The description follows: "Did the bearded men whose portraits are carved on the massive pillars of the fortress [Castillo Pyramid] at Chichén Itzá, belong to the Mayan nation? The Maya language is not devoid of words from Assyrian" (Salisbury 1877:99). The statement was probably allowed in print by Haven because Salisbury is named as author, but the actual author is Augustus Le Plongeon and the article is a reprint of his letters from Yucatán.

He also resented the Society's financial support of the photographer Désiré Charnay. Charnay's photographic work had received funding from the French government for what Le Plongeon considered imperialistic purposes, but adding to the controversy, Le Plongeon declared that he had heard from his Mexican colleagues that Charnay's writings and archaeological fieldwork were a kind of joke to the Mexicans.

Any support Le Plongeon received by aligning himself with the scholarship of the Americanist Brasseur de Bourbourg was seriously eroded after 1882. The influential historian Hubert Bancroft and other scholars were particularly critical of Brasseur's *Quatre Lettres sur le Mexique,* published in 1868 shortly before his death. Brasseur, whose earlier scholarship had been considered an important contribution to Americanist studies, and still is, fell from favor during this period. Bancroft wrote of Brasseur's *Quatre Lettres,* that they are "a chaotic jumble of facts and wild speculations that would appall the most enthusiastic antiquarian" (1882:128). Le Plongeon would soon face similar reviews of his writings.

Le Plongeon's feuds with Aymé, Charnay, and Valentini were followed by an even more outrageous conflict with Daniel Brinton. Brinton, one of the most powerful of Americanist scholars, was a major factor in his downfall.

After the Le Plongeons returned to New York in 1884, Augustus Le Plongeon wrote a number of journal articles, and in 1886 published his book, *Sacred Mysteries among the Mayas and Quiches, 11,500 years ago.* At the time of the publication he seems to have been on good terms with Brinton.

He then began work on *Queen Móo and the Egyptian Sphinx,* published in 1896. Based on his earlier work, *Sacred Mysteries,* it presented all his evidence that the Maya were the source of Egyptian civilization.

Throughout his writings, including "The Origins of the Egyptians" published posthumously in 1913, he compares modern and ancient Maya and

Egyptian ethnography, architecture, linguistics, iconography, and religious practices to prove that Maya culture diffused to Egypt. By using the comparative method he seems on the right track, and we should give him credit for making a number of insightful observations within the context of an exciting new field where few scholarly works could be drawn upon.

But, his explanation of the proposed cultural links between the Maya and Egypt does not fit what was known about the Maya or ancient Egypt in the late nineteenth century, and is written in a style that makes substantiation of his explanations extremely difficult. By the late nineteenth century most scholars, with Daniel Brinton in the vanguard, were convinced that he had failed to prove his diffusionist theory.

In 1885, Brinton, a noted scholar and first chair of archaeology at the University of Pennsylvania, had paid a visit to the Le Plongeons at their home in Brooklyn. He complimented them on the excellence of their photographs and drawings. But, Brinton took exception to "the analogies the doctor thinks he has discovered between the Maya culture and language, and those of Asia and Africa" (Brinton 1885:378).

The trouble intensified in 1887 when Le Plongeon concluded, with some evidence, that Brinton was behind the suspicious circumstances that prevented the Le Plongeons from giving papers at the annual meeting of the American Association for the Advancement of Science.

The dispute reached a serious level when a frustrated Le Plongeon charged that Brinton, who in fact had never done fieldwork in the Maya area, was a "mere closet archaeologist" (1896:203). The level of conflict became absurd when Brinton labeled Le Plongeon an "eccentric" for proposing the Maya used the meter as a standard of measure, and Le Plongeon countered that Brinton had proposed that the Maya used the cubit!

Brinton withdrew from the conflict when Le Plongeon challenged him twice to a public debate on Maya history and religion. Both challenges, one in 1893 and the second in 1894, were published in New York newspapers. The 1894 challenge was published to coincide with the annual meeting of the American Association for the Advancement of Science in Brooklyn, and may have been timed to embarrass Brinton who was then president of the Association.

From 1892 to 1894 Le Plongeon found his views rejected by other members of the academy, as well, and he responded as follows:

> I have been accused of promulgating notions on ancient America contrary to the opinion of men regarded as authorities on American Archaeology. And so it is, indeed. Mine is not the fault, however, although it may be my misfortune, since it has surely entailed upon me their enmity and its consequences. But who are those pretended authorities? Certainly not the doctors and professors at the head of the universities and colleges in the U.S.; for not only do they know absolutely nothing

of Ancient American civilization, but, judging from letters in my possession, the majority of them refuse to learn anything concerning it
(1896:xxi).

Brinton's unwillingness to debate or react to Le Plongeon led to his isolation, and we find him seldom mentioned in scholarly journals after this time.

Augustus Le Plongeon's support of the women's movement during this period should also be mentioned. Alice Le Plongeon was asked to participate in
a feminist symposium at the Columbian Exposition in Chicago in 1896, but
could not afford the travel expense. In a letter to the organizer she explained
that the movement not only had her support, but that Augustus Le Plongeon
had long been an active promoter of women's rights. While no written evidence has been found to support discrimination against Alice and Augustus Le
Plongeon for their involvement in the movement, it seems reasonable to assume that it may have added to their problems.

One of the few professional statements on Le Plongeon's work after the
turn of the century is a review in 1904 of *Queen Móo and the Egyptian Sphinx*
in the *American Antiquarian and Oriental Journal* by C. Stanisland Wake.

Wake wondered, as we do, "Why, then, have they [scholars] practically
agreed to taboo the work he has done?" With great insight for the times, he
then suggested: "Specialists are very apt to look with an unfavorable eye on
anything outside their own particular specialty, particularly . . . the work of
an 'amateur,' or, let us say, a non-professional." And, he compliments Le
Plongeon for "the good work he has done in collecting information which will
aid largely someday in deciding the important question of American origins"
(1904:361).

While Wake clearly understood the effects of archaeological professionalism on the self-taught generation, he also understood a deeper problem associated with Le Plongeon's work: "[T]here is something radically wrong with
the author's [Le Plongeon's] explanation of the facts" (Wake 1904:361).

Augustus Le Plongeon defended his explanation of the facts to the end. He
died of heart failure in 1908. Alice Le Plongeon died prematurely at the age of
59, in 1910.

In 1931, Carnegie Institution archaeologist Sylvanus Morley, and Frans
Blom, director of the Middle American Research Institute at Tulane University,
were offered the photographs and manuscripts of the Le Plongeons by Maude
A. Blackwell, who had inherited the collection from Alice Le Plongeon in
1910. Morley and Blom failed to conclude the purchase and the photographs
and manuscripts were purchased by Manly P. Hall, president of the Philosophical Research Society in Los Angeles and sympathetic to Le Plongeon's views
(Desmond 1983:8–12).

In 1962, archaeologist Robert Wauchope brought Augustus Le Plongeon
back into the limelight in his book *Lost Tribes and Sunken Continents*.
Wauchope, an important scholar, appears to have been particularly incensed
by Le Plongeon and his theories. He devotes part of a chapter to a criticism of

all aspects of Le Plongeon's life, ending with the following statement: "[H]is [Le Plongeon's] arrogant flaunting of his own ego produced a lurid epoch in the history of American archaeology" (1962:8). Le Plongeon may have had more influence on American archaeology than has been credited to him if we are to accept Wauchope's perspective.

After Wauchope, writers seem to stretch their imaginations to characterize Le Plongeon, and one wonders how they come to their conclusions. Were he alive today, C. S. Wake might ask again if something might be "radically wrong."

In 1973, the historian Robert Brunhouse in his book *In Search of the Maya*, presented a chapter on Le Plongeon, and characterized him as a kind of scholarly chameleon: "mysterious, preposterous, opinionated, haphazardly informed, reckless, and a remarkable figure" (1973:137, 164).

More recently, Charles Gallencamp described him as a "French antiquarian and mystic" (1985:32), and the important scholar Mary Miller sees him as a "master of self-deception" (1985:7).

Mexican scholar Jaime Litvak King sees him as "bigger than life in his time, and today when the world is quite a bit blander, a reminder that things weren't always so" (Desmond and Messenger 1988:xiii).

"Bigger than life," stubborn, and outspoken, Augustus Le Plongeon refused to be silenced. He desperately fought to keep his diffusionist ideas alive, but even before his death he faced attacks on his character by archaeologists. There is little worse for an archaeologist than to be accused of falsifying data, and more damning than to be convicted by an invisible court.

C.S. Wake is correct in his assessment of Le Plongeon—he had the facts, but it is his explanation of them that does not fit. Charles Darwin in *The Descent of Man* (1871:385) takes the following position: "False views, if supported by some evidence, do little harm, as everyone takes a salutary pleasure in proving their falseness." Augustus Le Plongeon's views were easily disproved once archaeology developed a firm chronology for the Maya and Egypt, but merely demolishing his theories appears not to have been enough for the new field of scientific archaeology.

As Darwin pointed out, "False facts are highly injurious to the progress of science, for they long endure" (Darwin 1871:385). Ironically, the supposed facts of Le Plongeon's mysticism, fakery, and personality disorders, fostered by archaeologists, have long endured.

## References Cited

Aymé, Louis. 1884. Letter to Stephen Salisbury, Jr., June 11. American Antiquarian Society, Worcester.

Bancroft, Hubert H. 1882. *The works of Hubert Howe Bancroft*, vol. V. San Francisco: A. L. Bancroft and Company.

Brinton, Daniel. 1885. "Notes on American Ethnology." *The American Antiquarian and Oriental Journal* 8 (6): 378.

Brunhouse, Robert L. 1973. *In Search of the Maya*. Albuquerque: University of New Mexico Press.

Darwin, Charles. 1871. *The Descent of Man and Selection in Relation to Sex*, vol. II. London: John Murray.

Desmond, Lawrence G. and Phyllis M. Messenger. 1988. *A Dream of Maya*. Albuquerque: University of New Mexico Press.

Desmond, Lawrence G. 1983. "Augustus Le Plongeon: Early Maya Archaeologist." Ph.D. diss. University of Colorado, Boulder.

Gallencamp, Charles. 1985. *Maya: Treasures of an ancient civilization*. New York: Harry N. Abrams.

Giles, Sue and Jennifer Stewart, eds. 1989. *The Art of the Ruins*. Bristol: City of Bristol Museum and Art Gallery.

Le Plongeon, Alice. 1884. "Dr. Le Plongeon's latest and most important discoveries among the ruined cities of Yucatán." *Scientific American* Supplement 448 (August 3), 7143–7144.

Le Plongeon, Augustus. 1879. "Archaeological communication on Yucatán." *Proceedings of the American Antiquarian Society* (72): 65–75.

———. 1886. *Sacred Mysteries among the Mayas and Quiches, 11,500 years ago*. New York: Macoy Publishing.

———. 1896. *Queen Móo and the Egyptian Sphinx*. New York: Privately printed.

———. 1913. "The Origins of the Egyptians." *Word Magazine* (Theosophical Publishing Company) 17: 9–20, 70–83, 161–176, 196–209, 273–281, and 345–360.

———. 1913–14. "The Origins of the Egyptians." *Word Magazine* (Theosophical Publishing Company) 18: 47–60, 67–84, 181–190, 224–228.

Mayer, Brantz. 1857. *Observations on Mexican history and archaeology, with special notice of Zapotec remains*. Smithsonian Contributions to Knowledge, vol. 9. Washington, D.C.: Smithsonian.

Miller, Mary E. 1985. "A re-examination of the Mesoamerican Chacmool." *Art Bulletin* 67 (1): 7–17.

Salisbury, Stephen Jr. 1877. "Dr. Le Plongeon in Yucatán." *Proceedings of the American Antiquarian Society* (69): 70–119.

Squier, Ephraim G. 1877. *Peru: Incidents of Travel and Explorations in the Land of the Incas*. New York: Harper and Brothers.

Thompson, Charles O. 1880. Letter to Stephen Salisbury, Jr. American Antiquarian Society, Worcester.

Valentini, Phillip J. 1882. "The Olmecas and the Tultecas." In *Proceedings of the American Antiquarian Society* (new series) II: 193–230.

Wake, C. Stanisland. 1904. "The Mayas of Central America." *American Antiquarian and Oriental Journal* 26: 361–363.

Wauchope, Robert. 1962. *Lost Tribes and Sunken Continents*. Chicago: University of Chicago Press.

# 6

## American Palestinian and Biblical Archaeology

## End of an Era?

William G. Dever

### Introduction

Archaeology in the "Lands of the Bible" (as the Levant was often called in the nineteenth century) could rightly claim to be the oldest branch of American archaeology. The serious search for material remains of Biblical civilizations began with topographical surveys in Syria and Palestine in 1838 by Edward Robinson of Union Theological Seminary, a great American pioneer, and the founder of Palestinology. When actual digging began in the Middle East shortly thereafter, Americans could not immediately compete with the European powers—which may be just as well, because most of their activity was little more than looting the ancient treasures of Egypt and Mesopotamia for national museums. But when more systematic excavations finally began at Nippur in 1878, and then in Palestine itself at Tell el-Hesy in 1890 under the legendary William M. F. Petrie, Americans soon wanted in on the act. A report in the first issue of *The Biblical World*, a journal established in 1893 by the University of Chicago, asked: "As one thinks of the many *tells* of Palestine, and of what they may contain, the question involuntarily arises, How long must we wait?" (Kent 1893)[1]

It must be emphasized that, from the very beginning, American motivation in the archaeological recovery of the Ancient Near East was largely biblical and theological, rather than merely romantic "Orientalism," or nationalistic pride in the race to plunder the past. The enormous, incredible popularity of "Biblical archaeology" throughout these early years, and indeed up until the present, has made "Biblical archaeology" part of the mainstream of American cultural life. Yet, as I shall try to show, steady progress in the growth of both Americanist and Near Eastern archaeology as professional and academic disciplines has culminated in recent years in pushing "Biblical archaeology" to the sidelines, as an amateur, marginal enterprise, one perhaps even threatened by extinction.[2] Perhaps there is a lesson here.

## The Heyday of "Biblical Archaeology" (ca. 1920–1950)

It is commonly accepted that, despite American excavations in Palestine as early as 1893, and again in the years before World War I (by G. A. Reisner at Samaria, for instance), "Biblical archaeology" did not find its Nestor until the great Orientalist of Johns Hopkins, William F. Albright, emerged on the scene. In the 1920s through the 1940s Albright simply dominated American archaeology in Syria-Palestine, and even further afield in the Middle East. This was due partly, of course, to his own pioneering excavations, his methodological innovations, and his innumerable masterful syntheses of archaeology and history. Perhaps even more significant, however, was Albright's intellectual achievement in shaping not only "Biblical" and Syro-Palestinian archaeology, but also a half-century of American Biblical scholarship. Only in the last decade can these disciplines arguably be said to have entered a "post-Albrightian" era.[3]

Why did Albright have such an impact in America? (In Europe, he was regarded as something of a maverick, although he was nevertheless respected for his vast erudition.) In retrospect, it is clear that Albright—and indeed the entire American "Biblical archaeology" movement that he founded—was a *reaction* against what were thought to be the extremes of European critical theories of the Old Testament, which seemed to undercut the historical basis of Biblical faith. The specter suddenly loomed of the Bible as a "pious fraud." It is not merely coincidence that in the "Fundamentalist-Modernist" controversy, which shook American religious life and institutions to their very foundations, many ultraconservative and evangelical scholars sought refuge in "Biblical archaeology." Many came to Hopkins to study with Albright, and others followed him into the field in Palestine.

So profound was Albright's influence over two generations of Biblical scholars, many of them conservative, that the respectable journal, *The Christian Century,* once described him as "a galloping Fundamentalist." But he was nothing of the sort. His lifelong conservative tendency, however, plus a certain Olympian style, gave Albright's interpretation of the results of archaeology a decidedly authoritarian status. The main thrusts of the "Biblical archaeology" movement under his tutelage follow: (1) the reconstruction of an authentic, early second millennium historical background for the "Patriarchal era" of Genesis; (2) the documentation of a "Mosaic Age" that would place the formative period of Israelite faith centuries earlier than Biblical critics would allow; (3) the attempt to illustrate archaeologically the Israelite Exodus from Egypt and military conquest of Canaan in the thirteenth century BC, toward the end of the Bronze Age; and (4) the portrayal of Israelite religion as unique and to be seen in a favorable light, especially as compared with Canaanite belief and practice. Apart from these specific objectives, the general aim of Albright and his students was to set the Bible in historical context. As he put it in an early work, *The Archaeology of Palestine and the Bible* (1935):

Archaeological research in Palestine and neighboring lands during the past century has completely transformed our knowledge of the historical and literary background of the Bible. It no longer appears as an absolutely isolated monument of the past, as phenomenon without relation to its environment. The excessive skepticism shown toward the Bible by important historical schools of the 18th and 19th centuries has been progressively discredited. Discovery after discovery has brought increased recognition of the value of the Bible as a source of history (Albright 1935[1974]:137–138).

Contrast Albright's statement with another by a Biblicist named Newton:

Not a ruined city has been opened up that has given any comfort to unbelieving critics or evolutionists. Every find of archaeologists in bible lands has gone to confirm Scripture and confound its enemies . . . Not since Christ ascended back to heaven have there been so many scientific proofs that God's word is truth.[4]

In the popular imagination, however, there can be little doubt that the apparent success of "Biblical archaeology" in the 1920s through the 1950s led to the still widespread misconception of Syro-Palestinian archaeology as an enterprise whose chief aim is to "prove that the Bible is true." As the original title of Werner Keller's best-seller, *The Bible as History in Pictures,* has it, *Und die bibel hat doch Recht*—"the Bible was right after all" (Keller 1964). But today, all of Albright's confident reconstructions of ancient Israel's history are widely challenged, and many of them have been rejected altogether.[5]

## The Post-War Environment and Positivist Theology

Albright remained a historian, not a churchman, and, by his own definition a "radical empiricist," although in his later years he toyed with certain speculative and philosophical schools of history writing, and even tried his hand at Biblical commentaries.[6] By the post-war era, however, American religious life found itself in a crisis with the collapse of Protestant liberalism and its world view.

In Europe's war-ravaged Church the existentialist theology of Rudolph Bultmann and others could offer no historical verities, only the believing community's "experience of a new reality," and no moral assurance except "situational ethics." Even critical Biblical scholarship was reduced to minute literary analysis, not the recovery of the actual course of events in Israel's ancient history, or the core of Israelite faith, both of which now seemed increasingly problematic.

One major response to existentialism in America was neo-orthodoxy. In the specific form of the Biblical theology movement of the 1950s and 1960s, which sought to revive Biblical authority, the central theme emerged as the issue of "faith and history." The Bible could not any longer be regarded as "objective history," in the modern post-critical era, of course. But it was argued that the Bible was originally, and should still be, *Heilsgeschichte,* or "salvation-history," the proclamation of the saving acts of God in actual *history,* where he reveals himself, not in subjective individual or community "religious experience."

A leading Biblical theologian of that era was G. Ernest Wright, Albright's principal protégé, Parkman Professor of Divinity at Harvard, and America's leading Syro-Palestinian archaeologist (my own teacher). In 1952 Wright put it succinctly: "In biblical faith, everything depends upon whether the original events actually occurred." The "original events" here refer to the Exodus, the giving of the Law by Moses, and the conquest of Canaan under Yahweh, God of Israel. To his credit, Wright at least implicitly repudiated this position when he returned to archaeology in the 1960s and 1970s and perceived its limitations.[7] Nevertheless, the notion is still widespread that archaeology confirms Biblical history in some sense, and thus validates the religious and moral inferences drawn by the Biblical writers from their experiences, which in turn becomes the basis of modern belief.

If this fundamentally *theological* approach to the archaeology of Palestine appears astonishingly naïve today, it was nonetheless dominant in America from the 1950s until recently.[8] For example, when I began fieldwork in 1962 in Jordan under Wright, the current American projects were all being carried out at Biblical sites, by excavation staffs made up almost exclusively of Biblical scholars, with an agenda drawn from issues in Biblical history, and with funding from religious institutions and individuals. In Israel, the few American projects could be similarly characterized.

It may be asked: "Where was the *secular* school?" After all, such a school had existed from the beginning of American archaeology in the Holy Land, from Harvard's early work at Samaria, through the excavations of Chicago, Pennsylvania, Yale, and other universities at several sites in the 1920s and 1930s. As I have shown elsewhere, however, these two "parallel streams" of American archaeology never converged; and by the post-war years, the secular stream had disappeared altogether.[9] Why?

There were, of course, many complex factors. But, in my view, the main reason for the collapse of the secular school of Palestinian archaeology was simply that it never caught the popular imagination of the quasi-religious culture in America, and thus never found public support at the time when this branch of archaeology might have established itself as a serious, professional, academic discipline. *Later,* the religious connection would become a liability, but at the time it was certainly seen as an essential asset. Most observers seemed to assume then, and a few still do, that "poor Palestine" had little to offer culturally (except, of course, the origins of Judaism and Christianity, and thus Western traditions!); that without religious motivations there would be neither rationale nor support for American excavations in that part of the world.

This position seems incredibly parochial to us now. It simply ignored the development, in this same period, of vigorous secular schools of Syro-Palestinian archaeology in Britain, Europe, and finally in the indigenous national schools in Israel and Jordan. This approach was also oblivious to prehistory, classical archaeology, and the wider world of anthropological archaeology in America, all of which were incomparably more sophisticated at the time. Sadly enough, the intellectual isolation of American "Biblical"—and, indeed, of most Palestinian—archaeology continued until the late 1960s or early 1970s, when the disciplines belatedly discovered the "New Archaeology" that was by then burgeoning in America. To that we now turn.

## The Impact of the "New Archaeology" in the 1970s

It is obvious in retrospect that both the historical and theological foundations of the "Biblical archaeology" movement were weak. At the same time, there were external factors, quite beyond the control of the movement, that brought it to a virtual end by the 1970s. Let us look at these briefly in turn.[10]

The first failing was the poor quality of much early fieldwork done by "Biblical archaeologists" in Palestine, as well as the scandalous lack of scholarly publication that has plagued this school from the beginning.

The amateurish nature of most "Biblical archaeology," however, was exhibited even more clearly by a second factor, its failure to develop a coherent body of properly *archaeological* methods and theory. To be sure, in the 1950s and 1960s advanced field methods—borrowed mostly from Dame Kathleen Kenyon and the British—led to more precise stratigraphy, higher technical standards of observation and recording, and thus a much wider array of retrieved data. Yet these improvements were largely pragmatic, *ad hoc* adjustments in field methods, rather than far-reaching intellectual reformulation. That is, "method" in this simplistic sense was construed to mean nothing more than excavation technique; it did not embrace either the challenge of interpreting archaeological remains, nor of setting overall goals for the archaeological enterprise. Archaeologists of this persuasion operated without even a *minimal* definition of "history," much less of "culture" or "cultural change." There was nothing even resembling true theory, in the sense of guiding principles, or propositions to be tested; no awareness whatsoever of the vast, controversial theoretical literature in the larger world of archaeology; and no notion of objectives except to discover whatever happened to turn up in the dirt. At best this unsystematic inquiry into the past was antiquarianism; at worst it was treasure hunting. Whatever the level of the efforts made, Biblical archaeology in this period remained unsophisticated, isolated from the mainstream of archaeology.

A further complication was the reactionary nature of Biblical archaeology from its inception. This meant that when the Liberal theological positions against which it defined itself and its agenda disappeared in the 1940s, and then the Biblical theology movement with which it allied itself also died in the late 1960s, Biblical archaeology was left without an adequate rationale for its existence. All this came about when this school was already otherwise weakened internally. The final blow came in the early 1970s, when trends in Biblical scholarship in America culminated in a "post-positivist" attitude, an anti-Albrightian stance that simply did not *need* archaeological confirmation, or even any longer a dialogue with archaeologists. The divorce between two disciplines so long allied was now inevitable.[11]

In retrospect, it is evident that the final factor to be considered in the collapse of Biblical archaeology would have been sufficient in itself to discredit the movement, that is, its failure after fifty years to achieve the goals it had set for itself. As seen above, these goals revolved around the general attempt to demonstrate the essential "historicity" of the Bible, especially the Old Testament, and specifically in the case of the Patriarchal and Conquest eras of early Israel. Without going into detail, I can state categorically that today not only have these goals remained elusive, but the task has been abandoned by both the mainstream of Palestinian archaeology and Biblical studies. In the case of the so-called Israelite "conquest" of Canaan in the thirteenth and twelfth centuries BC, a model lifted literally from the Book of Joshua, American and Israeli archaeologists in the last decade have proven almost beyond doubt that no military invasion ever took place. The early Israelites were mostly indigenous, that is, displaced Canaanites peacefully settling the hill country frontier. Furthermore, *archaeologically* speaking there is no evidence of a sojourn in Egypt—much less an Exodus—, crossing of the wilderness, and conquest of Canaan.[12] No more devastating blow to "Biblical archaeology" can be imagined, for these historical events lay at the very heart of Israel's faith, at least in the theoretical construct presented in the Hebrew Bible. (There are, of course, several theological ways out of the dilemma, but that is another story.)

The American public, and even most of the religious establishment, is still unaware of this impasse. But the most telling statement came several years ago from a leading Biblical scholar, one of Albright's most prominent protégés, Professor David Noel Freedman of Michigan. At a colloquium honoring Albright himself, Freedman made the following, admirably candid remarks:

> Albright's great plan and expectation to set the Bible firmly on the foundation of archaeology buttressed by verifiable data seems to have foundered, or at least floundered. After all the digging, done and being done and yet to be done, how much has been accomplished? The fierce debates and arguments about the relevance of archaeology to the Bible and vice versa indicate that many issues remain unresolved. Can anyone say anything with confidence about the patriarchs or the patriarchal age? The fact that skeptical voices now dominate the scene indicates that the Albrightian synthesis has become unglued, and we are further from a solution than we ever were. Archaeology has not proven decisive or even greatly helpful in answering the questions most often

asked, and has failed to prove the historicity of Biblical persons and events, especially in the early periods.[13]

It is obvious, of course, that Biblical archaeology was simply asking the *wrong questions,* that is, it was dealing with issues that were theological, not properly archaeological at all.

At the very time that "Biblical archaeology" was running out of steam, so to speak, there were larger trends in motion, both in the Middle East and in Americanist archaeology, that would in themselves probably have over-whelmed the movement. Because I have dealt extensively with these else-where,[14] I only enumerate them briefly here. All of the following were trends of the late 1960s and the 1970s.

First, the momentum of improved methods of digging and recording noted above inevitably led to the retrieval of more varied kinds of data from the archaeological record, and thus to the first truly multidisciplinary staffs and research designs in Palestinian archaeology. This was at first a purely prag-matic move to improve field projects; but in the sense of Thomas S. Kuhn's *The Structure of Scientific Revolutions* (1970) it led to a real "paradigm shift," an in-tellectual about face that brought this school more into line with mainstream archaeology.[15]

Second, the new projects became vastly more expensive and thus quickly outgrew the resources of seminaries and other religious institutions. To their credit, former Biblical archaeologists soon became sophisticated enough to write new research and award-winning grant proposals for the National En-dowment for the Humanities and other public agencies. Nothing did more to secularize Biblical archaeology than these changed sources of support and funding.

Third, rising costs and a shortage of skilled laborers in Israel and Jordan resulted in the advent of the "field school" so typical of all digs in the region today. Again, this began as an *ad hoc* solution to a practical field problem, rather than a deliberate educational venture. Having, however, to deal with the impertinent questions of American student volunteers in the 1970s liter-ally forced excavators from Biblical backgrounds to make explicit what they were doing and why. The result was an unexpected but salutary challenge that was probably more far-reaching than we know.

Fourth, the rapid growth of indigenous, largely independent national schools of archaeology in the Middle East demonstrated beyond doubt that other, much more radically secular approaches to the archaeology of the re-gion were not only viable, but threatened soon to dominate (as they now do, of course). Even in Israel, the secular approach was taken for granted, for there the Bible is used in archaeology not as confessional literature, but merely as a document of national history.[16] In both Israel and Jordan, Biblical archaeology of the classic *American* style has never really been understood in terms of its intellectual background and theological presuppositions and was simply toler-ated at best. I have gone further to show that indeed the Biblical archaeology movement is almost exclusively American and the product of American religious life. In that sense, it differed profoundly from the British, French, German, and other European schools, as well as those now in the ascendancy in the Middle East.[17]

Next to the above developments, however, the impact of the New Archaeology deriving from Americanist circles in the 1970s was even more profound. It is no longer necessary to outline the essential characteristics of the New Archaeology, which is already becoming *passé* in this era of the "post-processualist" archaeology of Ian Hodder and others.[18] Yet at the time, the more sophisticated anthropological and sociological theories of the new archaeology, together with its promise of more precise analytical procedures borrowed from the natural sciences, were extraordinarily broadening and invigorating. Most Biblical archaeologists of my generation became new converts relatively quickly and painlessly (and, of course, with all the naïveté and dogmatic stance that usually accompanies quasi-religious conversions). For the first time in the history of American Palestinian archaeology, the focus shifted from simplistic, particularistic, historical descriptions to larger explanations of cultural change.

A final factor does not seem to have been noted yet, namely the need to train younger American specialists in Syro-Palestinian archaeology as the transitional generation is in passing. Simply take a cursory look at graduate programs at centers like Arizona, Chicago, Duke, Harvard, or Toronto; or a glance at the papers now published or delivered by bright young graduate students at annual meetings of the parent body, the American Schools of Oriental Research, and at other national meetings. Despite the skepticism of some critics, or the fond nostalgia of a few others, the "new look" is here to stay.

## Syro-Palestinian Archaeology as a Discipline

In summary, American Biblical archaeology, after nearly a century, has passed from the scene as nothing more than an historical curiosity, or an amateur pursuit by armchair archaeologists who remain fascinated with the Biblical world.

Biblical archaeology has been effectively replaced by a vigorous, though small, school of Syro-Palestinian archaeology (as it was originally called by Albright in the 1930s) that is regarded simply as one branch of Near Eastern, and indeed of general, archaeology. This archaeology is conceived as an autonomous, professional discipline, free from the domination of Biblical and theological studies, entitled, indeed obligated, to pursue its own appropriate *archaeological* aims and methods. The school is still allied with Biblical studies in the necessary dialogue between texts and artifacts in historical archaeology, but it is no longer ancillary, the "handmaiden of history." It is also closely and increasingly allied with anthropology and the natural sciences, both in theory and method as well as academic affiliations. The watchwords of the revolution are "specialization," "professionalism," and "secularization." In short, biblical archaeology has at last emerged from the cloister into the academy, and even the marketplace—or from amateur into professional status in American cultural life.

Where will the future take us? Although I confess to being an inveterate trend spotter, I can only hazard a guess or two. Certainly among the unresolved issues are such questions as the following: (1) Can the fledgling discipline survive, given the perilous situation in the Middle East and the retrenchment in the humanities on the American academic scene? (2) What are the possibilities of a rapprochement of the newer anthropological archaeology with more traditional historical or Classical archaeology, on the one hand, or with the current style of Biblical studies on the other?[19] (3) Larger theoretical issues would include, of course, the overall relationship that should obtain between the study of artifactual and material-cultural remains and textual remains. (4) Finally, there is what I believe to be the *real* challenge of archaeology in the near future, the intellectual issue, or epistemology. How we can know anything with certainty concerning the past; moreover, what relevance may such knowledge have to the conditions of human life today? Has the lifelong study of failed civilizations taught us anything pertinent about the possible collapse of our own, or do archaeologists constitute merely an elitist establishment unresponsive to the larger needs of society, hermetically sealed from the social context of knowledge? I have few answers.[20] I am convinced, however, that the long, turbulent cultural history of this area of the world has more significance for us today than ever before, and the story is not yet finished.

## Conclusion

I have tried to show that Palestinian and Biblical archaeology have long captured the imagination of the American public, because of their obvious connection with the Holy Land. However, Palestinian (or more properly Syro-Palestinian) archaeology has recently distanced itself from Biblical and theological studies, to become an independent academic and professional discipline. Meanwhile, Biblical archaeology of the older style has faded, at least as anything more than a popular pastime, or more seriously as a dialogue between archaeology and Biblical studies.

If Palestinian archaeology has thus come closer to the mainstream of American archaeology with its emphasis on anthropological theory and scientific analytic method, Biblical archaeology has to the same degree been marginalized. It is thought in many circles to be Biblicist, even fundamentalist— "proving the Bible"; as antiquarian and unscientific at best; and, of course, as too wedded to notions of the Judeo-Christian heritage of Western culture to be politically correct. That was perhaps the inevitable accompaniment to the professionalization of the parent discipline, but it is nevertheless unfortunate.

The Bible remains a significant cultural, if not religious, resource; and modern archaeology has done wonders in illuminating the Biblical world. Furthermore, unless the new professional discipline of Syro-Palestinian archaeology can retain public appeal and support in mainstream America, which still holds the Bible and the lands of the Bible in high esteem, it will not likely survive. A new alliance between a small cadre of professionals and the public at large must be forged, in which both professional standards and general enthusiasm can be maintained.

## Notes

1. The editor of *The Biblical World* was the great Orientalist William Rainey Harper; the quotation here is from Kent (1893). On the early history of the discipline, see also Wright (1970:4–40) and King (1983[1935]).

2. For more detailed critical history of the "Biblical archaeology" movement, see Dever (1981:15–29; 1985:31–74; 1988:337–352; forthcoming).

3. For a biography and bibliography of Albright, see Running (1975) and Wright (1970:n. 1, 22–28).

4. This translated statement by Newton appears in Prescott (1933:65). Additional information to identify the Biblicist Newton does not appear in Prescott.

5. See, for instance, the entire issue of the *Biblical Archaeologist* vol. 56 (1993), with articles by myself and others—all highly critical of Albright's syntheses, despite his towering achievements.

6. See, for instance, Albright (1964) and Albright with C. S. Mann (1971).

7. See, for example, Wright (1971:70–76), and especially his last article, published posthumously (Wright, 1974:104–115).

8. See the extensive critique in my work cited above in n. 2, and Dever (1980: 1–15).

9. See references in n. 2.

10. *Ibid.*

11. The analogy of a "divorce" between the two disciplines of Syro-Palestinian archaeology and Biblical studies—together with a call for a renewed, *genuine* dialogue—was first made in Dever (1974).

12. See also Dever (1990:39–84), and especially Finkelstein (1988).

13. See Freedman as reported by Shanks (1985:6).

14. See references in nn. 2 and 11 above.

15. See Dever (1988:337–341) with respect to Kuhn (1970).

16. See, for example, Dever (1989:44–51) and references.

17. See especially Dever (1985:31–61).

18. Note especially Hodder (1986). The more radical treatment appears in Shanks and Tilley (1987). A good orientation will be found in the essays in Preucel (1991).

19. Elsewhere I have proposed a *new* style of relating archaeology to Biblical studies, following some aspects of Hodder's "contextual archaeology." See Dever (1993).

20. See further my tentative remarks in Dever (1994:105–117).

## References Cited

Albright, William F. 1974[1935]. *The Archaeology of Palestine and the Bible.* Cambridge, Massachusetts: American Schools of Oriental Research.

———. 1964. *History, Archaeology, and Christian Humanism.* New York: McGraw-Hill.

Albright, William F. with C. S. Mann. 1971. "Matthew." In *Anchor Bible Dictionary.* Garden City, New York: Doubleday.

Dever, William G. 1974. *Archaeology and Biblical Studies: Retrospects and Prospects.* The Winslow Lectures. Evanston: Seabury-Western Seminary Press.

———. 1980. "Biblical Theology and Biblical Archaeology: An Appreciation of G. Ernest Wright." *Harvard Theological Review* 73: 1–15.

———. 1981. "The Impact of the 'New Archaeology' on Syria-Palestinian Archaeology." *Bulletin of the American Schools of Oriental Research* 242: 15–29.

———. 1985. "Syro-Palestinian and Biblical Archaeology." In *The Hebrew Bible and Its Modern Interpreters,* edited by Douglas A. Knight and Gene M. Tucker, 31–74. Philadelphia: Fortress Press.

———. 1988. "Impact of the 'New Archaeology.'" In *Benchmarks in Time and Culture: An Introduction to Palestinian Archaeology,* edited by Joe F. Drinkard, Gerald L. Mattingly, and J. Maxwell Miller, 337–352. Atlanta: Scholars Press.

———. 1989. "Yigael Yadin: Prototypical Biblical Archaeologist." *Eretz-Israel* 20: 44–51.

———. 1990. *Recent Archaeological Discoveries and Biblical Research.* Seattle: University of Washington Press.

———. 1992. "Archaeology, Syro-Palestinian and Biblical." *Anchor Bible Dictionary,* edited by David Noel Freedman. New York: Doubleday. Vol. 1, Pp. 354–367.

———. 1993. "Biblical Archaeology—Death and Rebirth?" In *Biblical Archaeology Today, 1990,* 706–722. Proceedings of the Second International Congress on Biblical Archaeology, Jerusalem, June 1990. Jerusalem: Israel Exploration Society.

———. 1994. "Archaeology, Texts, and History-Writing: Toward an Epistemology." In *Uncovering Ancient Stones: Essays in Memory of H. Neil Richardson,* edited by L. Hopf, 105–117. Winona Lake, Indiana: Eisenbrauns.

Finkelstein, Israel. 1988. *The Archaeology of the Israelite Settlement.* Jerusalem: Israel Exploration Society.

Hodder, Ian. 1986. *Reading the Past: Current Approaches to Interpretation in Archaeology.* Cambridge: Cambridge University Press.

Israel Exploration Society. 1993. *Biblical Archaeology Today, 1993.* Proceedings of the Second International Congress on Biblical Archaeology, Jerusalem, June 1990. Jerusalem: Israel Exploration Society.

Keller, Werner. 1964. *The Bible As History in Pictures.* New York: Morrow. (Rev. ed., London: Hodder and Stoughton, 1984.)

Kent, Charles F. 1893. "The Present Possibilities of Excavation in Palestine." *The Biblical World* I.

King, Phillip J. 1983[1935]. *American Archaeology in the Middle East: A History of the American Schools of Oriental Research.* Philadelphia: American Schools of Oriental Research.

Kuhn, Thomas S. 1970. 2nd ed. *The Structure of Scientific Revolutions.* Chicago: University of Chicago Press.

Preucel, Robert W., ed. 1991. *Processual and Postprocessual Archaeologists: Multiple Ways of Knowing the Past.* Carbondale: Southern Illinois University.

Prescott, A. H. *The Spade and the Bible: Archaeological Discovers Support the Old Book.* n.p. 1933.

Running, Leona. 1975. *William Foxwell Albright: A Twentieth Century Genius.* New York: Two Continents Publishing Group.

Shanks, Hershel. 1985. *Biblical Archaeology Review* 11: 1, 6.

Shanks, Michael and Christopher Tilley. 1987. *Re-constructing Archaeology: Theory and Practice of Archaeology.* Cambridge: Cambridge University Press.

Wright, G. Ernest. 1970. "The Phenomenon of American Archaeology in the Near East." In *Near Eastern Archaeology in the Twentieth Century: Essays in Honor of Nelson Glueck,* edited by James A. Sanders. Garden City: Doubleday.

——. 1971. "What Archaeology Can and Cannot Do." *Biblical Archaeologist* 34: 70–76.

——. 1974. "The 'New Archaeology.'" *Biblical Archaeologist* 38: 104–115.

# 7

## Brahmins and Bureaucrats

## Some Reflections on the History of American Classical Archaeology

Stephen L. Dyson

It is both surprising and not surprising that no history of modern Classical archaeology, and especially of Classical archaeology in the United States exists. Surprising in that we do have recent histories of most other branches of archaeology from Danish and Central European prehistory to Egyptology (Daniel 1967, 1976; Bernal 1980; Kristiansen 1981; Christenson 1989; Wilson 1964). Not surprising in that North American Classical archaeology has proved to be a discipline singularly lacking in self reflection and analysis. It is the same attitude that has kept American Classical archaeologists out of the theoretical debates that have convulsed North American archaeology (both prehistoric and historic) and British prehistory for the past generation.

I have already expressed elsewhere my views on the problems caused Classical archaeology by its failure to engage in such theoretical debate (Dyson 1981, 1985, 1989, 1993). I regard the lack of sophisticated research in the history of the discipline as a complementary failure. Academic disciplines, like all other branches of cultural activity, are products of a particular past. This provides positive traditions, but also limitations and restrictions. What I would describe as historically reflective disciplines consider their past, continue to use methods and approaches which seem useful in contemporary circumstances, but at the same time abandon those which have outlived their usefulness. In contrast, customary groups pass on traditions from one generation to the next with minimal self-reflection. I would argue that Classical archaeology basically belongs in the latter category.

The skeptic might respond at this point that there are many studies which deal exclusively with the history of Classical archaeology or treat it as an important part of the larger discipline of archaeology. However, most of these histories deal with what I would call the prehistory of the discipline, that is, Classical archaeology from the Renaissance to the middle years of the nineteenth century. Classical archaeology as an academic discipline with professional societies, graduate programs, overseas research centers, organized long-term excavations, journals, and formal academic positions only emerged in the last decades of the nineteenth century (Levine 1986). For a history of the past one hundred years, we have useful preliminary works in the form of institutional histories, such as those of the American Academy in Rome and the American School of Classical Studies in Athens; accounts of major excavations such as Dura and Sardis; university histories; and numerous obituaries (Lord 1947, Hanfmann 1972, Hopkins 1979, Meritt 1984). Singularly lacking for the Classical archaeologists of North America, however, are biographies and autobiographies.[1] Moreover, there is little synthetic-analytical history, comparable to those of sister disciplines like anthropological archaeology and history (Willey and Sabloff 1980, Patterson 1986, Novick 1988).

Why do we need such history? Issues related to the internal importance of such a study will form the central focus of much of the rest of this chapter. Here I want to reflect briefly on the external importance of such research. Two groups of scholars will find the history of Classical archaeology relevant. The first is obviously the growing body of students of the history of archaeology. Classical archaeology is by far the oldest branch of the discipline. The celebrations of the 100th anniversary of the Archaeological Institute of America and the 50th of the Society of American Archaeology were roughly contemporary (Meltzer, Fowler, and Sabloff 1986). Classical archaeology is not only the oldest branch of archaeology, but it has been for most of its history the largest and most financially well endowed. Classical archaeologists were for long the most active in research of both field and museum varieties, and were, for the earlier decades, the intellectual leaders of the profession.

However, the development of Classical archaeology is of interest to a wider group of scholars studying the history of American education and American educational and cultural institutions. The study of the classics was at the core of American education during the nineteenth century, when Classical archaeology began to change from an amateur, antiquarian activity to a profession (Reinhold 1984). In such areas as the introduction of German scholarship into the United States and the development of formal graduate programs, Classical archaeologists played a key role (Herbst 1965). Classical archaeology has even a wider appeal to students of American culture. It is an expensive, often obscure scholarly pursuit, largely played out in dark libraries, musty museum storerooms, and distant lands. Sometimes Classical archaeologists discover objects of great beauty, but generally they do not. Yet because of its Romantic appeal, the importance of the Classical style in American culture and association with the roots of Western civilization, Classical archaeologists have been able to attract massive funding and exert considerable popular appeal. Few other scholarly disciplines have been able to draw such support from the likes of John D. Rockefeller, Jr., John Paul Getty, and David Packard. Certainly there is something here of considerable interest to the students of the history of institutions.[2]

The next question is what an ideal history of Classical archaeology should be like. Clearly another *Gods, Graves and Scholars* (Ceram 1986[1951]) is not called for. Neither is the genre that is a cross between an archaeological *Liber*

*Pontificalis* and the chronicles of an Oxford senior common room in which lists of digs and scholars are interspersed with folksy anecdotes about eccentric academics and faithful servants.

A powerful model is obviously Gordon Willey and Jeremy Sabloff's *A History of American Archaeology* (1980). Willey and Sabloff provide an intellectual-structural history of the development of American archaeology. Employing a Thomas Kuhn-style dominant paradigm approach to the subject, they divide their history into three major periods: 1840–1914, Classificatory-Descriptive; 1914–1960, Classificatory-Historical; and 1960s onward, Explanatory. These eras represent a movement from philatelic style ordering of archaeological material to the development of sophisticated models which use the archaeological data to explain changes in human social systems.

The major problem with applying the Willey-Sabloff approach to Classical archaeology is that Classical archaeology has not undergone the radical paradigm shifts that the authors see as central to the development of American archaeology. I would argue that Classical archaeology has remained fixed somewhere between the Classificatory-Descriptive and Classificatory-Historical with no real Explanatory period. During the last one hundred years, Classical archaeologists have immensely improved techniques of excavation and analysis, but fundamental models and modes of analysis have changed much less.

As an avid reader of the evolutionary biologist Stephen Jay Gould, I am fascinated by evolutionary backwaters, where time seems to have stood still. Static as well as changing behavior requires its own explanation. Why has Classical archaeology changed its intellectual framework so little, when other branches of archaeology such as European and North American prehistory have changed so much? One can argue the "great man" theory of history and say that Classical archaeology has produced no Lewis Binford, an individual who changed the thinking and direction of a discipline (Binford 1972:1–14).

Great man theories of history are now rather out of fashion, as we look for causation in social and economic phenomena. Thomas Patterson has demonstrated that one can apply Marxist-derived models of socioeconomic analysis to the history of archaeology (Patterson 1995). Taking a slightly different tack, one can argue that it is institutions and not individuals that are key to understanding why Classical archaeology has developed in a particular way. A Lewis Binford in Classical archaeology would not have emerged as the Lewis Binford that we know from the field of American prehistory. Institutions such as undergraduate and graduate programs, journals, professional meetings, overseas research institutes, and major excavations of long duration make possible the emergence of one type of archaeologist and severely limit the possibility that another type will appear. Each institution has its own rules, traditions, and bureaucratic procedures which in the eternal world of bureaucracies tend toward a certain conservatism. These institutions intersect, drawing strength from the collective tradition of the field and in turn enhance that tradition. This is the second point of reference in the title.

In an essay of this length, only a small part of the institutional history of Classical archaeology can be explored. I intend to focus on one topic, the structure of fieldwork in Classical archaeology with its premises both structural and social, economic and political. This paradigm developed in the period between the wars and reached its zenith in the two decades immediately after World War II. To establish a better context, it will be necessary to look both backward and forward in time.

North American Classical archaeologists inherited the institution of the major excavation from their European and especially French and German colleagues. The "big dig" was generally centered on a major site of great historical and cultural importance. Olympia, Delphi, Pergamon, and Ephesus provide good examples. Its object was to illuminate the Classical texts (the Greek travel guide of the second century AD Pausanias was a central figure in much of this research), and recover architecture and other works of art that would illustrate the Classical culture and especially Greek culture.

North American Classical archaeologists were already involved in tentative enterprises of this sort by the 1880s. The Archaeological Institute of America was founded in 1879 to promote such research. While the leaders of these early efforts were in many respects Brahmin amateurs, their pioneering field projects significantly advanced the professionalization of American Classical archaeology. Assos and the ill-fated 1910 expedition at Cyrene provide examples of such aborted research efforts (see Clarke 1898 on Assos). By the 1890s the American School of Classical Studies at Athens had obtained the concession for excavations at ancient Corinth, an enterprise that has continued with interruptions to the present day (Lord 1947:88–97, 100–108, 170–172, 183–189, 195–196, 212–215, 220, 246–248; Meritt 1984:151–174).

By the interwar period, the American archaeological presence was well established in the Mediterranean. In many areas the Americans came too late to use archaeology as a means of swelling museum collections. Syria and Egypt with their *de facto* colonial situations were the exceptions, and those countries were the scene of most of the museum sponsored excavations of the period (Wilson 1964, Hopkins 1979). Excavations in other areas benefited in other ways from what may be called a "capitalist-imperialist-colonialist archaeology" (Trigger 1989).

Archaeology of this type has several salient characteristics. First of all, the archaeologists benefit from a major disjuncture between the power of the country that sponsors the dig (in this case the United States) and the country where the dig takes place. These benefits were manifested in a variety of ways from cheap labor to the right to export antiquities or receive tax or other benefits not enjoyed by the natives. This is not to say that the archaeologists did not appreciate the natives or their culture. In the case of Greece, an abundance, even an excess of Helleno-Romanticism was present. However, the implied power relationships of imperialist versus subject were never far below the surface.

Since the sites selected were generally large and complex, and the cost of labor was cheap, these excavations generally operated on a large scale. They required not only hundreds of sweating natives, but also a staff organized on what may be called the corporate model. Here again the Americans drew heavily on the continental models of how an excavation was to be run. The director came to assume many of the qualities of the German Herr Professor with elements of the American corporation executive thrown in. As archaeology became a more specialized discipline, staff specialization became more important. Increasingly the director presided over a group of experts, who labored in their particular vineyard without ever seeing or wanting to see the larger picture.

Such digs had to be financed, and here again archaeology, colonialism, and capitalism intersected, establishing a mode of doing archaeology which has continued until the present. Before World War II, little institutional funding of American Classical archaeology existed. Unlike the German, French, and Austrian governments, that of the United States did not pay for Classical archaeology. Most money came from individual philanthropy with some contributions from private foundations, access to whose coffers was severely limited. There is no better testimony to the close link between Classical archaeology and the most secure wealth in America than the fact that American projects overseas flourished during the height of the Great Depression. While North American archaeologists were working for the WPA, their classical brethren were digging with the financial support of the American elite, which had insulated itself well from the collapse of world capitalism. In fact, they benefited from it, since the depression and other disasters kept costs low. This was especially true of human labor. David Robinson at Olynthus could do an awful lot with $10,000 raised from the comfortable folks in Baltimore, especially if his diggers were refugees from the calamities of the Greco-Turkish War.

The most important American excavation commenced in this period took place in the Athenian Agora. The prospect of excavating the citadel of democracy in the center of Athens had long intrigued American archaeologists. After long and complicated negotiations with the Greek government, and an intensive search for funds, excavations started in 1931. This project was complicated by the fact that not only was the area to be investigated a zone of immense archaeological richness, but also located at the center of a modern city. Large numbers of people had to be displaced by the excavations and what would now be called an historical quarter of the city of Athens destroyed[3] (Miller 1931).

The 1930s excavations by the Americans in the Agora had many parallels with those undertaken by Benito Mussolini in the center of Rome (Insolera and Perego 1983, Manacorda and Tamassia 1985). In both cases, large sectors of the historical fabric of the city were destroyed in order to explore important Classical remains. The destruction was justified on the grounds that these later remains represented corrupt and decadent descendants of a glorious Classical past. Moreover, the Americans were investigating the roots of democracy, while Mussolini was glorifying imperial Rome. Still the parallels deserve more research than they have received.

The point should be made here that the excavations in the Athenian Agora made very important contributions to the development of scientific Classical archaeology. In their methods, and especially recording systems, the Agora excavators were well ahead of their colleagues in other branches of American archaeology (Miller 1931, MacKendrick 1962:386–390). The Agora archaeologists were interested in a limited range of problems, but this was true of most archaeologists of the period. What set the Agora apart was the fact that it became the central model for the way that archaeological excavations should be conducted, especially in the period immediately after World War II. The reasons for this development will be explored shortly.

While the big dig was becoming the dominant mode of doing Classical field archaeology in the 1920s and 1930s, other intellectual and institutional developments contributed to a growing isolation of Classical archaeology. In part this was caused by the coming to maturity of other branches of archaeology, especially that of the Americanists. North American archaeologists, who had depended on the Archaeological Institute of America for the foundation of such fundamental institutions as the Center for Archaeological Research in Santa Fe, now went their own way with the founding of the Society of American Archaeologists in 1935 (Hinsley 1986). The same thing happened with other groups such as the medievalist art historians who followed the College Art Association in their own separate activities (Smith 1913). This is reflected in the programs of the annual meeting of the Archaeological Institute of America. In 1920, there was a sense of the openness of the boundaries of archaeology. The focus was Classical, but the interests of the participants extended well beyond the time periods of the Classical world and the shores of the Mediterranean. By 1940, AIA archaeology had become mainly Greek archaeology with a strong emphasis on architecture and elite material culture. Roman Italy was a world hardly heard from, the Roman provinces almost mute, and the world of archaeology and art history in other areas and time periods largely *terra incognita* (Dyson 1985).

The reasons for these changes were complex and not all the fault of Classical archaeologists. The result, however, was to create a certain dominant mode of doing Classical archaeology, and to create a nexus of communication in which Classical archaeologists talked almost exclusively to themselves and their associates, the classicists, who studied ancient literature. This did not matter much in the 1930s, for the other branches of archaeology had little to teach the classicists. It was to matter greatly after World War II, when the balance of intellectual dynamism changed (Willey and Sabloff 1980:130–210, Trigger 1989).

The pattern of Classical field archaeology that emerged after World War II was very much that which had been set in the 1930s. It is true that political colonialism almost completely disappeared in the eastern Mediterranean and with that the possibility of excavations that produced exportable objects.

Significantly, art museums largely lost interest in fieldwork. Projects like Antioch and Dura Europos came to an end. However, economic imperialism and American dominance remained very much in force in the Mediterranean. One could still move a lot of dirt in the Mediterranean for relatively little money. Americans had international economic and political power. These factors combined to produce the golden age of big dig archaeology.

The tradition of Classical archaeology, which combined explication of Classical texts and the recovery of public architecture and beautiful objects, was still very much in force. The American School in Athens rapidly assumed its role as the center of North American Classical archaeology in the Mediterranean, and the Agora became its field showpiece (Meritt 1984). New projects like Morgantina, Cosa, Aphrodisias, Gordion, and Sardis were conceived and executed in the same mold (Brown 1949, Hanfmann 1972, Erim 1986). Their funding was to come largely from private philanthropy or through foundations, where connections rather than open competition determined allocations of money. The excavations were planned on a massive scale and were intended to continue for a long period of time. Often considerable investments were made in buildings and equipment which reinforced the need to continue at a site for as long as possible. The most extreme example of this development was certainly the reconstruction of the Stoa of Attalus in the Athenian Agora, which served not only as a museum, but also as a permanent laboratory and storage space for the American excavations. The hierarchical, corporate model for the organization of excavation staff remained very much in force, reinforced in fact by the ever heightened respect for American management techniques and the growing mass of archaeology graduate students that filled the lower ranks on these excavations. It was in many respects "IBM become archaeology."

At the top of this organization was the director, who organized and managed the project. It was the director who understood the aims and results of the excavations. One day the director would explain it all, when the reports of the various specialists had been laid on his or her (mainly his) desk. Meanwhile, the director spent the field season in the manifold tasks of management and the off-season in the tasks of publicity production, fund raising, and participating in the time-consuming operations of the Classical archaeological power elite of which the major excavation directors were a major part.[4]

Below decks were the increasingly large staffs of specialists. One needed architects, a variety of pottery specialists, numismatists, lamp experts, glass analysts, epigraphers, and many more. The Agora staff became the ideal to which most major excavations aspired. As the number of major excavations increased, so too did the number of Classical archaeologists who were involved in this backroom activity. Each of these persons could stake out a satisfying subspecialty, which could bring publications, tenure, and frequent trips to the Mediterranean. However, relatively few were encouraged to strike out on their own. In fact, the whole system, from the permit system in Greece, which limited the number of excavations, through archaeological field training, which

stressed specialization at the expense of an overall vision of proper field techniques and field strategies, to the daunting cost and complexity of organizing
a big dig, discouraged initiative. Moreover, the professional power elite who
controlled both the major excavations and access to awards and advancement
in so many areas of Classical archaeology had little inducement to send a good
lamp person off to dig a farmhouse or undertake an independent field survey
on Roman Spain or even Classical Greece (McDonald 1984).

However, not even Classical archaeologists are in a position to control the
great political and economic cycles of history. What ended the golden days of
American Classical field archaeology in the Mediterranean was not the assaults
of Lewis Binford and the New Archaeologists, but the contraction of American
economic and political power and local, nationalist reactions against archaeological as well as other types of neocolonialism. Archaeologists long had to
contend with growing nationalism and anticolonialism in the Mediterranean
and the Near East, although these produced new manifestations in countries
like Greece in the 1970s and the 1980s. Export permits for antiquities had
long since ended in most areas, but now Americans found it difficult and uncomfortable to conduct basic research and especially excavation in some areas.

Growing nationalism was accompanied by radical economic change.
Prices and wages rose in the Mediterranean, while the buying power of the
dollar shrank. In their annual reports worried directors noted double-digit in-
flation and massive rises in daily labor costs for workers. In my own time as a
field archaeologist, the cost of hiring a worker for a day in Italy has risen from
a little over ten dollars to more than one hundred dollars. Travel expenses also
increased, making the cost of sending a staff of twenty to Greece or Italy three
or four times what they had been in the 1950s or early 1960s. A budget of
$100,000 in the 1970s could buy considerably less than David Robinson's
$10,000 in the 1930s.

The funding picture was also changing. The exit of museums from active
field research has already been mentioned. They still spent money on archaeology, but it was on the purchase of objects in the legal and illegal antiquities
market (Potter 1979:1–18). Private philanthropy was still available, as the list
of acknowledgments accompanying every dig report still shows. However, in
an age of growing national and international social and cultural concerns,
there was increased competition for the dollars of millionaires and private
foundations.

However, new funding sources appeared. The biggest new influx of funds
came from the establishment of the National Endowment for the Humanities
(NEH) in 1965. The NEH made a major commitment to the support of Classical archaeology early in its history. Finally the discipline had the backing of a
government agency which could be expected to sponsor open competitions
and in the Jeffersonian tradition provide opportunities for the "little" men
and women of Classical archaeology. Nor was NEH alone. The Fulbright program was started, and for Greece that meant many personal grants for Classical archaeologists. The support programs of the American Council of Learned

Societies, which had started before the war, were now expanded. They did not provide major grants, but did become a very valuable supplementary source of funding. National Geographic was now more active in financing archaeology, and Classical archaeologists working in certain areas and on certain time periods might even get some support from the National Science Foundation (NSF).

Another new funding source for Classical archaeologists without a tame millionaire on the string were the Smithsonian Foreign Exchange Programs. The money for these came from the payback of American aid funds in nonconvertible local currencies. Some of it was used to sponsor archaeology in countries like Tunisia and Yugoslavia, lands which held considerable interest for Classical archaeologists. It is true that these were not Greece or Italy, but for a while the money was abundant and the archaeological challenges interesting.[5] In 1971, Earthwatch, an organization that combined elements of profit and nonprofit research sponsorship, began funding archaeological projects.[6]

One would have thought that the combined realities of a declining American economic and political position in the Mediterranean, new directions in funding opportunities, and the new types of research agendas posed by the New Archaeology would have forced some fundamental rethinking about the future of field research in Classical archaeology. Sadly they did not, and no program illustrated that better than the first phase of the archaeology program at the NEH. A centerpiece for NEH archaeology support became the matching grant. A dollar of government money would be released only for archaeological research when it was matched by a dollar raised from outside the institution of the project director. This naturally played into the hands of those who had a tradition of access to friendly millionaires and private foundations. A young scholar without such connections faced the prospect that even if his or her project were approved for funding, the chances of getting significant NEH support were limited indeed.

Moreover, this same young person was caught in a number of other "catch 22" funding complications. NSF did provide outright grants, but only Classical archaeologists working in prehistory could reasonably hope for such support. The National Geographic Society was generally interested only if a project promised to find something exciting and photogenic. ACLS could provide funding for a trip to Greece or Turkey to work on the coins or inscriptions from a particular site, but did not offer money to sponsor even relatively small field projects. The Smithsonian programs did attract some interesting new projects. However, the dominant ethos in Classical archaeology had focused the young scholar on Greece and Italy. By the time that archaeological interest in the areas financed by counterpart funds had increased, the financial backing of the program was in decline. By the late 1970s and early 1980s, North American Classical archaeology faced a fieldwork crisis. Many of the major excavations were closing down or entering into an interminable sequence of study seasons. Few new projects were being started. It is true that there were many decades of cataloging and report writing ahead. However, these activities were not going to promote the creation of a new generation of field researchers, and fieldwork should be a central part of what archaeologists do.

Several potential solutions were possible. One was to concentrate a high proportion of the shrinking funding pool on a limited number of high profile projects which would keep the old traditions alive and carry the flag for American Classical archaeology in the Mediterranean. On the whole, this was what happened. Projects with a well-developed constituency and long traditions like the Athenian Agora, Corinth, and Isthmia continued, although with changes in direction and breaks in operation. They continued to receive massive funding from the same combination of private, semi-private, and public sources that they had before.

Another variation on the familiar Classical archaeology field team that assumed greater prominence was the use of the tame, more personally guided millionaire. Those who had a sugar daddy dug, and those who didn't, regardless of the worth of the project and the creativity of the archaeologists involved, didn't. This approach to fieldwork had the additional problem that everything depended on the interests and personal circumstances of the individual who footed the bills. Most of these were strongly interested and responsible individuals who made important research contributions to the discipline. However, shifts in personal interests or a bad year on the stock market could bring the project to a sudden halt.

A third solution would have been to rethink the goals of American Classical field archaeology. The conditions for doing archaeology in the Mediterranean had changed radically in that post-imperialist, post-colonialist age. The professional structure of American Classical archaeology was also changing in significant ways. The profession was larger, but its members were more scattered. Many young archaeologists found themselves at small institutions, where they could never hope to undertake a project like Sardis or Aphrodisias. Often their only archaeological colleague on campus was a young "New Archaeologist" in the anthropology department. The potential for sharing ideas and field projects existed and had great potential. Sadly it was seldom realized. As a lecturer on the Archaeological Institute of America tour during that period, I often found that even at small colleges, the Classical archaeologist and the anthropological archaeologist had virtually no communication.

The legacy of big dig archaeology in the United States has also been a mixed one. The results of projects like the Agora have been impressive indeed. More common has been an excavation, where publication has lagged years behind and consumed both massive amounts of money and the best years of a new generation of archaeologists, who were often picking up the pieces of the past. In many instances, the directors who were the intellectual and organizational heart of these complex, centralized operations have died, leaving the projects without direction and the great synthesis that was the expected final goal of so much research.

The British Classical archaeologists faced some of the same challenges during this period. It is true that they had never become accustomed to the opulent excavations undertaken by the Americans, Germans, and French. This penury became a greater reality after World War II. The British reacted to these circumstances in creative ways. They learned to combine innovative research designs with a few pounds sterling, a battered van, and many tins of tea and jam to produce significant results. Many of these projects were surveys, but others involved limited excavation, often using squads of volunteers.

The British model has a number of other attractions for the Americans beyond those of mere cost control. Potentially, it allows more scholars to get into the field. We face a crisis in the field training of American Classical field archaeologists. British archaeology students can get field training at both pre-historic and Classical sites in their own country. Some American Classical ar-chaeologists learn the rudiments of fieldwork at Native American or historical sites, but that is a form of archaeological education not generally encouraged among classicists. Few places are available on the limited number of major digs. The result is often despair and a retreat into the library, museum, or ex-cavation storeroom. Another result of this is a growing gap between the teach-ing world of Classical archaeologists, which in most cases has become more broad and general, and the research, which has become more narrow.

The prospect for future American fieldwork is not totally bleak. A confer-ence on survey archaeology in the Mediterranean which was held at the American School of Classical Studies in Athens in 1981, showed an impres-sive range of American research in this type of archaeology (Keller and Rupp 1983). This was in contrast to the skepticism, even scorn, that greeted the pio-neering survey projects of William McDonald and Richard Hope-Simpson in the 1950s (McDonald 1984).

However, the funding and fieldwork situation does not offer great hope. The future of the National Endowment for the Humanities, which through increasingly flexible funding policies, has become the main hope of younger Classical archaeologists, is threatened with severe cuts, even extinction. New opportunities are very few. One result is that the field training of the emerg-ing generation of American Classical archaeologists is woefully inadequate by contemporary British or even Italian Classical archaeology standards.[7] The big, old excavations still tend to grab major grants, preparing another genera-tion of archaeologists for a type of archaeology that almost none of them will practice.

### Notes

1. Except for a rather sentimental biography of Harriet Boyd Hawes pub-lished in 1992, I know of no full length biography or autobiography of a major figure in North American Classical archaeology since Charles Eliot Norton. For some of the problems of current archaeological biography, see Dyson (1994).

2. A major chapter in the history of Classical archaeology that needs

be written is that of the role of private philanthropy and the major foundations in shaping the discipline. Such information can be gleaned from a variety of sources including the footnotes of annual excavation reports and the
annual reports of foundations, universities, and major foreign schools.

3. For an overview of the results of the Agora excavations, see Camp
(1986).

4. Hanfmann (1972) provides a good picture of the life of a major archaeological director during the period in question.

5. Activities of the Smithsonian Counterpart Fund Program (technically
designated as Foreign Area Program Grants) were reported annually in *Smithsonian Year* beginning in 1966.

6. For the early history of Earthwatch, see Earthwatch (1982).

7. Two Italian projects that have done much to encourage field training
for Italian university students are the Settefinestre villa excavation in Tuscany
and the Crypta Balbi excavations in Rome. For Settefinestre, see Carandini and
Settis (1979). For the Crypta Balbi, see Manacorda (1982).

## References Cited

Bernal, Ignácio. 1980. *A History of Mexican Archaeology.* London: Thames and
    Hudson.
Binford, Lewis. 1972. *An Archaeological Perspective.* New York: Seminar Press.
Brown, Frank E. 1949. Cosa: Exploration in Etruria. *Archaeology* 2:2–10.
Camp, John M. 1986. *The Athenian Agora.* London: Thames and Hudson.
Carandini, Andrea and Salvatore Settis. 1979. *Schiavi e padroni nell'Etruria ro-
    mana.* Bari: De Donato.
Ceram, C. W. 1986[1951], *Gods, Graves and Scholars: The Story of Archaeology.*
    2nd rev. ed. New York: Vintage.
Christenson, Andrew L., ed. 1989. *Tracing Archaeology's Past.* Carbondale:
    Southern Illinois University Press.
Clarke, Graham. 1989. *Prehistory at Cambridge and Beyond.* Cambridge: Cam-
    bridge University Press.
Clarke, Joseph Thacher. 1898. *Report on the Investigation at Assos, 1882, 1883.*
    New York.
Daniel, Glyn. 1967. *The Origins and Growth of Archaeology.* Harmondsworth:
    Penguin.
———. 1976. *One Hundred and Fifty Years of Archaeology.* Cambridge: Harvard
    University Press.
Dyson, Stephen L. 1981. "A Classical Archaeologist's Response to the 'New
    Archaeology.'" *Bulletin of the American Schools of Oriental Research* 242:
    7–13.
———. 1985. "Two Paths to the Past: A Comparative History of the Last Fifty
    Years of *American Antiquity* and the *American Journal of Archaeology.*"
    *American Antiquity* 50: 452–463.
———. 1989. "Complacency and Crisis in Late Twentieth Century Classical
    Archaeology." In *Classics: A Discipline and Profession in Crisis,* edited

by Phyllis Culham and Lowell Edmunds, 211–220. Lanham: University Press of America.

———. 1993. "From New to New Age Archaeology: Archaeological Theory and Classical Archaeology—A 1990s Perspective." *American Journal of Archaeology* 97: 195–206.

———. 1994. "Archaeological Lives." *American Journal of Archaeology* 98: 159–62.

Earthwatch. 1982. *Earthwatch: The First Ten Years.* Belmont, Massachusetts: Earthwatch.

Erim, Kenan T. 1986. *Aphrodisias: City of Venus Aphrodite.* New York.

Grayson, Donald K. 1983. *The Establishment of Human Antiquity.* New York: Academic Press.

Hanfmann, George M. A. 1972. *Letters from Sardis.* Cambridge: Harvard University Press.

Herbst, Jurgen. 1965. *The German Historical School in American Scholarship.* Ithaca: Cornell University Press.

Hinsley, Curtis. 1986. "Edgar Lee Hewett and the American School of Prehistoric Research in Santa Fe 1906–1912." In *American Archaeology, Past and Future,* edited by David J. Meltzer, Don D. Fowler, and Jeremy A. Sabloff, 217–233. Washington, D.C.: Smithsonian Institution Press.

Hopkins, Clark. 1979. *The Discovery of Dura Europos.* New Haven: Princeton University Press.

Insolera, Italo and Francesco Perego. 1983. *Archeologia e citta: storia moderni dei fori di Roma.* Bari-Roma: Laterza.

Keller, Donald R. and David W. Rupp. 1983. *Archaeological Survey in the Mediterranean Area.* BAR International Series 155. Oxford: Oxford University Press.

Kristiansen, Kristian. 1981. "A Social History of Danish Archaeology." In *Towards a History of Archaeology,* edited by Glyn Daniel, 20–44. London: Thames and Hudson.

Levine, Philippa J. A. 1986. *The Amateur and the Professional.* Cambridge: Cambridge University Press.

Lord, Louis E. 1947. *A History of the American School of Classical Studies at Athens, 1882–1942. An Intercollegiate Project.* Cambridge, Massachusetts: Harvard University Press.

MacKendrick, Paul L. 1962. *The Greek Stones Speak.* New York: St. Martin's Press.

Manacorda, Daniele. 1982. *Archeologia urbana a Roma: il progetto della Crypta Balbi.* Firenze: All'insegma del Giglio.

Manacorda, Daniele and Renato Tamassia. 1985. *Il piccone del regime.* Roma: Armando Curcio.

McDonald, William A. 1984. "The Minnesota Messenia Survey: A Look Back." In *Studies Presented to Sterling Dow on his Eightieth Birthday.* Durham: Duke University Press.

Meltzer, David J., Don Fowler, and Jeremy Sabloff, eds. 1986. *American Archaeology Past and Future.* Washington, D.C.: Smithsonian Institution Press.

Meritt, Lucy Shoe. 1984. *History of the American School of Classical Studies at Athens, 1939–1980.* Princeton: Princeton University Press.

Miller, Walter. 1931. "The Athenian Agora and the Northwest Slope of the Acropolis: I." *Art and Archaeology* 32: 99–108.

Novick, Peter. 1988. *That Noble Dream: The 'Objectivity Question' and the American Historical Profession.* Cambridge: Cambridge University Press.

Patterson, Thomas C. 1986. "The Last Sixty Years: Toward a Social History of Americanist Archaeology in the United States." *American Anthropologist* 88: 7–26.

———. 1995. *Toward a Social History of Archaeology in the United States.* Fort Worth: Harcourt Brace.

Potter, Timothy. 1979. *The Changing Landscape of South Etruria.* New York: St. Martin's Press.

Reinhold, Meyer. 1984. *Classica Americana: The Greek and Roman Heritage in the United States.* Detroit: Wayne State University Press.

Smith, H. 1913. Problems of the College Art Association. *Bulletin of the College Art Association* 1:1–5.

Trigger, Bruce G. 1989. *A History of Archaeological Thought.* Cambridge: Cambridge University Press.

Willey, Gordon R. and Jeremy Sabloff. 1980. *A History of American Archaeology.* 2nd ed. (Third edition 1993.) San Francisco: W. H. Freeman.

Wilson, John Albert. 1964. *Signs and Wonders upon Pharaoh.* Chicago: University of Chicago Press.

Wylie, Alison. 1991. Feminist Critiques and Archaeological Challenges. In *The Archaeology of Gender,* edited by Dale Walde and Noreen D. Willows. Calgary: The Archaeological Association of the University of Calgary. Pp. 17–23.

to

# II

# Professionals May Not Be Women

Alice B. Kehoe

The three papers in this section present life experiences in archaeology that are remarkably similar for a set of otherwise dissimilar women. Nancy J. Parezo detailed the histories of the same sort of women under the apt title, *Hidden Scholars* (1993a, c). Jesse Jennings, one of the more powerful leaders of the profession in twentieth-century America, mentions in his autobiography (1994) only one woman, Harriet Smith, who excavated a mound in the Mississippian city of Cahokia, in Illinois. For a photograph he publishes of one of his field crews, he can name every young man, but none of the young women who probably worked as "lab chicks." Jennings' poor memory for women colleagues is typical, and demonstrative of the problem of preparing adequate histories of archaeology. *Opportunities* were never absolutely lacking, as the three subsequent chapters indicate; women's *contributions* simply were ignored. The image of the professional archaeologist is the picture of a man, "hairy-chested [or] hairy-chinned" (Kidder quoted in Cordell 1993:203). Kidder—of the generation before Jennings, and like him, a leader in the profession—gave an *idealized cognitive model* (Lakoff 1987:68) of the type George Lakoff calls an *image schema*. Such mental schemata are

> not rich (that is, fully detailed), and they do not have specific knowledge associated with them. . . . They are neither context-bound, nor specific, nor conscious, nor effortful. . . . [I]mage schemas structure both our perceptions and our rich images (Lakoff 1987:453).

Professionals preempt, institutionalize, and legitimate in the public sphere, and are autonomous in regard to other classes of public persons. None of these actions and conditions collocate with the image schema WOMAN. Ergo, professionals cannot *be* "women."

In the third edition of his co-authored *A History of American Archaeology*, Jeremy Sabloff states, "If the number of women cited herein is low—and it is obvious that it is—this should be attributed to the bias of the field up until very recent times rather than the biases of the present authors" (Willey and Sabloff 1993:94, n. 20). Despite this apologia, there can be no defensible reason for a 1993 edition to omit Florence Hawley Ellis, whose extensive, methodologically solid, innovative work in Southwest archaeology earned her a 1974 festschrift. The indefensible reason, I suspect, was that Hawley Ellis believed she must always be

> pleasantly dressed—a pleasant thing to look upon—and doing every lit-
> tle thing that is seen to be pleasant femaleness. And you have to show
> that you're not going after them [men]. You are just being a pleasant
> piece of the landscape. . . . You may go home and do a lot of weeping
> first and then wipe your tears and settle down to your paper and pencil
> (1985 interview quoted in Parezo 1993c:339).

Abby Leach was womanly, and created an uncontested niche teaching in a woman's college. Matilda Coxe Stevenson, in Levine's study, began her professional work as helpmate to her husband. His early death left her with field notes to be prepared for publication, and the need for a salary. While Colonel Stevenson was at her side, Mrs. Stevenson was admired for her ability to add valuable material to his researches; after his death, the same behavior was castigated as dominating, insensitive, and too independent (Parezo 1993b:46), for the leadership, commitment to fieldwork, and competence praised in the husband were unseemly in the woman, once these were seen to be her own qualities rather than a wife's reflection of her husband. "Pleasant femaleness" is not an attribute of the professional in our society.

Susan Bender's portrayal of Marian White illustrates the anomaly of the professional WOMAN. Clearly it never occurred to White to comport herself as a pleasant piece of the landscape. Her métier turned out to be fieldwork conducted with non-professionals who valued her training and credentials. To them, her gender could be ignored because they felt they needed this person's professional competence. Her fellow professionals didn't need her; worse, she was a competitor for jobs and research funds. If she lent her abilities to projects with non-professionals, she shifted, in professionals' perception, into a social worker role, a nurturant helper. This was appropriate for a WOMAN. White is an example of a human being whose social persona is bent two ways: towards her gender by the men with whom she might otherwise compete, and towards her professional status by the men who competed in other arenas. (Hawley Ellis, her contemporary working in the Southwest, parallels White's situation; see Jonathan Reyman's citations in his essay in Section III of the helpful field manuals she prepared for use by avocational as well as professional archaeologists.)

The effect of the 1964 Civil Rights Act in the United States, and comparable social action in other countries, has been a modification of the WOMAN and PROFESSIONAL image schemas so that these categories now overlap. They overlap, but do not coincide: a high proportion of professional women archaeologists have rejected motherhood (Levine 1994:27; Parezo 1993a:8, 19, and 1993c:342–343), or have limited their reproduction to one child. The campaign "take your daughter to work" one day only out of the work year reveals that, although PROFESSIONAL may include WOMAN, it definitely includes FATHER, but it still doesn't encompass MOTHER. The images are so far apart that childlessness as a price to be paid for professional status is almost absent as an issue in the voluminous discussions of women's problems as professionals. This inequity should not be ignored in reading the lives of women archaeologists.

## References Cited

Cordell, Linda S. 1993. "Women Archaeologists in the Southwest." In *Hidden Scholars,* edited by Nancy J. Parezo, 202–220. Albuquerque: University of New Mexico Press.

Jennings, Jesse D. 1994. *Accidental Archaeologist.* Salt Lake City: University of Utah Press.

Lakoff, George. 1987. *Women, Fire, and Dangerous Things.* Chicago: University of Chicago Press.

Levine, Mary Ann. 1994. "Presenting the Past: A Review of Research on Women in Archeology." In *Equity Issues for Women in Archaeology,* edited by Margaret C. Nelson, Sarah M. Nelson, and Alison Wylie, 23–36. Archeological Papers of the American Anthropological Association, no. 5. Washington, D.C.: American Anthropological Association.

Parezo, Nancy J. 1993a. "Anthropology: The Welcoming Science." In *Hidden Scholars,* edited by Nancy J. Parezo, 3–37. Albuquerque: University of New Mexico Press.

———. 1993b. "Matilda Coxe Stevenson: Pioneer Ethnologist." In *Hidden Scholars,* edited by Nancy J. Parezo, 38–62. Albuquerque: University of New Mexico Press.

———. 1993c. "Conclusion: The Beginning of the Quest." In *Hidden Scholars,* edited by Nancy J. Parezo, 334–367. Albuquerque: University of New Mexico Press.

Willey, Gordon R. and Jeremy A. Sabloff. 1993. *A History of American Archaeology.* 3rd ed. New York: W. H. Freeman.

# 8

## Women and Classical Archaeology at the Turn of the Century

## Abby Leach of Vassar College

James Halporn

In the administrative structures of American universities classical studies often subsumes the disciplines of the ancient history of Greece and Rome, as well the art and archaeology of these cultures. Whatever other factors may enter into the distinctions in classics, however, the central focus of classics, or better put, classical philology or even *Altertumswissenschaft*,[1] remains texts. At various periods, Greek and Latin classical texts enjoyed a privileged position: at one time these texts served as models for later authors to follow in writing texts in the ancient languages; at another time privilege attached to presenting classical texts as the source of proper educational and moral principles (what the Germans call *Bildung*); at still another time, the use of classical texts to illuminate ancient culture as a whole claimed the position of privilege.

The growth of the research imperative in the universities of Germany in the nineteenth century led, to use the terms of Anthony Grafton, from "Polyhistor" to "Philolog" (1983:159–192). That is, antiquarians who taught classics as a static body of facts and doctrines were supplanted by a generation of researchers who focused on reconstructing the lost texts of antiquity, freeing the discipline from the burden of the scholarly tradition and making it "new." They could restore the text externally by developing a methodology of textual criticism, often referred to as the "method of Lachmann," or internally by a study of the morphology, syntax, and metrics of the ancient languages. With the growth of the research imperative came also the development of professionalism. It is valuable to consider how the professionalization of the field affected the women who decided to enter the field of classics at the end of the nineteenth century.

The sociologist M. Sarfatti Larson (1977) has defined professions as "occupations with special power and prestige. They have special competence in esoteric bodies of knowledge linked to central needs and values of the social system, and are devoted to the service of the public, above and beyond material incentives" (xi). Professionalization, however, as the noun suggests, is "the process by which producers of special services sought to constitute *and control* a market for their expertise" (xvi). It is "an attempt to translate one order of scarce resources—special knowledge and skills—into another—social and economic rewards" (xvii).

Professionalization became widespread in the United States because the American university was especially open to new fields of learning and there was support for general access to higher education in American society. To the elites of the new middle class, the university provided a common socialization, which preceded, in fact, their rise and assertion in the new social order. The dominant, and almost the unique, meaning of these professional movements was the conquest and assertion of social status (Larson 1977:153, 155). This move towards professionalism and professionalization had profound effects on aspiring teachers and scholars, male and female.

Women found many obstacles to achievement and limitations on the development of professional identities. Professions that did welcome women attracted them in large numbers, but they had to sacrifice claims to high status, competitive salaries, and career advancement. This was especially true of the most popular profession, teaching. The high status occupations were reserved for men, and women entered professions which extended their previous functions in the home, such as teaching, librarianship, and nursing (Antler 1987:379).

The world of professionalism sketched briefly here was the world which women were to enter in the late nineteenth century. Of course, there had always been women's schools and seminaries in which the study of Latin was pursued as a humanistic subject. Greek, however, was regarded as much too difficult for the female mind. For the few who dared to attempt Greek, and who wished to follow the new calling of the professoriate, there seemed little hope. It is a familiar tale. Their way was blocked by the rules of the universities. Women were unable to study regularly with that patron saint of American classical scholarship, Basil L. Gildersleeve. In the fall of 1877, M. Carey Thomas, a resident of Baltimore (and whose family had been involved in the founding of the university) enrolled at Johns Hopkins University. She had received her undergraduate degree at Cornell, and sought an advanced degree from Johns Hopkins. However, she was accepted at Hopkins only on restricted terms. She was offered a syllabus and attendance at certain lectures, and such assistance as she could obtain from an individual professor, but was not permitted to attend classes (nor the Greek Seminarium under the direction of Gildersleeve). It is perfectly clear that had Gildersleeve seriously wanted to accept her as a pupil he could have done so (Dobkin 1979:149f). Carey Thomas left Hopkins after three years to study at Leipzig, Stuttgart, and Zürich, where she was finally granted her Ph.D.

Just as serious as the lack of opportunities to study with recognized scholars was the unavailability of scholarly resources. We need only recall the famous paragraphs of Virginia Woolf in *A Room of One's Own*. She writes that one day, when crossing the quadrangle at "Oxbridge," she was puzzling out questions about Milton, Lamb, and Thackeray:

"It then occurred to me that the very manuscript itself which Lamb
had looked at was only a few hundred yards away, so that one could follow Lamb's footsteps across the quadrangle to that famous library where
the treasure is kept. Moreover, I recollected, as I put this plan into execu-
tion, it is in this famous library that the manuscript of Thackeray's
[*Henry*] *Esmond* is also preserved. . . . [H]ere I was actually at the door
which leads into the library itself. I must have opened it, for instantly
there issued, like a guardian angel barring the way with a flutter of
black gown instead of white wings, a deprecating, silvery, kindly gentleman, who regretted in a low voice as he waved me back that ladies are
only admitted to the library if accompanied by a Fellow of the College
or furnished with a letter of introduction" (1945:9).

If this situation of 60 years ago seems both foreign and out-of-date, consider that in 1980 Harriet F. Adams could write, "only 20 years ago when I was
in boarding school in Boston women could not set foot in Harvard's Widener
Library" (1984:135).[2] A wealthy classics professor recently suggested in an article that no one could do classical philology without a private library of at
least 10,000 volumes. Without even access to such a library, imagine the difficulties that a woman at the turn of the century encountered, if she wanted to
pursue text criticism and editing, disciplines that require an extensive reference collection and entry into manuscript collections! The world had moved
a long way from the time when Maggie Tulliver had to sneak a glance into her
brother's Latin books, but the world in which men maintained their culture of
male bonding through classical studies was intact.[3]

Furthermore, in higher education women did not have great opportunity
for self-initiated scholarship, being bogged down in routine teaching duties.
For most of them a self concept as members of a highly trained professional
discipline was lacking. Historically, most women went into teaching as a
means of earning a livelihood while waiting to be married. Achievements
of women professionals remained largely idiosyncratic; traditionally defined
spheres of gender activity remained remarkably resistant to change. By 1920,
women's search for a new identity remained largely as unfulfilled as in 1890
(Antler 1987:412, 423).

The career of Abby Leach, first woman president of the American Philological Association (1899–1900), is exemplary in the history of collegiate education for women in America and in the study of the place of women in
American classical scholarship. Leach's arrival in Cambridge, Massachusetts
marks the beginning of the notion that women could have a professional career in classical studies, and not merely a role as teacher of classical languages.
Born in 1855 into a manufacturing family from Brockton, Massachusetts,
Leach received the typical education for women of the New England middle
classes. She attended high school in Brockton, and then studied at the Oread
Collegiate Institute in Worcester, one of those finishing schools that usually
marked the end of formal education for women in that period. It was at Oread
that Leach began her study of Greek. Both she and her sisters were encouraged

to continue their education. Higher education for women was a possibility but still a rarity in the last quarter of the nineteenth century. Even Bryn Mawr, founded in 1885, the most scholarly of the women's institutions, did not require Greek for entrance.

Although no college program for women then existed at Harvard, Abby Leach went to Cambridge in the fall of 1878, at the age of twenty-three, to attempt private study with the faculty of the classics department. She is said to have persuaded William W. Goodwin to take her on as a private pupil by her ability in sight translation of Greek, after he had initially rejected even the idea of such a strange request. Goodwin is familiar to all classicists today as the author of what is still a standard school Greek grammar. He also produced a major reference work on the Greek verb, *Syntax of the Moods and Tenses of the Greek Verb* (2nd ed., 1890) as well as an epoch-making edition of Demosthenes' *On the Crown* (1901). He was interested in archaeology from his student days and was therefore a suitable choice to serve as the first director of the American School of Classical Studies in Athens (ASCSA) when it was founded in 1881.[4]

Of this period, Charles B. Gulick remarks in his memoir of Leach (1933: 72), "It is difficult to realize the courage and tact then required to overcome not only masculine and even feminine prejudices against such instruction, but also the many practical difficulties which impeded liberal-minded men like William W. Goodwin and James B. Greenough in their desire to help her."

She proved to be a successful student for both Goodwin and Greenough. The latter said of her to Arthur Gilman, who was attempting to develop instruction for young women from the Harvard faculty in 1878, that this young lady "was to be the nucleus of a University" (comment of James B. Greenough to Arthur Gilman, November 26, 1878, Radcliffe Archives). In terms that may sound to us condescending, Le Baron Russell Briggs, president of Radcliffe College, described her, some fifty years later, as a "normal, vigorous, and capable girl, . . . who knew what she wanted, deserved it, got it, and used it well . . . " (1929:106). More seriously, Goodwin wrote of her, "I am confident that, if she had been a regular student of the College, she would have graduated with the highest honors in Classics" (Goodwin letter dated June 20, 1884, Radcliffe Archives). Her example encouraged Arthur Gilman and others to set up the Committee for the Private Collegiate Instruction of Women at Harvard, which was at last incorporated as Radcliffe College in 1894.

Leach and other women students who studied at Harvard were subject to extreme difficulties in their pursuit of learning. They were not permitted the use of the Harvard College Library and books had to be brought to them by messenger to the reading room set up for them in a private house. Indeed, President Eliot of Harvard seems to have taken such a dislike to the presence of women that they were quickly removed from the Harvard Yard by the custodians if Eliot was seen crossing the area.

During the 1879–1882 period, Leach was a special student at the Harvard Annex, which was the popular name for the women's branch. She did not take the program leading to the certificate (it was several years before degrees were offered), but simply took Greek and Latin courses. During these years she also taught at the Girls' Latin School in Boston in order to pay for her studies.

There is no record of the work that Leach did as a private pupil in 1878–1879, but in the first year of the Harvard Annex, she enrolled in some five courses. She was one of twenty-six students in 1879–1880, ranging in age from 17 to 32. This was a considerable number of students for a beginning institution, since most women's colleges in this period had less than fifty enrolled in the collegiate department. Leach was the most advanced student in Greek and Latin. In these years she studied Greek with John Williams White and W. W. Goodwin, and Sanskrit with J. B. Greenough. Although advanced study, especially in Greek, was regarded as beyond the capability of women, Leach was able to show to the satisfaction of some of the most distinguished of American classicists that she could meet the standards set for men students.[5]

In 1883, she was appointed teacher and instructor of Greek at Vassar College; in 1885 she achieved the B. A. and M. A. degrees at Vassar by examination, and was elected to Phi Beta Kappa. In that same year, she studied during the summer at Johns Hopkins, taking private instruction from Basil L. Gildersleeve. The next year, she was appointed as assistant professor of Greek language at Vassar, and in the summer of that year she traveled to Bonn. During the year 1886–1887, she remained abroad, studying at Leipzig and traveling in Italy and Greece. It is likely that during this European tour she went to England and visited Anne Jemima Clough, the English educator, at Cambridge. In 1888, she was appointed associate professor of Greek at Vassar; in 1889, professor of Greek; and in 1890, chair of the newly constituted Department of Greek, a position she held until her death in 1918.

Leach's general interest in higher education for women was focused on her service to the Association of Collegiate Alumnae (later the American Association of University Women) of which she was president from 1899 to 1901. She attended meetings of the American Philological Association assiduously from the time of her initial membership in 1888, and was elected president in the society's thirtieth year. Her presidential address, delivered at Madison, Wisconsin, in July 1900, appeared in the *American Journal of Philology* under the title, "The Athenian Democracy in the Light of Greek Literature." She also served the field of classics as a member of the Committee of Managers of the American School of Classical Studies in Athens from 1888–1918, and fostered the interests of women's graduate education as a member of the fellowship committee of the Association of Collegiate Alumnae.

The annual reports she submitted as chair of her department to President Taylor of Vassar College show her intense concern for the growth of classical studies in Greek for women on the undergraduate and graduate level, and especially her interest in seeing that the newly developing field of classical archaeology be well supported and represented at Vassar.[6]

Her reports to President Taylor of Vassar began in 1889–1890, in which year 61 pupils were enrolled in the Greek Department. She then submitted her first request for books, photographs, and back numbers of philological journals. She repeated the request for more books and journals in her report for 1890–1891, and, mentioning Vassar's connection with the American School of Classical Studies in Athens (ASCSA), requested an appropriation for photos of "every new find." In the immediately succeeding years, she repeated her desire for an appropriation for acquired photographs. By 1894 there were 164 students enrolled in the Greek department (she reported total Vassar enrollment as 1129). In the 1895 report she stressed the need for more work in archaeology, and mentioned her graduate students. Her requests for books, photos, and slides continued. In her report for 1898 she mentioned a new course in Pausanias requiring additional slides and photos. At this time she asked for a course in Modern Greek, to enable her students to compete for Archaeological Institute of America fellowships. In the 1899 report she mentioned that the course in Pausanias was given in the second semester, and that, "since archaeology is growing in importance," Professor Leotsakos presented a one-hour course in the first semester in Modern Greek, and she hoped to have the same course in the coming year. Four of her M. A. students studied Attic inscriptions with her, and three of her students would be at the ASCSA. In 1900 both the course in Modern Greek and the course in Pausanias were repeated, and a new course in archaeology was to be added. This she observed was important, "because women now can compete for archaeology fellowships."[7]

In 1900 her prominence in the profession was marked by several offices: chair of the ASCSA's Committee on Fellowships, president of the Collegiate Alumnae Association, and president of the American Philological Association.

In 1902 Leach stressed the development of the archaeology program both for its "widespread interest" and because "some knowledge of it is demanded of teachers in the best secondary schools." In 1908, in spite of a decline in the study of Greek both at Vassar and in preparatory schools, Leach maintained her interest in archaeology. In 1910 she noted a marked increase in archaeology student numbers. To emphasize the attractiveness of her archaeology program, she added, "my electives proportionally are as large and numerically bear favorable comparison with the advanced electives in the scientific course."

This brief discussion of the career of Abby Leach shows that her interest was to encourage women to work in the newly developing field of archaeology rather than in the central (and most prestigious) field of classical philology with its focus on text criticism, grammar, and writing scholarly commentaries.[8] The same was not true of women who entered the fields of English and modern foreign languages. How, then, are we to explain the gravitation to this ancillary classical discipline?

I would suggest several reasons. First, women were not admitted to seminars in the strongest classical philology programs, including in European universities. In Europe, however, women had the right at least to attend lectures.

Second, the prestige of American scholars as philologists and text critics was overpowering, and this helped to create an exclusionary environment. Third, women teaching in the established college programs realized that the recruitment of undergraduates to their courses required a broad study of antiquity that included archaeology. I believe that all of these factors played a part, but that another factor provided the major impetus: the newness of the field. As a developing field in this period, archaeology was open to new talent. The sheer newness of the discipline enabled women to apply their scientific interest in the analysis of artifacts to the discovery and recovery of an ancient civilization that could serve as a source of study in the contemporary world. Furthermore, the absence of superior scholars in archaeology on the American scene may also have contributed to making the field more accessible to newcomers.

Something similar happened in the social sciences in general. An example is the University of Chicago at the time of its establishment. The president of the university, William Rainey Harper, a specialist in Hebrew, wanted to build strong departments in Semitics, classics, and philosophy. He was unable to recruit faculty in these traditional areas. Instead, he assembled a faculty weighted toward science and social science rather than towards classics and philosophy. While the attempt was made to keep women out of the new disciplines like sociology by shunting them off into social work,[9] women did find opportunities in political science, anthropology, and archaeology. Because representatives of these fields were so sparse, there was little danger of their feminization, as was feared for the liberal arts curriculum and for education.[10] The prediction of James R. Angell of the University of Michigan was realized: when women were encouraged to study at the graduate level and when they no longer felt obliged to "conform their collegiate work to immediate bread and butter issues [i.e., becoming high school teachers]," they would demonstrate broader interests and greater talents than they had been able to display up to that time (Rosenberg 1982:64).

Despite the efforts of Abby Leach, the number of women who took up the professional study of classics rapidly declined in the early decades of the twentieth century. The elimination of the Latin requirement for college entrance after World War I was partly responsible, but the decline in enrollments on the college level in Greek was also substantial. In 1893, Abby Leach was able to produce Sophocles' *Antigone* at Poughkeepsie, an event that received wide coverage in the New York City newspapers and attracted a large audience, including many of the major scholars from the Eastern universities. Such an event would have been unthinkable in later years. Was the reason in part the increased professional standards that came into the field as time went on?

Richard Jenkyns (1980) and Frank M. Turner (1981) have suggested that a partial explanation for the interest in Classical civilization during the late nineteenth century is the attempt by the educated class of society to create an ethical system outside the Judeo-Christian tradition. This is an assertion worth exploration with regard to classical studies in the United States. Abby

Leach was invited to give the address at the twentieth-fifth annual commence-ment exercises of Radcliffe College in 1908. Her subject was "What Makes Up the Essential Life; How to Make the Individual Life Give the Best Returns and Prove its Intrinsic Worth" (Leach 1908/1909:105–108). She attacks the grow-ing interest women had in the life of service to others, and in social work. She wonders why social work, which she also regards as good, is to be the supreme work for all. She asks then if the essential life has to be practical, because the age is a practical age, and demands tangible results, at all events on the mate-rial side. No, she asserts, the truly practical is that "which enlarges one's pow-ers and leads to rich fields of productive thought and high intellectual culture, and no knowledge outrivals the knowledge of Greek in what it has to offer for the enrichment of thought and feeling." Anything, she says, that becomes part and parcel of one's life is practical. She notes the open contradiction be-tween being and seeming, between profession and practice, between stand-ards praised, and standards followed. She takes her example from democracy. "Democracy with its blatant insistence upon equality—where are place and power and privilege more eagerly sought for? Democracy praises equality and craves distinction. It lauds principle and bows down before success" (107). Like a latter day Antigone, she concludes, "the life to strive for is the life of perfect poise and noble beauty, and this comes from the power to see life steadily and see it whole [as Matthew Arnold had said of her favorite author, Sophocles]. . . . [S]ome steadfast truth beyond the mysterious chances and changes . . . abides . . . , some lofty and unchanging principle, beyond life's facts, its verities—the laws that are not of to-day or yesterday, but live on for-ever. The vision to see and the will to do, there is the essential life" (108). How distant this earnestness of 1908, this secular elitist faith seems to us now, al-though perhaps this faith was part of the essential life of the classicist, and perhaps it has to be. If such passion is necessary to the classicist, it is a message that no one since has listened to very carefully or even cared to notice.

## Acknowledgments

Material on the life and work of Abby Leach, her fellow students, and her stu-dents at Vassar came from the archives of Radcliffe College and Vassar College, as well as the working files for *Notable American Women* at the Schlesinger Li-brary in Cambridge, Massachusetts. In particular, I made use of the papers of Ann Townsend Zwart, author of the *NAW* biography of Abby Leach. I want to thank J. Knowles of the Radcliffe Archives and L. Browar of the Vassar Library for their kind assistance.

## Notes

    1.  In spite of our tendency to translate the German term "Wissenschaft" as science, this inevitably gives the wrong slant to the concept. Fritz Ringer (1969:102f) provides an excellent summary of the meaning and intention of the term:

The German *Wissenschaft* is not the equivalent of the English 'science,' for the latter implies certain methodological commitments. In German usage, any organized body of information is referred to as *eine Wissenschaft,* with the indefinite article.

At the same time, all formal knowledge, and the collective activity of scholars in obtaining, interpreting, and ordering it, may be rendered *Wissenschaft* or, more commonly *die Wissenschaft,* with the definite article. Thus *die Wissenschaft* must be translated as 'scholarship' or 'learning,' rarely as 'science,' and *eine Wissenschaft* simply means a 'discipline.' In English, it is possible to argue about whether sociology or history is 'a science.' In German, history is *eine Wissenschaft* by definition, and to ask whether sociology is *eine Wissenschaft* is to wonder about its status as a distinct and clearly circumscribed discipline, not about its more or less 'scientific' methods.

To call a certain historical investigation *wissenschaftlich* is to praise it for its sound scholarship and perhaps for its past-mindedness.

A humanistic discipline by definition is a *Geisteswissenschaft.* This was an immense advantage to the humanist, who could always argue against an opponent that his scientific approach was *naturwissenschaftlich* or *positivistisch,* thus showing that his approach to the humanistic study was false in its conceptions of knowledge and learning. Naturally, the tie of this term with the term of German idealism, *Geist,* was both obvious and employed. Wissenschaft must be impractical: as Werner Jaeger put it, '*Wissenschaft* and empiricism [*Empirie*], the latter word taken in the antique sense of practical experience, are two fundamentally different things, and Wissenschaft has no place where *Empirie* is required, for theory kills the instinct' (Jaeger, "Stellung und Aufgaben," 73, as translated by Ringer, 110).

2. Adams is not entirely correct, but she is right in suggesting that women were not made welcome in the Harvard libraries. Women undergraduates had restricted use of the Widener Library until about 1938, when they were admitted to the main reading room; graduate students had access to the stacks. It was not until 1966, after the Hilles Library was opened on the Radcliffe Quad, that women were finally admitted to the undergraduate Lamont Library. It is unclear when undergraduates, men and women, were admitted to the Widener stacks. (See Carpenter 1986:186–189 and Metcalf 1987:87.)

3. For attempts to maintain the superiority of the male mind in the study of Greek and Latin and the dangers to women, especially in terms of their "feeble minds" and the unsuitability of the learned woman as a wife, see Fowler (1983). Such views were prevalent even among educated women. Note the observation by Alethea Hayter (1988:1248): "Dorothy Bradby's dictum that women ought not to 'strain their feebler intellects and ruin their health

in a vain attempt to compete with men in learning,' [was] a bizarre comment from a woman who herself got a First in English at Oxford, and whose younger sister Barbara . . . was the first woman ever to achieve a First in both Mods and Greats at Oxford."

4. See Danker (1988:61f). William Watson Goodwin: Born Concord, MA 1831. Ph.D., Göttingen 1855. 1860, Eliot Professor of Greek, Harvard (ret. 1901). President of the APA 1871 and 1884. Died 1912.

5. For the importance of maintaining a male curriculum while at the same time protecting the health and well-being of the supposedly more frail female students, the program at Vassar was a model. (See Rothman 1978:26–42.) Although the "mental discipline" notion of the importance of classical training seems to have died out in the 1870s, it was still important in defending the introduction of new disciplines, such as English studies. (See Graff 1987:37ff.)

6. Yet she always remained conscious of the central position of language study in the curriculum. Her strongest academic objection towards her colleague, Grace Macurdy, against whom she exhibited a strong personal animus, was her weakness as a teacher of beginning Greek, and her lack of ability in Greek prose composition.

7. Of her students then in Athens, Leach remarked that a Miss Stevens had to leave Athens because of her brother's illness. In this period women typically saw themselves first as members of the family and only second as professionals (Antler 1987:176, 178).

8. For the period in question, the volumes of *Notable American Women* include eight professional women classicists, not including Leach herself. Five of the eight, including Lida Shaw King, Leach's pupil, became professional archaeologists. Of the rest, one was an art historian and two were ancient historians. In her early thirties, King, together with Ida Thallon (Vassar, 1897), excavated in Attica. Because in her later years she was professor and dean at Pembroke College, for whose growth and success she was largely responsible, she has not been included in Sherman's survey (1981).

The American archaeologists, excepting King, were Edith (Hall) Dohan, Hetty Goldman, Harriet Ann (Boyd) Hawes, and Esther Van Deman. The ancient historians included Grace Macurdy and Lilly Ross Taylor, and the art historian was Mary Hamilton Swindler. Two other women classicists are mentioned: Edith Hamilton, the popular writer on Greek subjects, and Helen Magill White, the first woman to receive a Ph.D. (which was in classics), but whose professional career ended at age 37 when she married the president of Cornell, Andrew Dickson White. *The Biographical Cyclopaedia of American Women* (1925:II.106ff) lists Mary Crowell Wells as the secretary of the Consumer's League, a reform organization. Wells, a graduate of Smith with a Yale Ph.D., also studied at Leipzig and the ASCSA. For further information on Hawes, Dohan (who was one of Hawes' assistants at Gournia), Goldman (who worked together with Alice Leslie Walker, a pupil of Leach) and Van Deman, see Sherman (1981:32–34).

9. Women graduate students in any case tended to be more interested in social work than theoretical sociology, for social work paralleled in the pub-

lic sphere the kind of work they had been reared to perform in the home. Scientific expertise was only a tool rather than a goal (Rosenberg 1982:49f). On men's fears of feminization and the loss of "manliness" in this period, see Filene (1986:74–78). It has been suggested that Harper was unable to find semiticists for his program because of the prevalent anti-Semitism in academe at that time. This seems to me to have introduced an endemic problem of the Eastern academic establishment into the Midwest where it hardly existed.

10. My colleague Eleanor W. Leach has suggested that women may have avoided literary studies in classics generally because they were too close to the traditional area of feminine cultural "accomplishments" to be attractive to them as scholars. For the close relation of sociology to literature, see Lepenies (1988).

## References Cited

Adams, Harriet F. 1984. "Work in the Interstices: Woman in Academe." *Women in Academe,* edited by Resa L. Dudovitz, 135–141. Oxford: Pergamon Press. [Also published in *Women's Studies International Forum* 6 (1983): 135–141.]

Antler, Joyce. 1987. *The Educated Woman and Professionalization: The Struggle for a New Feminine Identity, 1890–1920.* New York: Garland.

Briggs, Le Baron R. 1929. "An Experiment in Faith: Radcliffe College." *Atlantic Monthly* 143 (January): 105–109.

Danker, Frederick W. 1988. *A Century of Greco-Roman Philology.* Atlanta: Scholars Press.

Carpenter, Kenneth E. 1986. *The First 350 Years of the Harvard University Library: Description of an Exhibition.* Cambridge: Harvard University Library.

Dobkin, Marjorie H., ed. 1979. *The Making of a Feminist: Early Journals and Letters of M. Carey Thomas.* Kent: Kent State University Press.

Filene, Peter G. 1986. *Him/Her/Self: Sex Roles in Modern America.* 2nd ed. Baltimore: Johns Hopkins University Press.

Fowler, R. 1983. "'On Not Knowing Greek': The Classics and the Woman of Letters." *Classical Journal* 78: 337–349.

Graff, Gerald. 1987. *Professing Literature: An Institutional History.* Chicago: University of Chicago Press.

Grafton, Anthony. 1983. "Polyhistor into *Philolog:* Notes on the Transformation of German Classical Scholarship, 1780–1850." *History of Universities* 3: 159–192.

Gulick, Charles B. 1933. "Abby Leach." In *Dictionary of American Biography,* vol. 11, edited by Dumas Malone. New York: Scribner's.

Hayter, Althea. 1988. "Review of Anne Ridler, 'A Victorian Family Postbag.'" *Times Literary Supplement* (November 11–17): 1248.

Jaeger, Werner. 1960. 2nd ed. "Stellung und Aufgaben der Universität in der Gegenwart." In *Humanistische Reden und Vorträge,* 68–86. Berlin: de Gruyter.

Jenkyns, Richard. 1980. *The Victorians and Ancient Greece.* Cambridge: Harvard University Press.

Larson, Magali Sarfatti. 1977. *The Rise of Professionalism: A Sociological Analysis.* Berkeley: University of California Press.

Leach, Abby. 1908/1909. "What Makes Up the Essential Life; How to Make the Individual Life Give the Best Returns and Prove its Intrinsic Worth." *Harvard Graduates' Magazine* 17: 105–108.

Lee, Erma C., ed. 1925. *The Biographical Cyclopaedia of American Women,* vol. II. New York: Franklin W. Lee.

Lepenies, Wolf. 1988. *Between Literature and Science: The Rise of Sociology,* translated by R. J. Hollingdale. Cambridge: Cambridge University Press.

Metcalf, Keyes D. 1987. *My Harvard Library Years, 1937–1955.* Cambridge: Harvard College Library.

Ringer, Fritz K. 1969. *The Decline of the German Mandarins: The German Academic Community, 1890–1933.* Cambridge: Harvard University Press.

Rosenberg, Rosalind. 1982. *Beyond Separate Spheres. Intellectual Roots of Modern Feminism.* New Haven: Yale University Press.

Rothman, Sheila M. 1978. *Woman's Proper Place: A History of Changing Ideals and Practices, 1870 to the Present.* New York: Basic Books.

Sherman, Claire R. 1981. "Widening Horizons (1890–1930)." In *Women as Interpreters of the Visual Arts, 1820–1979,* edited by Claire R. Sherman with Adele M. Holcomb, 27–36. Westport: Greenwood Press.

Turner, Frank M. 1981. *The Greek Heritage in Victorian Britain.* New Haven: Yale University Press.

Woolf, Virginia. 1945. *A Room of One's Own.* Harmondsworth: Penguin.

# 9

## Uncovering a Buried Past

## Women in Americanist Archaeology before the First World War

Mary Ann Levine

The last 20 years have witnessed the rise of studies that seek to reinstate women in the history of Americanist archaeology. However, the first generation of female archaeologists—women who contributed to archaeology in the late nineteenth and early twentieth centuries—have received less scholarly attention than subsequent generations of women archaeologists. Most studies have focused on the second generation of female archaeologists—women born early in the twentieth century who launched their careers in the inter-war years, the 1920s and 1930s (Levine 1994b:25–26). Although women are absent from much of the literature on the early history of the discipline, they have been contributing to the development of Americanist archaeology since at least the 1870s. At roughly the same time that archaeology was becoming professionalized, women not only played an active but a leading role in shaping the discipline.

In this chapter I call attention to archaeology's nearly forgotten foremothers, the first generation of women to have contributed to archaeology. For the purposes of this essay, I do not explore women in classical studies, but rather examine women's contributions and experiences in Americanist archaeology prior to World War I. Although I do not attempt to offer an exhaustive history of women in pre-war archaeology, I hope to provide a more comprehensive and thorough account than is presently available.

I specifically report on four women—Matilda Coxe Stevenson (1849–1915), Alice Fletcher (1838–1923), Mary Hemenway (1820–1894), and Zelia Nuttall (1857–1933) as well as an organization to which they all belonged, the Women's Anthropological Society of America. I reconstruct this largely unrecorded chapter in the history of the profession to expose the institutionalized forms of sexism encountered by women who wished to contribute to archaeology, to document the strategies taken by these women to overcome the barriers, and to consider their substantial and notable contributions to the development of the discipline.

## Women, Higher Education, and the Scientific Professions

The participation of women in Americanist archaeology prior to World War I must be seen within the broader framework of women's entrance into higher education and the scientific professions. Rossiter (1982:1) reports that one of the major developments of the nineteenth century was the rise of higher education for women. The first half of the nineteenth century witnessed a remarkable growth in educational opportunities for women as female academies, seminaries, and a few female colleges were established (Rossiter 1982:7). Opportunities for full collegiate level education expanded after the Civil War with the establishment of Vassar College in 1865, Smith College in 1871, Bryn Mawr in 1885, and Barnard College in 1889 (Rossiter 1982:10). By mid-century, the United States led the world in the amount of education it made available to women (Rossiter 1982:1). Those who supported higher education for women believed that formal schooling would result in the creation of better wives and mothers who would raise moral and patriotic sons. However, women became less constrained by motherhood in the 1880s and 1890s and began to make advances in what had previously been a male monopoly on intellectual discourse (Rossiter 1982:313). New barriers rapidly surfaced to curb this threatened feminization of science. One such barrier was the requirement for a doctoral degree for academic posts during a time when women were denied access to such degrees (Rossiter 1982:313).

Women's admission to male dominated graduate schools came as early as the 1870s at Boston University and as late as the 1960s at Princeton University (Rossiter 1982:29). By 1889, ten institutions including Boston University, Syracuse University, the University of Wooster, the University of Michigan, and Cornell University had awarded 25 doctoral degrees to women (Rossiter 1982:32). After 1889, women's admission to graduate school attracted a great deal of public interest and by the early 1890s, six more institutions (Yale, Pennsylvania, Columbia, Brown, Stanford, and the University of Chicago) decided to admit women to their graduate programs (Rossiter 1982:33–34). However, Yale and Pennsylvania continued to deny women entrance into their undergraduate colleges. Female graduate students were finally admitted to Johns Hopkins University in 1907 and in 1902 Harvard formed the Radcliffe Graduate School so that Radcliffe, not Harvard, awarded women the Ph.D. degree (Rossiter 1982:44).

Rossiter (1982:51) notes that by 1910, women could earn degrees from almost every American university that awarded them to men. She also points out that such educational reforms did not open full careers in science to the few women who had acquired university degrees. The same institutions that granted degrees to women institutionalized unequal gender based employment policies. In the 1880s, women's opportunities in scientific research institutions were limited; they were primarily in marginal positions that may be referred to as a hierarchical kind of "women's work" (Rossiter 1982:60). In an attempt to combat sex segregated employment policies, women created separate forms of employment for female scientists (Rossiter 1982:51). It must be noted that even from these subordinate positions, women made sizable contributions to science.

In the case of anthropology, women in the 1880s began to hold marginal positions in museums. Rossiter (1982:58) notes that women were loosely affiliated field workers who were generally unpaid but were allowed to publish in museum proceedings. A small number of more affluent women assumed the role of financial patrons at late nineteenth century museums (Rossiter 1982:59). Following a discussion of the Women's Anthropological Society of America I report on four women who contributed to Americanist archaeology in the late nineteenth century in these capacities.

## Women's Anthropological Society of America

In the last decades of the nineteenth century, the number of scholarly organizations in Washington increased dramatically (Moldow 1987:147). These organizations were all male, afforded their members the opportunity for intellectual stimulation, buttressed professional identities, and effectively brought together leaders of the new professional elite (Moldow 1987:9). The Anthropological Society of Washington (est. 1879) was one such newly founded scholarly organization. Prohibition against female membership to this society served to marginalize women from the mainstream of professional life in anthropology. Women recognized the benefits that membership could offer and tackled the problem by establishing their own society, the Washington based Women's Anthropological Society of America. Although the professional ethos of the time may have presented aspiring female archaeologists with a constellation of obstacles, women did contribute to the development of Americanist archaeology in the nineteenth century and began to devise strategies to counter male hegemony in the discipline. The establishment of the Women's Anthropological Society of America may be viewed as one such strategy to combat the "old boy network" and infiltrate the mainstream.

The impetus for the creation of a separate professional association stemmed from the rejection of Matilda Coxe Stevenson's membership application to the all male Anthropological Society of Washington (Rossiter 1982:80). At the time of her unsuccessful attempt to join a society to which her husband belonged (Moldow 1987:148), Stevenson had already undertaken numerous ethnographic studies and published reports on some of these expeditions (Parezo 1988:337–338). The decision to deny her membership was formed on the basis of her gender and presumed lack of field experience (Rossiter 1982:80). According to Moldow (1987:148), Stevenson responded to this verdict by issuing "a call for 'intellectual women' to join her in the study of science." Stevenson's husband believed that the project would fail since he could not imagine that there were a half-dozen women with a keen interest in science to respond to this call to form the society's core (Moldow 1987:148). On June 8, 1885, Stevenson met with nine other women to found their own scientific society—the Women's Anthropological Society of America (McGee 1889:240). On that day, officers were chosen and a committee was appointed to draft a constitution (Mendenhall 1893:4). By the end of their first year the society had 34 active members, 1 corresponding member, and 3 honorary members (Mendenhall 1893:5). Like its all male counterpart, the Women's Anthropological Society included scholars from anthropology in addition to researchers from a multitude of related fields.

In response to the question "why should there be two anthropological societies in Washington?," Anita Newcombe McGee, recording secretary, issued the following statement on behalf of the society: "[W]e have no desire to perpetuate a distinction of sex in science; and were we all professional scientists, or possessed the education fitting us to enter the race for intellectual attainment without handicap, we doubt whether a second society would ever have been formed. Under existing conditions, however, we are satisfied to work out our own problems in anticipation of the time when science shall regard only the work, not the worker" (1889:240–241). Anita Newcombe McGee, daughter of Simon Newcombe, America's foremost astronomer, was married to William John McGee, a Bureau of American Ethnology scientist (Hinsley 1981:233). Recognizing her intellectual prowess, Mr. McGee encouraged his wife to pursue medicine and anthropology (Hinsley 1981:233). She became an M. D. in 1892, joined the Women's Anthropological Society when it was founded, and regularly accompanied her husband in the field (Hinsley 1981:233).

For fifteen years, the society, consisting of female anthropologists from all subfields including archaeology, met regularly. Americanist archaeologists as well as classicists such as Sarah Scull and Sophie Schliemann were represented in the society (Anonymous 1889:13). They met "to present papers to each other as a means of mutual encouragement . . . " (Rossiter 1982:82). For example, Stevenson presented a paper entitled "The Religious Life of a Zuñi Child" in 1886; Erminnie A. Smith offered "Reminiscences of Life among the Iroquois Indians in the Province of Quebec"; and Mary Parke Foster delivered a report called "The Ancient Ruins of Mexico" (McGee 1889:241–242).

The society assumed a decidedly professional code of conduct. Biweekly meetings were held in reception rooms provided by Columbian University (now George Washington University) rather than in members' homes (McGee 1889:241). In addition, their constitution declared that "[n]o refreshments shall be provided at the regular meetings of the society" (Anonymous 1889:10). As Lurie (1966:35) notes, this was certainly no pink tea gathering. Potential members were carefully screened and all papers for presentation were previewed to assess their suitability (Moldow 1987:150). In 1886 the Committees on Publications and Communications were established to review papers for publication (May 1988:69–70). By 1889 the Society boasted 67 members (Anonymous 1889:13–15) and in 1893 it celebrated its one hundredth meeting (Mendenhall 1893). Members declared with satisfaction that the society neither sought nor ever received any direct encouragement or aid from societies of scientific men (Moldow 1987:148). They were proud that the society had grown "in spite of prophecies to the contrary . . . without a single unfriendly disagreement or any presage of dissolution" (McGee 1889:24).

With time, the society did significantly alter its constitution. When the society was initially formed, its objectives were "first, to open to women new fields for systematic investigation; second, to invite their co-operation in the development of the science of anthropology" (McGee 1889:240). Moldow (1987:150) argues that in the early days, the leadership placed the activities of the society within the realm of the traditional womanly role. It was asserted that female anthropologists could make unique contributions to the study of women and children. By 1889, McGee, in addition to several other members, felt that women had the right to participate in any scholastic undertaking and should not be confined to endeavors related to their maternal role (Moldow 1987:152). With McGee as secretary, the society amended the objectives section of the constitution to omit any reference to the gender of the members. Some members felt that drawing attention to "feminine" research in science served to foster a distinction that ought not to exist (Moldow 1987:152). The society's constitution now declared that the aim of the association was to "promote Anthropology, by encouraging its study and facilitating the interchange of thought among those interested in anthropological research, and by arranging and preserving systematically all information relating to it, and also by holding regular meetings for its discussion" (Anonymous 1889:5).

Throughout the 1890s, the two Washington based societies met jointly on occasion (Lamb 1906). During this time two important events occurred: Anita McGee and other members of the women's society were negotiating a merger with the men's group, and in 1891, the Anthropological Society of Washington opened its membership to women (Moldow 1987:153). That year, Stevenson was finally elected into that society by a bare majority and after heated debate (Moldow 1987:153). By 1899, McGee felt that women had demonstrated their worthiness and further believed that the existence of two separate societies was no longer necessary (Moldow 1987:153).

The societies merged in 1899, terminating the existence of the Women's Anthropological Society of America. By this time the power that the male society had once wielded had waned as influence shifted away from Washington and the Bureau of Ethnology to university centered anthropology departments (Moldow 1987:153). Therefore, the society was unable to bestow on women the prestige and recognition it had once granted to its male members (Moldow 1987:153). Only forty-nine members of the Women's Anthropological Society joined the Anthropological Society of Washington. May (1988:90) has calculated that as many as seventy women may have chosen not to join the new society in 1899. The Women's Anthropological Society should not be remembered for its bittersweet end, but for the important role it played in affording women an opportunity to recognize their own self-worth. It also served to buffer a sense of isolation and difference that many of these women had probably silently endured. Through the alliances forged by this "old girl net-work," female anthropologists made important steps toward changing the balance of power in the discipline.

In the face of membership barriers it was not uncommon for nineteenth century female intellectuals to fortify their existing yet oftentimes invisible subculture of women's networks and in some cases, such as in anthropology, to create a separate scientific society (Rossiter 1982:74). Fortunately, restrictions placed on gaining access to higher education, joining scientific associations, and obtaining employment did not stop all women from contributing to science, including archaeology, during the 1880s and 1890s. Although some nineteenth-century male researchers were loath to treat female scientists as equals, others were quite sympathetic to the involvement of women in archaeology.

Unfortunately, claims that women were well suited for archaeological research were reasoned from biological determinism. One researcher stated: "[i]n those sciences, such as archaeology, antiquarianism, genealogy and heraldry, where the chief elements of success are infinite patience, conscientious study, and a fine memory and broad general culture, women have always manifested signal ability" (Anonymous 1895:83). In spite of the institutionalized forms of sexism that women in archaeology struggled against, women were instrumental figures in professionalizing the discipline. Matilda Coxe Stevenson, the founder of the Women's Anthropological Society, Alice Fletcher, charter member and vice president, Mary Hemenway, honorary member, and Zelia Nuttall, corresponding member, are among those scholars who made important contributions to the early development of Americanist archaeology.

## Matilda Coxe Stevenson

Matilda Coxe Stevenson was born in 1849 and was raised in Washington, D.C., where her father was an attorney. Parezo (1993:39) has described her family as members of the privileged middle-upper class who provided private governesses for their children before they could attend private schools. After attending Miss Annable's Academy, a female seminary in Philadelphia, she returned to Washington to study law, chemistry, and geology. In 1872 she married Colonel James Stevenson, a self-taught geologist, naturalist, and anthropologist (Parezo 1993:40). The couple, who had no children, became the first husband-wife team in anthropology. Although Stevenson is often remembered for her role in founding the Women's Anthropological Society, her contributions to archaeology are not as well documented in standard histories of the discipline.

After her marriage, Matilda Coxe Stevenson assisted her husband with fossil and ornithological collection and the study of geysers. In the mid-1870s, on one of their trips out West, Stevenson undertook her first ethnographic study among the Ute and Arapaho (Parezo 1993:40). When the Bureau of Ethnology was established in 1879, James Stevenson was appointed leader of an expedition to the Southwest. Matilda Coxe Stevenson joined the expedition as "volunteer coadjutor in ethnology" (Parezo 1993:40). Although best known as an ethnologist and the first woman to do such work in the American Southwest (Parezo 1988:337), Matilda Coxe Stevenson also carried out some archaeological research (Holmes 1916:553).

During the 1880s, archaeologists were primarily concerned with the acquisition of materials for newly established museums. During their first expedition to the Southwest the Stevensons collected ethnographic objects, surveyed local archaeological sites, and gathered materials from caves and shrines (Parezo 1993:40). Patterson (1994:54) notes that in 1881 alone, James Stevenson sent ten thousand pounds of archaeological objects from Moki Pueblo and twenty thousand pounds from Zuñi Pueblo to the U.S. National Museum. This expedition provided the data for Matilda Coxe Stevenson's first ethnographic publications on the Zuñi as well as her first publications in archaeology.

She published a manuscript on archaeological ceramics entitled *Zuñi Pottery* (Stevenson 1881) and a report on the location of archaeological sites entitled "The Cliff-Dwellers of the New Mexican Canyons" (Stevenson 1883). In 1887 and 1888, Matilda Coxe Stevenson and Alice Fletcher lobbied Congress to protect many Southwestern archaeological sites (Fletcher and Stevenson 1889) However, Stevenson's insight into archaeological issues was sometimes wrongly dismissed or ignored by her male contemporaries (Reyman 1992:77–78). The Southwest expedition also resulted in many unrecognized publications; Stevenson wrote many of the reports that were published under her husband's name (Parezo 1993:54).

Parezo (1988:339) notes that after her husband died in 1888, Stevenson was hired to put "her husband's" notes in order, a task that required additional fieldwork. Matilda Coxe Stevenson was thus the first woman to be paid as a government anthropologist. Her salary was always lower than her male contemporaries and about half as much as what her husband earned at the time of his death (Parezo 1993:43). Stevenson never succeeded in securing outside funding for her research. In fact, she was unsuccessful in her attempt to have Mary Hemenway fund a project to bring Native American artisans to the 1893 World Columbian Exposition (Parezo 1993:43). Until her death in 1915, Matilda Coxe Stevenson continued to undertake fieldwork among the native peoples of the Southwest and publish extensively. A complete list of her publications and contributions to ethnology can be found in Lurie (1966, 1971) and Parezo (1988, 1993).

## Alice Cunningham Fletcher

Alice Fletcher was born in 1838 in Cuba, where her parents were visiting to improve her father's health. Her parents, well-educated New Englanders, were both descendants of seventeenth-century colonists (Mark 1988:3–4). Her father, a promising New York lawyer, died when she was only an infant. Following his death, the family moved to the exclusive Brooklyn Heights area of New York where Fletcher enrolled in the Brooklyn Female Academy. Her mother was then remarried to a strict and authoritarian man named Oliver Gardiner. There is considerable evidence to suggest that Gardiner may have sexually abused the adolescent Fletcher (see Mark 1988:10–13). According to Mark (1988:13), Fletcher, who never married or had children, yearned for male companionship and a home, but avoided any form of physical intimacy.

Fletcher, a pioneer in Native American ethnology and archaeology, began her anthropological career at the age of forty. Although she is chiefly known for her widely published ethnographic work among the Omaha, Fletcher's archaeological legacy is considerable. Prior to her involvement in anthropology, she was active in Sorosis, one of the earliest women's clubs in the United States, and was instrumental in the establishment of the Association for the Advancement of Women. Her participation in these associations afforded her the opportunity to learn how to run an organization, to debate publicly, to meet with other suffragists, and to interact within a network of women scientists (Mark 1988:17–27).

Toward the end of the 1870s, Fletcher created a niche for herself as a public lecturer. She prepared a successful set of presentations on ancient America that quickly expanded from four to eleven lectures (Mark 1988:32). She reported on the earliest traces of humankind, the moundbuilders, the peoples of the pueblos, and the antiquities associated with caves, rock shelters, and shell middens. She soon contacted Frederic W. Putnam, director of Harvard's Peabody Museum, who encouraged her to study at the museum, an invitation that she readily accepted. Under Putnam's instruction she read extensively, assisted with the excavation of east coast shell middens, and joined the Archaeological Institute of America (Mark 1980:64; Temkin 1988:101).

Among her lasting contributions to archaeology were her efforts to preserve the Great Serpent Mound, the much celebrated effigy earthwork in Ohio. In 1885 Putnam returned from Ohio bearing news about the imminent danger facing Serpent Mound (Putnam 1973:114). Through a public lecture on American archaeology, Fletcher alerted a group of wealthy women in Newport, Rhode Island, to the potential destruction of Serpent Mound. The women created an association for the preservation and investigation of American antiquities and provided the funds that Putnam needed to purchase the mound. The site was turned over to the state of Ohio where it was made into a state park (Mark 1988:141). The law passed to preserve Serpent Mound was the first law in the country concerned with the preservation of American antiquities (Mark 1988:141). In 1886 Putnam appointed Fletcher "assistant" at the Peabody Museum and in 1891 Mary Copley Thaw endowed a life fellowship for her at the Peabody (Hough 1923:254–255; Wilkins 1971:631).

Inspired by the success of the Serpent Mound conservation protect, Fletcher (1888) formally proposed that the American Association for the Advancement of Science lobby Congress to pass legislation on the preservation of archaeological remains. Alice Fletcher and Matilda Coxe Stevenson (1889) were nominated to the "Committee on the Preservation of Archaeological Remains on the Public Lands" and prepared a bill that sought to preserve a number of sites in the American Southwest. Although that bill did not pass, Mark (1988:143) notes that it was used as a prototype for the "Act for the Preservation of American Antiquities" in 1906.

Fletcher's interest in North American archaeology did not end with her efforts to preserve prehistoric sites. In the early 1900s, she became more actively involved in the Archaeological Institute of America, an institution that had traditionally granted privilege only to the study of Old World civilizations. Alice Fletcher, an advocate for the study of prehistoric Native American culture, was the driving force behind the institute's controversial decision to establish the School for American Research in Santa Fe in 1908 (Mark 1980:75–87). She served on the Board of Regents of the School of American Research until 1912. It was to this school that she willed her estate valued at $35,000 at the time of her death in 1923 (Mark 1988:346).

Fletcher held many important professional posts. She was a charter member and vice president of the Women's Anthropological Society, president of the Anthropological Society of Washington after it admitted female members, president of the American Folklore Society, and vice president of American Association for the Advancement of Science. Although Fletcher achieved prominence in her chosen profession, as an older female who lacked a Ph.D. and a permanent position, she occupied the fringes of the academic world (Mark 1988:348).

Joan Mark (1988:xv) argues that Fletcher struggled against male power and male authority throughout her life. For example, Paul Radin, a graduate student at Columbia, read Fletcher's manuscript proofs without her permission and then printed a critique of her paper before it was officially published. Fletcher was understandably furious and complained about Radin's conduct. In an interview forty years later, Radin dismissed Fletcher as a dreadfully opinionated woman (Mark 1988:337).

Dexter (1978) calls attention to a separate incident that sheds some light on how Fletcher was treated by the male establishment. Although Putnam provided opportunity and encouragement to a number of women including Fletcher and Zelia Nuttall, none of his female students were invited to an anniversary celebration in his honor. Fletcher was very disappointed but thanked Putnam for having sent copies of the Festschrift which included contributions from both her and Nuttall (Dexter 1978:6). Fletcher wrote: "I'm glad to know why I was left out of the dinner. I forgot I was a woman. I only remembered I was a friend and a student" (quoted from Dexter 1978:6).

## Mary Porter Tileston Hemenway

Mary Hemenway was born in New York in 1820, the daughter of a shipping merchant, and was educated in private schools (Brackett 1932:518; Tileston 1927:3). In 1840 she married Augustus Hemenway. The couple had five children (Keller 1971:179). Her husband was a Boston based merchant, considered by many as one of the city's greatest businessmen (Eustis 1955). His business interests included a large sugar plantation in Cuba (Tileston 1927:21) and mining and smelting operations in South America (Tileston 1927:4). As his self-made fortune increased, he became preoccupied with his business affairs and with the acquisition of even more wealth (Keller 1971:180). He suffered a nervous breakdown in 1860, was committed to a sanitarium for fourteen years, and died in 1876 (Keller 1971:180). In addition, Mary Hemenway's eldest daughter died in 1865 (Keller 1971:180). Her husband's failing health demanded that she direct and control her husband's sizable financial and commercial affairs (Crane 1894:708). It was during this time that Mary Hemenway began to devote herself to humanitarian and benevolent endeavors.

Mary Hemenway channeled her wealth and energies in many worthy directions including the study of American history and prehistory. In 1876 she offered $100,000, one quarter of the total sum required, for preserving the Old South Meeting House in Boston, and thus played an instrumental role in stopping the demolition of this historic landmark (Brackett 1932:518; Crane 1894:709). This was the first campaign for historic preservation in Boston (Mark 1988:31). The site was subsequently used as an institute to promote interest in American history. In 1886, Alice Fletcher spoke there on "Indian Music." Hemenway offered to make all of Fletcher's slides for a series of illustrated lectures planned for later that year. Fletcher traveled to Alaska instead of lecturing and Hemenway focused her philanthropy on Frank Cushing (Mark 1988:223).

A visit to Boston by Frank Cushing of the Bureau of Ethnology with four Zuñi and one Hopi introduced Mary Hemenway to the need for archaeological research and the preservation of prehistoric monuments (Tileston 1927:60–61; Keller 1971:181). In 1886, she established the Hemenway Southwestern Archaeological Expedition and commissioned it to conduct research on populations such as the Hopi and Zuñi. She provided a substantial endowment for travel costs, excavation, artifact curation, and publication of research results (Crane 1894:709). Woodbury and Woodbury (1988:46) note that some scholars consider the Hemenway Southwestern Archaeological Expedition the first institution avowedly dedicated to scientific research into that area's prehistory. With its concern for both contemporary and prehistoric people, the Expedition broke new ground and helped establish the Southwest as a distinct cultural area (McChesney 1991:282). For these reasons, McChesney (1991:282) describes Mary Hemenway as an instrumental figure in professionalizing anthropology. Hinsley (1985:54–55) contends that for this time period, securing the support of wealthy patrons for research on Native American prehistory was generally more difficult than obtaining funds for the collection of European classical antiquities. Because of this bias, Hemenway's contributions were especially timely and noteworthy.

Frank Cushing, from 1887 to 1889, and J. Walter Fewkes, from 1889 to

1894, conducted investigations into Hopi and Zuñi prehistory under the aegis of the Expedition (Tileston 1927:61–63; Brackett 1932:518). Fewkes's anthropological career was formed, supported, and directed by Hemenway's generosity and vision (Woodbury and Woodbury 1988:47). Cushing and Fewkes excavated in a variety of Southwestern locales. *The Journal of American Ethnology and Archaeology* printed five volumes of the investigative reports, and the Hemenway Room at Harvard's Peabody Museum housed the artifacts (Tileston 1927:61–63). Some artifacts were displayed at the Seventh Congress of Americans in Berlin in 1888 and the *Exposición Histórica-Americana* in Madrid in 1892–93 (Tileston 1927:61–63). Hemenway also commissioned Fewkes to record the Passamaquoddy peoples of Maine through the use of the newly invented phonograph (Tileston 1927:62). The impact of this study on Alice Fletcher's ethnomusicological work is reported in Mark (1988:223–228).

Hemenway shared Alice Fletcher's and Matilda Coxe Stevenson's interest in the conservation of archaeological sites. Hemenway joined in a petition to preserve a single site, Casa Grande in Arizona, which was successfully presented to Congress in 1889 (Tileston 1927:61–62). In 1890, she established an American ethnology and archaeology fellowship at Harvard's Peabody Museum, which has continued to the present (Woodbury and Woodbury 1988:47).

Field expeditions supported by Hemenway did not come to an end with her death in 1894. Her obituary in the March 7 issue of the *New York Times* (1894a) reported that at the time of her death, she was the richest woman in Boston (with an estate valued at $15,000,000). Her will included a trust fund for the various projects she supported while she was alive (Brackett 1932:519). After her will was filed, the *New York Times* (1894b) reported that "It is her wish that any men or *women* engaged in archaeological work at her expense at the time of her death shall continue the work on the same terms if the results attained by them shall warrant such continuance" (italics mine). This statement reflects a profound loyalty to archaeology as well as a commitment to the advancement of women in the profession. Including a provision for women in her will not only indicates that she was aware that women had contributions to make in archaeology, but it also reveals that she wished to protect their jobs and keep them employed in the discipline after her death.

Hemenway's influence may have opened opportunities for women interested in archaeology. Crane (1894:709) notes that one of the most promising members of Hemenway's scientific staff was Jeannette Webster Williams, whom she describes as a gifted and talented archaeologist. Williams was entrusted with the care of the "Hemenway Archaeological Collection of Prehistoric Antiquities" and barely completed an original memoir destined for publication in the *Journal of American Ethnology and Archaeology* a few months before Hemenway died (Crane 1894:709). Since it appears that Hemenway organized her own staff (Hale 1894:248), it is likely that she played a role in supporting Williams' interest in archaeology. Mary Hemenway's obituary in the *Boston Herald* (1894) noted that "many thousands are better and happier today . . . nearer the ideal of complete manhood, and womanhood, . . . because of what she has done."

## Zelia Maria Magdalena Nuttall

In contrast to Mary Hemenway, Zelia Nuttall did not contribute to the development of Americanist archaeology as a philanthropist, but rather as an independent researcher. Zelia Nuttall was born into fortunate circumstances in San Francisco in 1857. Her father was a physician and her grandfather was one of the city's wealthiest bankers (Parmenter 1971:640). In 1865 the family moved to Europe where Nuttall was educated in France, Germany, Italy, and at Bedford College in London (Tozzer 1933:475). They returned to San Francisco in 1876. Four years later, Nuttall wed Alphonse Louis Pinart, a French ethnologist (Tozzer 1933:475). Together they traveled to the West Indies, France, and Spain where she gained some field experience (Parmenter 1966:88). The couple separated in 1884 and a divorce was granted to Nuttall in 1888; she received custody of their only child and the right to use her maiden name (Tozzer 1933:475).

Nuttall's mother, who was born in Mexico, introduced her to archaeology at a young age by giving her Lord Kingsborough's multi-volume set, *Antiquities of Mexico* (Tozzer 1933:475). However, it wasn't until 1884 that Nuttall launched her long career in archaeology. Not unlike her male contemporaries including Alfred P. Maudslay and Sylvanus Morley, she was largely self-taught (Parmenter 1971:642). In 1884 she visited Mexico, worked at the National Museum, and embarked upon a study of terra cotta heads unearthed at Teotihuacán (Tozzer 1933:475–476). On the basis of that study, Nuttall (1886) revised the temporal placement of these effigies and suggested that they were used in funeral practices. Parmenter (1971:640) notes that this "won the respectful attention of scholars" including Frederic W. Putnam. That year, Putnam made her an honorary assistant in Mexican archaeology at Harvard's Peabody Museum. Nuttall held this position until her death in 1933. The Peabody Museum published several of her monographs including *The Fundamental Principles of Old and New World Civilizations* (Nuttall 1901). Although this work was initially received with qualified enthusiasm (Parmenter 1971:641) and described as "archaic" at the time of her death, it attracted many students to the field of Mesoamerican studies (Tozzer 1933:477). Nuttall's most enduring contributions to Americanist archaeology center on her archival research.

Nuttall alerted the professional community to two major codices. She discovered the Codex Magliabecchiano in 1890, at the Biblioteca Nazionale in Florence (Tozzer 1933:477). She later traced the Codex Nuttall from the Monastery of San Marcos in Florence to the library of Lord Zouche of Haynworth in England (Tozzer 1933:477). In *A History of Mexican Archaeology*, Bernal (1980:151) states that her interpretation of the Codex Nuttall was notable because she demonstrated the historical significance of the document. He explains that her colleagues were reading ritual or mythological codices and placing too much emphasis on the religious meaning of all codices while historical ones were not well understood (Bernal 1980:151). Bernal reports that although some of her contemporaries later published similar interpretations, "to Nuttall, the first woman to make an important contribution to this field, falls the honor of having been the pioneer" (152).

Nuttall's field experience was not extensive though she did discover a previously unrecognized kind of figurine near her home in the Valley of Mexico (Tozzer 1933:477; Parmenter 1971:641). She reasoned that these artifacts belonged to an archaic culture antedating both Toltec and Aztec remains; the accepted view had been that only those two cultures existed in prehistoric Mexico (Bernal 1980:162). Chiñas (1988:271) describes Nuttall's Isla de Sacríficios research as her only attempt at a thorough field project. Nuttall first surveyed the island and in 1909 requested permission and funding to excavate (Chiñas 1988:271). Although the Mexican government granted her two requests, she never undertook this project (Chiñas 1988:171). Unfortunately, her efforts were undermined by Leopoldo Batres, Mexico's inspector of monuments (Parmenter 1971:641). He managed to have her funding reduced and to have himself appointed as her supervisor (Chiñas 1988:271). He also tried to take credit for her discoveries on the island (Nuttall 1910:279; Parmenter 1966:641; Chiñas 1988:271). Batres published an official notice in a government newspaper claiming that he had discovered the island ruins that Nuttall had found and reported to officials months earlier (Nuttall 1910:279). Since Batres was known for his poor methods and had a history of plundering sites for personal gain, Nuttall protested publicly his interference in her work (Chiñas 1988:271). One week after the Batres piece was printed, an article appeared in an American paper published in Mexico that challenged the Batres account and vindicated Nuttall (Nuttall 1910:279). Nuttall also expressed her outrage by resigning from many posts including Honorary Professor of the National Museum. Tozzer (1933:479) argues that Nuttall's grievances were entirely justified and that her essay which documents the altercation (Nuttall 1910) is "in some ways . . . her greatest contribution to the knowledge of the field archaeology of Mexico" (Tozzer 1933:479).

In his obituary of Zelia Nuttall, Philip Ainsworth Means (1933:489) notes that it sometimes seemed to him that "Mexican and North American archaeologists engaged in Mexicanist studies went out of their way to annoy her." He recollects that "[s]he did not grieve about it unduly, however, and occasionally enjoyed a good scrimmage" (489). Unfortunately, the extent to which Nuttall's gender played a role in inspiring such a lack of collegiality or having her research undermined by Batres is unclear. Given what is known about the circumstances surrounding the establishment of the Women's Anthropological Society and the restrictions placed on women's entrance into higher education and the scientific professions, it is likely that Nuttall's gender played at least some role in producing negative sentiments among her male peers.

From Nuttall's (1910:280) point of view, the Batres incident was the only "discouraging experience" she had in her long career in archaeology. Although some members of the anthropological community may have been uneasy with Nuttall's gender, she did earn the respect of many archaeologists and colleagues in other fields. A 27-year-long correspondence with Franz Boas reveals that he held her in high regard (Parmenter 1966). D. H. Lawrence immortalized her as Mrs. Norris in his novel *The Plumed Serpent* (Parmenter 1971:641).

In addition to the posts held at the Peabody Museum and the National Museum of Mexico, Nuttall like Alice Fletcher was a member of the Advisory Council of the Department of Anthropology, University of California, Berkeley. She was the field director of the Crocker Archaeological Field Research Project and her exhibits earned her gold medals in expositions in Madrid, Chicago, and Buffalo. It was in Chicago at the 1893 World Columbian Exposition that Alice Fletcher and Zelia Nuttall became friends (Mark 1988:235). Fletcher advised Nuttall on how to deal with Putnam (Mark 1988:243), while Nuttall later introduced Fletcher to Phoebe Hearst, a wealthy philanthropist (Mark 1988:282). Fletcher also stayed for six months with Zelia Nuttall in Mexico where they occasionally went into the field together (Mark 1988:295).

Chiñas (1988:272) reasons that Nuttall's friendship with suffragist Mary Adelaide Nutting and her membership in the Women's Anthropological Society of America suggest that Nuttall may have sympathized with the cause of women's suffrage and may have considered herself a feminist as well. Nuttall appears to have been conscious of her role in the small but growing worldwide trend toward feminizing the profession of archaeology. By 1900, Nuttall regarded archaeology as a promising field for women (*New York Tribune*, June 30, 1900). As evidence for her conviction, she pointed to the Countess Pauline Ouvaroff, president of the Imperial Archaeological Society of Moscow; Alice Le Plongeon, a London-born archaeologist who excavated Mayan sites with her husband Augustus; Sara Yorke Stevenson, an Egyptologist who is best known for her role in founding the Museum of the University of Pennsylvania; Mary Hemenway; and Alice Fletcher (Anonymous 1900:5).

## Conclusion

Despite the obvious differences in the way that Matilda Coxe Stevenson, Alice Fletcher, Mary Hemenway, and Zelia Nuttall contributed to the development of archaeology, they nonetheless had much in common. All four pioneers were white non-immigrant women who were sufficiently affluent to make their chosen careers possible. They were all educated in private schools but never received formal training in archaeology. Trigger (1989:16) notes that few archaeologists (presumably male or female) were educated in the discipline until the twentieth century. It is also important to note that these four women essentially made their contributions to anthropology as single women. Although Matilda Coxe Stevenson initially carried out fieldwork as part of a husband-wife team, her husband died before she undertook much of her anthropological research. Mary Hemenway developed an interest in archaeology only after having become a widow. Alice Fletcher never married whereas Zelia Nuttall launched her archaeological career at roughly the same time as she became a divorcée.

These women shared some professional interests as well. For example, Stevenson, Fletcher, and Hemenway shared an interest in the conservation of archaeological sites. They were fifteen years ahead of President Roosevelt, who would eventually take up their cause (Mark 1988:143). All but Nuttall had a documented interest in the American Southwest. Stevenson and Fletcher undertook ethnological fieldwork whereas Hemenway provided funds for the collection of ethnographic data. Although the four women played a significant role in the development of archaeology, none of them conducted extensive archaeological fieldwork. And finally, they also share the dubious distinction of being absent from much of the literature on the early history of Americanist archaeology.

It must be apparent from even these few examples that women were not absent from the practice of Americanist archaeology prior to World War I and that their alleged absence results in part from the almost routine erasure of their existence in our received histories. Furthermore, this "absence" cannot be used to legitimize any current power structure in archaeology that attempts to marginalize women. Faced with this indisputable evidence that there was a significant female presence in archaeology during the professionalization of the discipline, we must reinstate women as active participants in archaeology and acknowledge the political conditions within which archaeology flourished. Although a small number of women were active in archaeology prior to World War I, their involvement was limited and circumscribed. In contrast to Lurie (1966:40), I do not suggest that there was a lack of opposition to women during these early days of American anthropology. Although this first generation of female archaeologists did not face an unconditionally prohibitive environment, their nineteenth century world was not particularly welcoming either.

The first generation of women in Americanist archaeology were excluded from both formal and informal networks of communication and were afforded few career opportunities. They maneuvered around these barriers by creating the Women's Anthropological Society of America. As members of this organization they helped to sustain the first anthropological society in the United States "organized and maintained by women alone" (McGee 1889:242). These women undoubtedly acted as role models as they defied social convention and expanded the boundaries for intellectual women in the late nineteenth century. They served as examples of women who devoted energy and effort toward realizing goals that were difficult to attain. In addition to being banned from participating in formal scholarly organizations, Alice Fletcher and Zelia Nuttall were excluded from such informal gatherings as the all male celebration for Frederic W. Putnam. There were other attempts to marginalize women from the professional mainstream. Matilda Coxe Stevenson's salary was smaller than those of her male counterparts. Reports that she and her husband prepared together were published only under one name—her husband's. Zelia Nuttall's work was undermined by Leopoldo Batres who reduced her funding, demoted her, and tried to take credit for her discoveries. As resistance to these injustices Nuttall protested publicly and was eventually vindicated.

The societal and professional milieu within which women lived seriously limited the number of career options available to them. The first generation of female archaeologists included such women as Matilda Coxe Stevenson, Alice Fletcher, Zelia Nuttall, and Mary Hemenway who all made significant contributions to Americanist archaeology but as loosely affiliated workers who were permitted to publish in museum proceedings or as financial patrons. This narrow range of professional pathways for female archaeologists widened in the 1920s while the socioeconomic and educational backgrounds for women expanded. Although women in the second generation were still underrepresented in the discipline and continued to face sizable obstacles to advancement and recognition they achieved greater visibility in academic and museum settings (Levine 1994a). The second generation of women in archaeology thus continued to infiltrate the mainstream, a slow process that their foremothers began.

## Acknowledgments

I wish to thank James Delle, Dena Dincauze, Mary Beth Emmerichs, Alice Kehoe, Blythe Roveland, Bruce Trigger, Martin Wobst, and Nathalie and Richard Woodbury for having commented on earlier drafts of this chapter. I am grateful for the suggestions each has offered. I am particularly indebted to Dena Dincauze and Martin Wobst for their guidance and support. Over the years, I have benefited greatly from many discussions we have had on the history of women in archaeology. Early drafts of this chapter were prepared while I was a recipient of a 1991–1992 Social Sciences and Humanities Research Council of Canada Doctoral Fellowship.

## References Cited

Anonymous. 1889. *Organization and Historical Sketch of the Women's Anthropological Society of America*. Washington, D.C.: The Society.
——. 1895. "A Woman Archaeologist." *Scientific American* 73 (6): 83.
Bernal, Ignácio. 1980. *A History of Mexican Archaeology: The Vanished Civilizations of Middle America*. London: Thames and Hudson.
Boston Herald. 1894. "A Great and Noble Woman." (March 7): 4.
Brackett, Jeffrey R. 1932. "Mary Porter Tileston Hemenway." In *Dictionary of American Biography*, vol. VIII, edited by Dumas Malone, 518–519. New York: Charles Scribner's Sons.
Chiñas, Beverly Newbold. 1988. "Zelia Maria Magdalena Nuttall (1857–

1933)." In *Women Anthropologists: A Biographical Dictionary,* edited by Ute Gacs, Aisha Khan, Jerrie McIntyre, and Ruth Weinberg, 269–274. New York: Greenwood Press.

Crane, Agnes. 1894. "The Noble Life of Mary Hemenway." *Leisure Hour* 43: 708–710.

Dexter, Ralph W. 1978. "Guess Who's Not Coming to Dinner: Frederic Ward Putnam and the Support of Women in Anthropology." *History of Anthropology Newsletter* 5: 5–6.

Eustis, Frederic A. 1955. *Augustus Hemenway 1805–1876: Builder of United States Trade with the West Coast of South America.* Salem: Peabody Museum.

Fletcher, Alice C. 1888. "On the Preservation of Archaeological Monuments." *Proceedings of the American Association for the Advancement of Science* 36: 317.

Fletcher, Alice C. and Matilda Coxe Stevenson. 1889. "Report of the Committee on the Preservation of Archaeological Remains on the Public Lands." *Proceedings of the American Association for the Advancement of Science* 37: 35–37.

Hale, Edward E. 1894. "A Record of Progress." *Lend a Hand* 12: 243–250.

Hinsley, Curtis M., Jr. 1981. *Savages and Scientists: The Smithsonian Institution and the Development of American Anthropology, 1846–1910.* Washington, D.C.: Smithsonian Institution Press.

———. 1985. "From Shell-Heaps to Stelae: Early Anthropologists at the Peabody Museum." In *Objects and Others: Essays on Museums and Material Culture,* edited by George W. Stocking Jr., 49–74. History of Anthropology, no. 3. Madison: University of Wisconsin Press.

Holmes, W. H. 1916. "In Memoriam: Matilda Coxe Stevenson." *American Anthropologist* 18 (4): 552–559.

Hough, Walter. 1923. "Alice Cunningham Fletcher." *American Anthropologist* 25 (2): 254–258.

Keller, Phyllis. 1971. "Mary Porter Tileston Hemenway." In *Notable American Women: 1607–1950,* vol. II, edited by Edward T. James, Janet Wilson James, and Paul S. Boyer, 179–181. Cambridge: The Belknap Press of Harvard University Press.

Lamb, Daniel S. 1906. "The Story of the Anthropological Society of Washington." *American Anthropologist* 8: 564–579.

Levine, Mary Ann. 1994a. "Creating Their Own Niches: Career Styles Among Women in Americanist Archaeology Between the Wars." In *Women in Archaeology,* edited by Cheryl Claassen, 9–40. Philadelphia: The University of Pennsylvania Press.

———. 1994b. "Presenting the Past: A Review of Research on Women in Archaeology." In *Equity Issues for Women in Archaeology,* edited by Margaret C. Nelson, Sarah M. Nelson, and Alison Wylie, 23–36. Archaeological Papers of the American Anthropological Association, no. 5.

Lurie, Nancy Oestreich. 1966. "Women in Early American Anthropology." In *Pioneers in American Anthropology: The Uses of Biography,* edited by June Helm, 29–81. Seattle: The University of Washington Press.

———. 1971. "Matilda Coxe Stevenson." In *Notable American Women: 1607–*

*1950,* vol. II, edited by Edward T. James, Janet Wilson James, and Paul S. Boyer, 373–374. Cambridge: The Belknap Press of Harvard University Press.

Mark, Joan. 1980. *4 Anthropologists: An American Science in its Early Years.* New York: Science History Publications.

———. 1988. *A Stranger in Her Native Land: Alice Fletcher and the American Indians.* Lincoln: University of Nebraska Press.

May, Laurie Donovan. 1988. "The Women's Anthropological Society, 1885–1899: 'Earnest in the Search for Truth.' " Master's thesis, George Washington University.

McChesney, Lea S. 1991. "Hemenway, Mary." In *International Dictionary of Anthropologists,* edited by Christopher Winters, 281–283. New York: Garland Publishing.

McGee, Anita Newcomb. 1889. "The Women's Anthropological Society of America." *Science* 13: 240–242.

Means, Philip Ainsworth. 1933. "Zelia Nuttall: An Appreciation." *The Hispanic American Historical Review* 13: 487–489.

Mendenhall, Susan A. 1893. "Statistical Sketch of the Women's Anthropological Society." In *Woman's Anthropological Society: Proceedings of the One Hundredth Meeting,* 4–9. Washington, D.C.: Gibson Bros., Printers and Bookbinders.

Moldow, Gloria. 1987. *Women Doctors in Gilded-Age Washington: Race, Gender, and Professionalization.* Urbana: University of Illinois Press.

New York Times. 1894a. "Interest on Mrs. Hemenway's $15,000,000 is so Bequested." (March 15): 4.

———. 1894b. "Mrs. Mary Hemenway." (March 7): 4.

New York Tribune. 1900. "Mrs. Nuttall Believes that a Promising Field in Archaeology is Open to Them." (June 30): 5.

Nuttall, Zelia. 1886. "The Terra-Cotta Heads of Teotihuacán." *American Journal of Archaeology* 2: 157–78, 318–330.

———. 1901. *The Fundamental Principles of Old and New World Civilizations.* Paper 2. Cambridge: Peabody Museum.

———. 1910. "The Island of Sacrifícios." *American Anthropologist* 12: 257–295.

Parezo, Nancy J. 1988. "Matilda Coxe Evans Stevenson (1849–1915)." In *Women Anthropologists: A Biographical Dictionary,* edited by Ute Gacs, Aisha Khan, Jerrie McIntyre, and Ruth Weinberg, 337–343. New York: Greenwood Press.

———. 1993. "Matilda Coxe Stevenson: Pioneer Ethnologist." In *Hidden Scholars: Women Anthropologists and the Native American Southwest,* edited by Nancy Parezo, 38–62. Albuquerque: University of New Mexico Press.

Parmenter, Ross. 1966. "Glimpses of a Friendship: Zelia Nuttall and Franz Boas." In *Pioneers in American Anthropology: The Uses of Biography,* edited by June Helm, 83–147. Seattle: The University of Washington Press.

———. 1971. "Zelia Maria Magdalena Nuttall." In *Notable American Women: 1607–1950,* vol. II, edited by Edward T. James, Janet Wilson James, and Paul S. Boyer, 640–642. Cambridge: The Belknap Press of Harvard University Press.

Patterson, Thomas C. 1994. *Toward a Social History of Archaeology in the United States*. Fort Worth: Harcourt Brace College Publishers.

Putnam, Frederic Ward. 1973[1890]. "The Serpent Mound of Ohio." Reprinted in *The Selected Papers of Frederic Ward Putnam,* edited by Stephen Williams, 113–130. New York: AMS Press.

Reyman, Jonathan E. 1992. "Women in American Archaeology: Some Historical Notes and Comments." In *Rediscovering Our Past: Essays on the History of American Archaeology,* edited by Jonathan E. Reyman, 69–80. Aldershot: Avebury.

Rossiter, Margaret W. 1982. *Women Scientists in America: Struggles and Strategies to 1940*. Baltimore: The Johns Hopkins Press.

Stevenson, Matilda Coxe. 1881. "Zuñi Pottery." Report of the Davenport Academy of Science.

———. 1883. "The Cliff-Dwellers of the New Mexican Canyons." *Kansas City Review* 6 (11): 636–639.

Temkin, Andrea S. 1988. "Alice Cunningham Fletcher (1838–1923)." In *Women Anthropologists: A Biographical Dictionary,* edited by Ute Gacs, Aisha Khan, Jerrie McIntyre, and Ruth Weinberg, 95–101. New York: Greenwood Press.

Tileston, Mary Wilder. 1927. *A Memorial of the Life and Benefactions of Mary Hemenway: 1820–1894*. Boston: Privately published.

Tozzer, Alfred M. 1933. "Zelia Nuttall." *American Anthropologist* 35: 475–482.

Trigger, Bruce G. 1989. *A History of Archaeological Thought*. Cambridge: Cambridge University Press.

Wilkins, Thurman. 1971. "Alice Cunningham Fletcher." In *Notable American Women: 1607–1950,* 630–633. Vol. I. Cambridge: The Belknap Press of Harvard University Press.

Woodbury, Nathalie F. S. and Richard B. Woodbury. 1988. "Women of Vision and Wealth: Their Impact on Southwestern Anthropology." In *Reflections: Papers on Southwestern Culture History in Honor of Charles H. Lange,* edited by Anne Van Ardsdall Poore, 45–56. Santa Fe: Archaeological Society of New Mexico.

# 10

## Alternative Networks in the Career of Marian E. White

Susan J. Bender

In her short novel, *A Room of One's Own,* Virginia Woolf explores the question of women in history. In the course of her considerations, she arrives at the conclusion that traditional scholarship treats women only as they fit into other categories of inquiry. Entirely lacking are texts that consistently set out to explain the experiences of women in the past. Woolf describes women not as the "second sex," but rather as the invisible sex, without a historical record of its own. In archaeology, women have indeed been the "invisible sex," both as subjects of inquiry and as scholars. The work of women archaeologists has, for example, been systematically undercited in major syntheses within the discipline for years (Kehoe 1989; Reyman 1989; Willey and Sabloff 1980). This chapter has been written to address these interrelated issues. It is an exercise in the history of archaeology of women. While examining the career experiences of one woman archaeologist, Marian E. White, it seeks to resurrect some of her important contributions to the discipline, defined in the broadest possible sense (cf. Dincauze 1989).

Marian E. White is distinguished as the first woman to receive her Ph.D in archaeology from the University of Michigan, in 1956. After receipt of the doctorate degree she pursued an extremely active and productive career at the State University of New York at Buffalo, specializing in Iroquoian archaeology. In nine years' time she advanced in the university hierarchy from the position of research associate (1959) to full professor in 1968. Such rapid advancement through the academic ranks was based upon White's extremely active field program (accounting for approximately seventy-five percent of all the university's current archaeological holdings) and upon her resultant set of publications which defined the prehistoric chronology and cultural traditions of western New York (Fenton 1976; Milisaukis 1977).

While in many respects White's story can be read as one of success, I would like to emphasize here that her career encompassed a broader range of experiences. Hence I pursue the hypothesis that Marian White's career took on a number of qualities shown to be characteristic of academic women's careers in a recent study by Aisenberg and Harrington (1988). In a world where the male model defines success, the true accomplishments underlying the distinctive career and scholarly style of women can frequently be undervalued. Certainly Gilligan's (1982) convincing demonstration that women's distinctive academic and intellectual styles are systematically underrated by male biased measures suggests that such an hypothesis would be a fruitful line of inquiry. Let us begin then with the notion that there is such a thing as a definable woman's career style, assess its expression in Marian White's career, and then consider some of the consequences of systematic undervaluation of such a career. Such a structure of inquiry will, I believe, help us to understand how the woman known as "Happy" among close friends could be labeled "the wicked witch of the West" by less sympathetic colleagues.

While this is not a study of gender discrimination, there can be no doubt that such discrimination was a part of the historical climate in which White pursued her career. Ample documentation of this climate is provided in Bernard's classic 1964 study, *Academic Women*. Several anecdotes selected from the various stages of White's career can serve to indicate that White's career experiences and style were shaped by many of the same obstacles faced by other academic women; only hers were, I believe, even more complicated by a commitment to an active research career based on field archaeology (cf. Dincauze 1989).

In graduate school, Marian White was the only woman working for a Ph.D in an archaeology program where some, but certainly not all, faculty had a reputation for actively discouraging women throughout the 1950s and 1960s. While White was in graduate school, she was the only woman working for a Ph.D., and she had no women role models or mentors in a departmental faculty and administrative structure devoid of women. It is clear that White must have had to learn to navigate and forge her own role in a male-dominated hierarchy.

In her early job search, White faced similar obstacles. Finding an academic post was not an easy task for her, as her 1957–1958 correspondence reveals. While Albert Spaulding was actively supportive of White's career aspirations, nominating her for a post-doctoral fellowship at Michigan in 1958, other members of her doctoral committee were not as actively helpful. In a 1958 letter to Spaulding, White writes of her enthusiasm about a job possibility at the University of Buffalo, observing that "They insist upon research, regard archaeologists as anthropologists, and are used to the idea of professional women. Without having to fight against all these things, one might have the time to work for something." Here I think she reflects some of the pressures she felt as an aspiring academic woman.

Having secured the position at Buffalo and begun a regimen of extremely active fieldwork, White's experiences with gender based discrimination continued in a way unique to archaeology. Many of her excavations were plagued by collector disturbances, and in White's *American Antiquity* obituary, Milisauskas makes what I believe to be an accurate observation about this particular source of frustration in White's career: "Because she was a woman, sometimes it was much harder to keep away unethical amateur males who were raiding her sites for interesting artifacts" (1977). He goes on to report a tale which has gained almost folkloric status in western New York archaeology:

> Once while she was excavating in central New York, one pot hunter was continuously sneaking in to rape her site. To stop the fellow from damaging the site she went to the local justice of the peace for help. This visit proved to be fruitless, since he was a friend of the pot hunter. Then one morning while she was cleaning up the damage at the site after the pot hunter's visit, Marian came up with an unorthodox defense strategy. She told the crew that when they saw the pot hunter's car parked near the site they should hide in the bushes nearby with their cameras ready. Then as the pot hunter returned to his car, Marian would appear next to him and start ripping away her clothes and scream "rape." At that moment the students were to start taking pictures of the incident. With such a defense strategy the site was reasonably well protected (1977).

Bill Engelbrecht, White's student and colleague, has observed to me with a smile that that is the only time he knew Marian White to use her sex to achieve what she wanted.

That such experiences left an imprint on White's career cannot be denied. One of her former female students, now a successful academic, has observed to me that although White never said so explicitly, she expected her women students to be tougher and work harder—both in the field and the classroom—than males. The essential correctness of her reading of White is, I believe, confirmed by the fact that she was mentioned to me as one of White's favorite students in other interviews. In this anecdote we see, I think, one of the elements of White's career strategy. That is, it was White's—in some respects perhaps naïve (cf. Wylie 1989)—belief that women archaeologists could succeed in academia by setting higher standards for themselves than those of their male counterparts. Commitment to superior standards is one of the clear hallmarks of White's career; it was a commitment in which she never faltered and one which sometimes led her into unhappy clashes with colleagues and students.

Such commitment combined with the other feminine aspect of White's career to produce a pattern of remarkable and distinctive productivity. I define this other aspect of White's career, following ideas from Bernard's (1964) and Aisenberg and Harrington's (1988) works. Both sources suggest that women's academic careers characteristically—although certainly not exclusively—take on aspects of commitment to community. While Bernard documents that women's academic careers since the mid-nineteenth century have systematically been teaching and service oriented, Aisenberg and Harrington (1988) suggest that

> . . . a large body of women's work in the academy is marked by common, distinct characteristics: . . . the placement of subject matter in a cultural context; the insistence on raising value-related, change-related

questions even if their study does not fit conventional definitions and
disciplines;. . . .

The net result of these points is the assertion that the high levels of activity encoded in women's professional careers go unnoticed because they do not
fit into the standard curriculum vitae categories which reflect traditional male
interests and activity patterns. This common women's career pattern is reflected in White's career style, a style founded in and defined by commitment
to community, where the community is defined by the intersection of archaeological and local communal interests.

Marian White's community was western New York, where she was born
and raised and introduced to archaeology by local amateurs. Here she spent
her entire professional life learning and teaching about the prehistory of that
region. Albert Spaulding recalls that in coming to Michigan as a graduate student, White had her program set. She knew she wanted to study the prehistoric Iroquois of western New York, and set about securing her professional
credentials to do so with maturity and competence. He describes White as
unusually self-reliant, noting with some good humor that "none of us (male)
full professors were going to deter her; she wasn't impressed." Spaulding's description is only the first record of a professional commitment that shaped
White's entire career.

After graduate school, White appears to have limited her job search to
western New York so that she could continue her local research interests. Her
ability to get a job in Buffalo in 1959, a time when women were receiving
teaching posts in ever fewer numbers (Bernard 1964:39–40), is a testament to
good luck, good local contacts with supportive female colleagues, and White's
usual perseverance in the face of uncertainties (her initial position being a
non-tenure track research associate line shared between the Buffalo museum and the University). Having found her foothold, however, White moved
quickly to consolidate her position in western New York archaeology.

In the next year she became a full-time member of the University of Buffalo faculty and won her first of three successive National Science Foundation
grants, a rare occurrence for a woman (cf. Kramer and Stark 1988). These
grants were secured to fund initial fieldwork on a series of Niagara Frontier
Iroquois village sites. Over the next 16 years, until she died, White continued
her field campaign, directing excavations at 30 sites, many under salvage conditions, and organizing two county-wide (Cayuga and Jefferson) surveys
(Hunt 1986).

Although all of this work was carried out in accordance with the highest
professional standards, it was not for Marian White a simple means of career
advancement. It was truly a labor of love and commitment. This characteristic
of her fieldwork is reflected in many different ways, but it can be seen primarily in the fact that White did not dig simply to have new data to publish and
to increase her professional visibility. She often delayed publication in order
to meet a heavy schedule of community commitment. White dug in order to

learn, and she felt a deep responsibility for sharing what she learned with communities that housed archaeological resources. Thus she devoted untold hours to giving talks at local historical societies, presenting mini-courses in public schools, and involving interested members of local Iroquois communities in active learning about their cultural past. A heavy load of such activities added up to a good deal of local visibility for White's work, but yielded little in terms of recognized items on her curriculum vitae.

White's deep sense of personal responsibility for her work extended also to an unfailing commitment to protection of the archaeological record. Here her efforts are legendary among the people who knew her, and again they are expressed in several different facets of professional activity. First, White recognized that professionals must work with amateur archaeologists to ensure that the results of amateur activity be useful and available to the professional community. Thus she is known to have breathed new life into the activities of the New York State (amateur) Archaeological Association, and she is the one who brought their now regularly-published *Bulletin* into being (cf. Brennan 1976). Second, White clearly recognized the threat to the archaeological record posed by construction projects. In a paper titled, "The Crisis in Western New York Archaeology," she observed that if the archaeological record is destroyed by construction activity, "then we have failed and the responsibility rests on both the archaeologist and the public" (1972:1). Not one to turn her back on responsibility, White enacted her conviction by working with other senior archaeologists in the state to form the New York Archaeological Council, a body conceived originally to organize and monitor the standards of CRM work in the state. Third, White personally organized a number of critical salvage efforts in western New York, working at twelve sites between 1958 and 1971 on a total budget of less than $4,000. In addition, she led western New York's official Highway Salvage program. That she infused all of this work with an emotional sense of mission is clear from commentary in numerous sources. Colleague Frederick Gearing's eulogy of her states that anthropology was Marian White's "life, vocation and religion."

What then was the net result of such commitment to professional responsibility and standards? The result was not only a life marked by extraordinary levels of activity (cf. Milisauskis 1977), but a career whose imprint has not extended far beyond the local network. At the center of local archaeological activity and a legend in local archaeological lore, White is poorly known in the national network. Her work tends not to be cited in major North American syntheses (cf. Willey 1966; Jennings 1974), and it is minimally cited in similar regional work (cf. Ritchie 1969; Ritchie and Funk 1973; Mason 1981). Moreover, despite her well-known capability for defining a problem and determining and implementing its solution, White did not hold office in any national anthropological organization until 1976, the year of her death (Fenton 1976).

When queried about the reason behind this relative invisibility in the "national network," colleagues' responses seem to converge on three reasons. First, they agree that her publication record wasn't strong enough; White is thought to have published too little and in outlets whose circulation was too tightly confined to the local or regional level. Second, they say that her work was too narrowly focused on the prehistory of western New York, and that it was too conservative in its interpretive stance. These "flaws" in White's traditionally construed career can be, I think, understood in terms of her feminine career style.

If White published too little and too locally, then such must be the result of her extraordinary level of field and community focused activity. Her efforts to protect archaeological sites, salvage those beyond protection, and share her understanding of local cultural resources with the public must have used up large portions of her time and energy. White chose to be an archaeological activist instead of a career tactician, forsaking moves that would have advanced her career for a larger sense of responsibility. Note how this pattern reflects observations cited earlier about women's career patterns. The narrow focus of White's work reflects, I believe, some of the same elements. How could White branch out when she perceived so much to be done in western New York? Moreover, I am quite sure that her conservative interpretations of data grew from her commitment to very high standards, the other aspect of White's career pattern resulting from her experiences as a woman.

Thus we see in Marian White's life a career of absolute commitment to professional standards and the personal responsibility attendant upon them. Marian White's career pattern was not strategically aimed at becoming nationally prominent, but rather targeted on doing her job well, in the broadest possible sense. As a result, her real contributions to our knowledge of the past have not been widely acknowledged, and her insistence on high standards has earned her, in some circles, the unflattering label alluded to earlier. The well-known sociologist David Reisman has observed that

> ... competitiveness is so very American or more broadly western in its style that I am led to wonder whether it bears some relation to our progress in scientific work, or rather whether, if women had a larger influence on that work, other sorts of discoveries might not be made, other "laws" emphasized, and altered patterns of scientific and academic organization preferred or discovered (cited in Bernard 1964:xix).

Perhaps through studying the career experiences of women such as Marian White, we can come to understand the motivation and value of alternative career patterns in our discipline. By incorporating such patterns into professional life, we might also broaden our understandings of archaeological achievement and inquiry.

## Acknowledgments

I owe thanks to many people for a variety of help with this chapter. Most especially I would like the acknowledge the support of the anthropology department and archival staff at SUNY-Buffalo. Their enthusiasm about my work on

Marian White gave me an immediate sense that I had defined an interesting and worthwhile research topic and their help with locating records was invaluable. Peggy Nelson, Lee Hunt, Shonnie Finnegan, and Chris Denzmore were particularly giving of their time. In addition, Bill Engelbrecht, Albert Spaulding, Shirley Stout, and Ethel White, Marian's sister, provided me with a rich variety of information about White in our interviews. I thank them as well for the generous contribution of their time and memories. Any failure to adequately describe the character of White's work is my responsibility alone.

## References Cited

Aisenberg, Nadya and Mona Harrington. 1988. *Outsiders in the Sacred Grove.* Amherst: University of Massachusetts Press.

Bernard, Jessie. 1964. *Academic Women.* University Park: The Pennsylvania State University Press.

Brennan, Louis A. 1976. "Marian White, An Appreciation." *The Bulletin of the New York State Archaeological Association,* 66: 31–33.

Dincauze, Dena F. 1989. "Exploring Career Styles in Archaeology." Paper presented at Women in Archaeology Symposium, annual meeting of Society for American Archaeology, Atlanta, Georgia.

Fenton, William N. 1976. "Obituary: Marian E. White, 1921–1975." *American Anthropologist* 78 (4):891–892.

Gilligan, Carol. 1982. *In a Different Voice.* Cambridge, Massachusetts: Harvard University Press.

Hunt, Eleazer D. 1986. "Marian E. White: researching settlement patterns of the Niagara Frontier." *North American Archaeologist* 7 (4):313–328.

Jennings, Jesse D. 1974. *Prehistory of North America.* 2nd ed. New York: McGraw Hill.

Kehoe, Alice B. 1989. "Contextualizing Archaeology." In *Tracing Archaeology's Past,* edited by A. L. Christenson, 97–106. Carbondale: Southern Illinois University Press.

Kramer, Carol F. and Miriam Stark. 1988. "The status of women in archaeology." *Anthropology Newsletter* (December): 1 ff.

Mason, Ronald. 1981. *Great Lakes Archaeology.* New York: Academic Press.

Milisaukas, Sarunas. 1977. "Obituary: Marian Emily White, 1921–1975." *American Antiquity* 42 (2): 191–195.

Reyman, Jonathan. 1989. "Women Archaeologists in the American Southwest, 1895–1945: Review and Reflection." Paper presented at the 22nd Annual Chacmool conference, University of Calgary, Alberta.

Ritchie, William A. 1969. *The Archaeology of New York State.* 2nd ed. Garden City: Natural History Press.

Ritchie, William A. and Robert E. Funk. 1973. "Aboriginal settlement patterns in the Northeast." *New York State Museum and Science Service Memoir,* no. 20.

White, Marian E. 1972. "The crisis in western New York archaeology." Manuscript on file, Department of Anthropology, State University of New York at Buffalo.

Willey, Gordon R. 1966. *An Introduction to American Archaeology*, vol. 1. North
    and Middle America. Englewood Cliffs: Prentice Hall.
Willey, Gordon R. and Jeremy A. Sabloff. 1980. *A History of American Archaeol-
    ogy*. 2nd edition. (3rd edition, 1993). San Francisco: W. H. Freeman.
Wylie, Alison. 1989. "Beyond Objectivism and Realism: Feminist Critiques
    and Archaeological Challenges." Paper presented at the 22nd Annual
    Chacmool conference, University of Calgary, Alberta. (Published 1991 as
    "Feminist Critiques and Archaeological Challenges," in *The Archaeology of
    Gender*, edited by Dale Walde and Noreen D. Willows. Calgary: Archae-
    ological Association of the University of Calgary. Pp. 17–23.)

**III**

# Southwestern Archaeology as Case Example

Alice B. Kehoe

We place the following two chapters in a separate section because the American Southwest has been a focus of archaeological research for over a century. Parezo (1993:355) notes that "by 1940, the Greater Southwest was the most systematically studied region in the world, and this fact was widely recognized." As Fowler states, the Southwest was seen to be an "anthropological laboratory" because there abounded an impressive variety of ruins (categorized as Anasazi, Mogollon, and Hohokam) and living Indian nations (Pueblos, Athabascans, Yumans, Uto-Aztecans). The metaphor became an institution funded by the Rockefeller Foundation, drawing students whose names are a roll call of the mid-century leaders of American anthropology. Add the budding eminences enrolled at the rival Chaco Canyon field school run by Edgar Lee Hewett (Mathien 1992), and it could be argued that in the first half of the twentieth century, most American prehistorians and ethnologists received training in the Southwest.

These two final chapters provide case examples of the principal issues in the professionalization of archaeology in America, the contest between "democratic science" and the academically credentialed, and the precarious position of women in the discipline.[1] Each author reveals dimensions to these issues that emphasize the importance of comprehending the social history of a discipline.

Edgar Lee Hewett, central figure in Don Fowler's study, personifies the all-American entrepreneur. With little formal education, Hewett fit well with other self-made men in a region newly incorporated as a state. New Mexico's exotic beauty and dry sunny climate drew wealthy Easterners, especially once Fred Harvey promoted his railroad holidays. Hewett shrewdly cultivated these potential philanthropists, re-creating in the Land of Enchantment their role as museum patrons. This was entirely congruent with the Archaeological Institute of America's composition and covert function of signaling patrons' high status and power by recovering palaces and respective furnishings from past societies. Hewett chose projects in Santa Fe's Palace of the Governors and in Chaco Canyon, the American Southwest's most urban prehistoric complex with relatively palatial ruins. Hewett and his patrons sought the finest of the barbaric American past-as-known trophies for display.

Meanwhile, back at the ranch, trained young professionals sought to apply internationally recognized scientific methods to discover data from prehistory. Not only Harvard University, but also Columbia's Franz Boas publicly deplored what they saw in Hewett's many projects as little better than looting; never mind the fact that Hewett lobbied hard for a federal Antiquities Protection Act. They feared that such legislation would only license politicians' cronies (read, Hewett). At bottom, the autonomy of the archaeological profession was at stake: should it pander to private patrons' preferences, its legitimacy as a disinterested, truth-seeking science would be jeopardized. Hewett demanded autonomy as well, but it was for his personal judgment, not for the collegial group. Over the course of decades, the professionalization of archaeology was played out in New Mexico. This process had a particular scientistic bias, but discussion of the bias throughout the professionalization of archaeology is beyond the scope of this book.[2]

Jonathan Reyman became sensitive to discrimination against women in archaeology as he dealt with the persistent rejection suffered by his own major professor, Walter Taylor. It was a roundabout route, from the wealthy iconoclastic Harvard man, Taylor, whose hard-hitting *A Study of Archaeology* (1948) lambasted the revered A. V. Kidder, to Marietta Wetherill. Reyman's experiences led him to perceive that the scientific worth of work such as Taylor's could be negated by personal qualities, and that particular pasts-as-known might fall into oblivion as a result. In the field, Reyman tested Wetherill's observations and in the mode of his major professor, pushed them toward the corpus of mainstream archaeological practice. Marietta Wetherill's legacy became, in Reyman's hands, a test case in the sociology of scientific knowledge.

In concluding this section, let us call attention to Reyman's plea for the retrieval of unpublished archaeological records. Field records and interpretive manuscripts, as well as personal correspondence and journals, are essential for understanding contemporary archaeology along with its history. In recognition of this need, the Wenner-Gren Foundation convened a conference in 1992, "Preserving the Anthropological Record: Issues and Strategies." The proceedings were published by the Foundation that year, and have been updated. Bringing the challenge into public view has accelerated the archiving of materials and should rescue many obscured results of good archaeological research. Professionalization always incurs the exclusion of unacceptable paradigms, some of which gain credibility as personalities, ideologies, and databases change. To understand the history of ideas, and to evaluate the breadth and depth of presently favored concepts, we need to bring essays such as those in this volume into archaeologists' consciousness.

## Notes

1. Mathien (1992) did not highlight the women students whose husbands became professional archaeologists, such as Emily Ross (Mrs. William) Mulloy,

Martha Morris (Mrs. Herb) Dick, and Adelaide (Mrs. Ripley) Bullen. Such women often became their husbands' principal assistants, sometimes emerging as professionals in their own right (e.g., Adelaide Bullen), sometimes continuing their husbands' work in widowhood (e.g., Emily Mulloy).

2.  See Ross (1991), although Ross does not include archaeology or anthropology, and Kehoe (1998).

### References Cited

Kehoe, Alice Beck. 1998. *The Land of Prehistory: A Critical History of American Archaeology.* New York: Routledge.

Mathien, Frances Joan. 1992. "Women of Chaco: Then and Now." In *Rediscovering Our Past: Essays on the History of American Archaeology,* edited by Jonathan Reyman, 103–130. Aldershot: Avebury.

Parezo, Nancy J. 1993. "Conclusion: The Beginning of the Quest." In *Hidden Scholars,* 334–367. Albuquerque: University of New Mexico Press.

Ross, Dorothy. 1991. *The Origins of American Social Science.* Cambridge: Cambridge University Press.

# 11

## Harvard vs. Hewett

## The Contest for Control of Southwestern Archaeology, 1904–1930

Don D. Fowler

There was an old duffer called Hewett
Who was head of the School—and he knew it
When anyone came
Who knew naught of his fame
He took out his trumpet, and blew it.
—*Beatrice Blackwood*

Above all, Hewett was, as are all great and secure individuals, a modest, unpretentious person. As he once remarked to one of my contemporaries, "I'm not much of an archaeologist, but I do try to be a man." That he most certainly was, in the fullest meaning of that word.
—*Edwin N. Ferdon, Jr.*[1]

### Introduction

Edgar Lee Hewett (1865–1946) played a pivotal role in the development of Southwestern archaeology. He was adept at forming networks and creating organizations through which he pursued his very personal vision of research and museology. From about 1904 until the early 1930s, Hewett was a dominant figure in Southwestern archaeology. Everyone who came to the Southwest to conduct archaeological research had to deal with him. From 1909 until his death he directed both the Museum of New Mexico and the School of American Research—key anthropological institutions, then, as now. In addition, from 1915 to 1928 he was also director of the San Diego Museum of Man, and professor of anthropology at San Diego State Teachers College. In 1929 he became professor of anthropology at the University of New Mexico, and in 1934 helped found the anthropology department at the University of Southern California. Given these various roles, Hewett was a very powerful figure within the nascent, but growing, field of American anthropology.

Between about 1904 and 1930, Hewett and his supporters often bitterly clashed with various archaeological and other members of the "Eastern Establishment" over policies, professional standards, and control of key institutions and the funds to operate them. Although Hewett was formally sponsored by powerful eastern institutions, especially the Archaeological Institute of America and the Smithsonian Institution, he was not *of* the Eastern Establishment. He was, *and saw himself as,* a Westerner (a member of the American "Core Culture" in Patterson's [1995:44] terms) with a very different orientation than his eastern colleagues. Hewett was often vilified, indeed slandered, by his bitter archaeological enemies who charged that his standards of research and professionalism were slovenly. He publicly ignored the charges. His equally bitter enemies within the frequently clamorous, bared-claw hotbed of Santa Fe public life leveled equally invidious charges. Hewett usually managed to publicly ignore them as well. On the other hand, Hewett was widely admired in many national circles, and in Santa Fe and in Southern California (Chauvenet 1983; Ferdon 1993). In the mid-1990s, fifty years after his death, opinions are still sharply divergent among old-time Santa Feans.

The synergistic conflicts between Hewett and his allies and various "eastern" archaeologists and their allies provide a case study of the functions of gossip (often of a slanderous or libelous nature), opportunism, and power politics in the professionalization of American anthropology and the development of institutions within which anthropological research was conducted between 1900 and 1930. The human relationships popularly called "networks" are central to the professionalization of a discipline, both of its individual members and the organizations in which, and through which, they work. "Networks" herein refer to sets or systems of *informal* interpersonal relationships which structure the allocation of "influence"—ideas, jobs, power and money—usually through *formal* institutional, political, or bureaucratic structures and procedures.

"Harvard vs. Hewett" is a prime example of the uses of such networks by individuals seeking to influence or seize control of intellectual, political, and monetary resources needed to professionalize and expand archaeology in the American Southwest as they (variously) conceived of it. A number of the protagonists in this ongoing contest were connected with Harvard University, a key node in any definition of the Eastern Establishment. A subset of the Establishment—anthropologists connected with Harvard and Columbia universities, the Smithsonian Institution and various related organizations—was often at loggerheads with Hewett and his allies. Hence, the title of this essay is simultaneously alliterative, substantive, and metaphorical[2] (Chauvenet 1983:33–96; Hinsley 1986; Stocking 1982).

Hewett entered the American anthropology scene at the turn of the twentieth century, a time of rapid theoretical and institutional change in the discipline. In 1877–78, Johns Hopkins University had adopted the German university system in which the Ph.D. became an advanced research degree in a single field of study. Other major universities followed suit over the next two decades

(Oleson and Voss 1979; Patterson 1995:47). Doctorates in anthropology began to be awarded in the 1890s at Harvard, Chicago, and Columbia universities. Anthropology at Columbia was created and dominated by Franz Boas, an archetypal product of the German university system (Stocking 1974). The job market for anthropologists remained centered in museums, as it had for the previous two decades. However, the young Ph.D.s brought new standards of professionalism and research that were very much a part of the larger ongoing institutionalization and reification of science so characteristic of the period (Bruce 1987; Elliott and Rossiter 1992).

The previous generation of American anthropologists were all self-taught and had come from disparate backgrounds. They had created an anthropology that was centered in nineteenth-century natural history museums and museum collections (Fowler and Fowler 1991). Their theoretical orientation derived primarily from Lewis Henry Morgan's (1877, 1881) social evolutionism. The focal point for American anthropology until about 1900 was the Smithsonian Institution. Most of the individuals in the United States who were paid to do anthropology, rather than participate in it as an avocation, worked either for the U.S. National Museum or the Bureau of American Ethnology, both administrative entities of the Smithsonian. The doyen and senior figure of this group was John Wesley Powell, scientific entrepreneur and administrator *par excellence* (Fowler in press:Chapter 3; Hinsley 1981:125–230) who died in 1902.

Edgar Lee Hewett was very much of the natural history generation of anthropologists. He was self-taught in archaeology and anthropology. He did acquire a doctorate—in sociology from the University of Geneva in Switzerland. His detractors, however, regarded the degree as little more than the product of a diploma mill.[3]

Hewett was a stubborn man. As noted previously, he engendered strong feelings, ranging from admiration to hate, in all who knew him and many who only knew of him. Adversaries and colleagues alike called him (behind his back), "El Toro," both for his physical strength and his perceived *modus operandi*. A key to his personality and actions is found in his autobiography, published just prior to his death. He was, he tells us, taught to box at an early age: " . . . Only a few times through life have I had occasion to use my instruction in boxing, but to this day, on provocation my hands and feet snap into position" (Hewett 1946:6). Throughout his careers, first as a pedagogue, and then as an administrative entrepreneur, Hewett was often provoked; he certainly provoked others. On balance, he probably won more rounds than he lost. The concern of this essay is with five of those rounds between 1904 and 1930.

Hewett was born and raised on a farm in the Midwest and educated to be a school teacher. His interest in Southwestern archaeology started about 1890 when he began teaching school in Florence, Colorado. He and his spouse spent their summers in a horse-drawn camp wagon, touring from Yellowstone to Chihuahua, hoping the open air and sunlight would cure her tuberculosis. Hewett was particularly intrigued by the ruins on the Pajarito Plateau, west of Santa Fe. He read voraciously in Old and New World archaeology, and began to lecture on the subject in Colorado and New Mexico.

In 1897, Hewett met a prominent citizen and attorney of Las Vegas, New Mexico—Frank Springer. The two became fast friends—a key node in Hewett's network. The following year Hewett published his first anthropology paper, "The Study of Anthropology" (Hewett 1898).[4] Soon after, through Springer's influence, Hewett was appointed president of the newly established New Mexico Normal School (now New Mexico Highlands University), in Las Vegas. In addition to administrative duties, Hewett taught anthropology and archaeology. Hewett's courses would place New Mexico Normal, along with Clark, Harvard, Columbia, and Chicago, among the first colleges to teach anthropology in the United States. Hewett thought that science was best taught through field trips and direct observation. With students and colleagues he spent weekends and summers at Pecos Ruin, on the Pajarito Plateau and, in 1902, in Chaco Canyon.

Hewett made his first trip to Washington, D. . in 1900. There he sought out the leaders of the anthropological community. He called on John Wesley Powell and met Frederic Ward Putnam, who happened to be in the city. Hewett also met and began long and close friendships with Alice Cunningham Fletcher and William Henry Holmes (Chauvenet 1983:42; Mark 1988:303–305) who would prove to be staunch supporters over time.

In 1898, Hewett joined with others to form the Archaeological Society of New Mexico (Chauvenet 1983:40–42). Soon the Society was petitioning the U.S. General Land Office to investigate the activities of the Hyde Expedition and, particularly, Richard Wetherill in Chaco Canyon. Under the auspices of the American Museum of Natural History, the Hyde Expedition had been excavating in Pueblo Bonito and other sites in and around Chaco Canyon since 1898.[5] The Society charged that Wetherill and the Hyde Expedition were engaged in "spoilation [sic] and destruction" of Chacoan sites and were selling artifacts taken therefrom. This led to an investigation by a Land Office agent, S. J. Holsinger (1901). Holsinger did not find evidence of "spoilation and destruction," nor of the selling of artifacts, but he did find improprieties in Richard Wetherill's homestead claim on the section of land containing Pueblo Bonito, Chetro Ketl, and Pueblo del Arroyo. In the end, the Hyde Expedition was permanently forbidden to excavate at Pueblo Bonito and, in March, 1902, Wetherill's homestead entry was suspended (McNitt 1966:198–208). In light of all this, Hewett's 1902 trip to Chaco Canyon takes on additional interest.

Hewett (1904a) had been pushing for the establishment of a national cultural park on the Pajarito Plateau to protect the many ruins there (Hewett 1904a; Altherr 1985). Now he added Chaco Canyon as a second candidate. Through his Washington connections, as well as local speeches and through the Archaeological Society of New Mexico, Hewett became identified as a spokesperson on matters archaeological in New Mexico and the Southwest. He wrote a major report on New Mexico antiquities which was published in 1903 by the U.S. Government Printing Office as part of the annual report of the Governor of the New Mexico Territory (Hewett 1903). The report brought him additional attention within the eastern anthropological community, and particularly to the attention of the Commissioner of the General Land Office, as will be seen below.

However, also in 1903, Hewett ran afoul of some citizens of Las Vegas and the new governor of New Mexico. Although apparently well-liked by students and faculty, local opinion makers looked askance at his unconventional teaching methods and his refusal to court them. His persistent efforts to get large tracts of public land set aside for national parks angered powerful ranchers and large landowners (Ferdon 1993:14). His contract was not renewed by the university regents for 1903–04. Springer, however, remained an adamant Hewett champion. His firing marked a major turning point for Hewett. At age thirty-nine he decided that he wanted to be an archaeologist. For that he needed an advanced degree if he was to be taken seriously within the emerging milieu of American anthropology. He sold his possessions, including a ranch at Pecos, and used the money to go to the University of Geneva to get his doctorate and to make an extensive archaeological tour of the Near East. Hewett returned to Washington, D.C., taking on whatever odd job anthropological work was available. While there, his wife died of tuberculosis in 1905. While mourning her, Hewett threw himself into the fight for passage of a federal antiquities act. His success therein brought him national attention and laid the groundwork for his subsequent career.

### Round One: The 1906 Antiquities Act

Passage of the 1906 Antiquities Act, to protect and control the excavation of archaeological sites on public lands, was the culmination of the efforts of many individuals for over a century to achieve a modicum of protection and conservation for American antiquities (Fowler 1986). The first step toward what became the 1906 Act was a petition submitted to Congress in 1882 by a committee of prominent Bostonians. Their interest was stimulated by Adolph Bandelier's (1881a, 1881b) reports to the Archaeological Institute of America on his Southwestern work, and perhaps also by Frank Hamilton Cushing's famous 1882 visit to Boston with his entourage of Zuñi Indians (Green 1990:218–236). The petition noted the decay of ruins in the Southwest and the problems of rampant vandalism. The petitioners prayed

> that at least some of these extinct cities or pueblos, carefully selected, with land reservations attached [that is, buffer zones around the sites] . . . may be withheld from public sale and their antiquities and ruins preserved, as they furnish invaluable data for the ethnological studies

now engaging the attention of our most learned scientific, antiquarian, and historical students. [Wilder and Slafter 1882:3777].

The petition quietly died in Congressional committee, but the concern within the Boston intellectual community for Southwestern antiquities had only just begun. In 1889, there was a successful effort, again spearheaded by Bostonians, to set aside Casa Grande in Arizona as a national monument (Lee 1970:23).

Rampant looting of Southwestern sites continued, however, throughout the 1890s, stimulating concern in many quarters. By 1899 new organizations began to coalesce to push for antiquities legislation. The American Association for the Advancement of Science appointed a Committee on the Protection and Preservation of Objects of Archaeological Interest. Members included Thomas Wilson of the U.S. National Museum, Frederic Ward Putnam of Harvard, George Dorsey of the Field Columbian Museum, and Grove Karl Gilbert, chief geologist of the U.S. Geological Survey. The Archaeological Institute of America also created a standing committee on American archaeology. Its members were Charles Bowditch, Putnam and Franz Boas. The committee was charged with developing an Americanist research program (as discussed below), but also to help seek antiquities legislation.

With Putnam as the link, the two committees joined forces to press Congress for passage of an antiquities bill. Wilson, with the help of S. V. Proudfit, a Department of the Interior solicitor and member of the Anthropological Society of Washington, drafted a bill which was introduced on February 5, 1900. The explanation accompanying the bill pointed out that European countries, as well as Mexico, Turkey, Greece, Egypt, Persia, and the Barbary States, all had strong antiquities legislation, while the United States had none. Two other bills also were introduced. The chief thrust of all the bills was to achieve some sort of protection for, and control over, archaeological sites on public lands. No action was taken and the bills died with the end of the Congress (Lee 1970:51–54).

After a period of regrouping, new bills were introduced in 1904. One bill, sponsored by Senator Henry Cabot Lodge of Massachusetts, placed all antiquities on public lands under the Department of the Interior. It empowered the Secretary of the Interior to issue permits for excavation and obligated the Secretary to issue a permit to any state or territorial museum that applied to dig sites in its own state, provided that the governor of the state or territory endorsed the application. The bill was widely supported by universities and museums, as well as by the Archaeological Institute of America.

A second bill was written by William Henry Holmes and others at the Smithsonian Institution. It gave control of antiquities on public lands to the Department of the Interior, but supervision of them and control of permits for their excavation to the Smithsonian. This was seen by many, including Hewett, as an attempted power grab by the "elitist" Smithsonian and a few eastern university cronies. The much more populist Lodge Bill passed the Senate and nearly passed the House of Representatives, but Smithsonian lobbyists managed to get it killed at the eleventh hour, and Congress adjourned. This move generated a good deal of animosity within the museum and archaeological communities (Baum 1904a, 1904b). However, rifts were mended and ranks closed and a new attempt was launched to develop an acceptable bill in 1905 (Lee 1970:66–67).

In the spring of 1902, Congressman John F. Lacey of Iowa, chair of the House Committee on Public Lands and an ardent conservationist, spent two weeks on a horseback trip with Hewett. The two were probably introduced by Frank Springer, who had grown up in Iowa. They visited various ruins in Colorado and New Mexico, and discussed the problems of vandalism and site protection around evening camp fires. Lacey was later to say that his interest in getting an antiquities bill passed was due to his trip with Hewett (Chauvenet 1983:42).

In mid-1904, General Land Office Commissioner W. A. Richards decided to review the entire problem of protecting antiquities on public lands as background to any subsequent legislation. A central concern was what needed to be protected, especially in the Southwest, the focus of concern. Richards was apparently aware of Hewett's 1903 report on New Mexico antiquities, and may have been influenced by Congressman Lacey. Richards asked Hewett to undertake the review. On Sept. 3, 1904 Hewett submitted his "Memorandum concerning the Historic and Prehistoric Ruins of Arizona, New Mexico, Colorado and Utah and their Preservation" (Hewett 1904c). Therein he presented a clear statement of what was known about ruins in those four key states. The report was subdivided into the Rio Grande, Gila, San Juan, and Little Colorado drainages, and further subdivided into approximately twenty archaeological districts. Hewett sketched the characteristics of each district and described many of the major ruins in each. The report was comprehensive, and allowed federal land administrators and the Congress to get a firm grasp of the problem for the first time.

When the American Anthropological Association (AAA) was formed in 1902, one of its first acts was to create a Committee on Antiquities (Hewett 1905:164). In 1905 Hewett was appointed to that committee. Seizing an opportunity, he became the committee's secretary and spokesperson in Washington, where there was sentiment for a further amended Lodge bill. Some informally proposed amendments apparently gave control of antiquities on Western public lands to the Smithsonian and/or a commission comprised of representatives of Eastern universities. There were also a variety of administrative and jurisdictional problems with the Lodge bill and other previous bills. At a joint American Archaeological Association/Archaeological Institute of America meeting in Ithaca, New York, on December 28, 1905, Hewett persuaded both groups that a bill was needed which would circumvent administrative and jurisdictional conflicts inherent in earlier bills, and would be politically feasible in Congress. At a joint business meeting, the two groups unanimously endorsed Hewett's bill (Hewett 1906:113). Hewett's definition of "politically feasible" meant a bill that would pass Congress, but would *not* give control of western archaeology to eastern archaeologists.

On January 9, 1906, Congressman Lacey introduced Hewett's bill in the House; a companion bill was introduced in the Senate on February 26. Everyone went to work to get the bill passed. To help with the lobbying, Hewett was joined in Washington by the flamboyant Charles F. Lummis, editor, archcheerleader for the Southwest, and founder of the Southwest Museum in Los Angeles (Bingham 1955; Fiske and Lummis 1975). But the two, particularly Lummis, rubbed many of their compatriots and others the wrong way. In their headlong haste to gain support for the Lacey bill, and prevent amendments giving eastern institutions some form of control over western antiquities, Lummis and Hewett offended a number of eastern sensibilities; certain owners of those sensibilities would remain offended for the next three decades.

In a February 3, 1928 letter to Byron Cummings discussing the then impending Laboratory of Anthropology (see below), Hewett wrote:

> That there is a concerted plan looking toward the control of our Southwestern field from the outside can no longer be doubted. It is the recrudescence of the plan that gained great headway in 1904–05. . . . It took the form at that time of a proposed act of Congress which was backed by a large group of eastern universities and museums and which would have put the whole thing in the hands of a commission of professors of those institutions with power that would have virtually excluded, or at least put under their control, the work of not only the Southwestern states and their institutions but of the National Government itself.
>
> As I was a free lance at that time, having just returned from my work abroad, it fell to me to defeat that Bill. That was a memorable fight in Congress, especially in the House of Representatives; and as a result not only the . . . [Lodge] Bill but all other pending Bills on the subject, all of which were bad, were defeated and the Lacey Act . . . became law. The New York and Cambridge groups did not accept their defeat graciously. . . . [Those] groups, frankly at first and covertly ever since, have sought to overturn what was then accomplished (ELHP).

Lummis would later claim that it was primarily he, Hewett, William Henry Holmes, and James Garfield, Secretary of the Interior, who got the Antiquities Act passed.[6] Whatever the truth of Lummis's hyperbole, two matters are relevant here. First, Hewett's and Lummis's rough and tumble tactics offended some eastern gentlefolk; doubtless, some refined Bostonians shuddered slightly at the antics of these two western bumpkins. The fact that they succeeded not only in getting an Antiquities Act passed, but one that blocked attempts by eastern universities and the Smithsonian to control western archaeology, made matters worse. Second, working on the Antiquities Act cemented a longstanding and close friendship between Hewett and Lummis— another important node in Hewett's network. On June 8, 1906, President Theodore Roosevelt signed the "Lacey Bill,"—the 1906 Antiquities Act, as it has come to be known. The wording is essentially Hewett's (Lee 1970:77). By the time the bill was signed, Hewett was in a new trajectory as a fellow of the very eastern Archaeological Institute of America (AIA).

## Round Two: The School of American Archaeology

When the AIA was founded by a group of prominent Bostonians in 1879, Lewis Henry Morgan, Francis Parkman, and others urged a commitment to Americanist work. But the organizers' eyes were on the glories of the ancient Mediterranean world, where they founded major research schools. Their only New World commitment was the rather meager support given to Adolph Bandelier.[7]

By the 1890s, however, Institute membership had begun to decline. A committee noted that many chapters in the United States had strong New World interests, and urged the appointment of an Americanist to the AIA Council. Charles P. Bowditch was chosen. A prominent Boston businessman, and major donor to the Peabody Museum at Harvard, Bowditch had become entranced with the Maya in the late 1880s. He soon began funding Peabody expeditions to Central America (Mark 1988:299). In 1899, the AIA appointed an Americanist committee, consisting of Bowditch, Frederic Ward Putnam, and Franz Boas, as previously noted. In the same year, Bowditch created a fellowship in American archaeology at Harvard. The first recipient was Alfred Tozzer, who set off the study the Maya and the Lacandones.[8]

In 1903, the Society of the Southwest, centered in southern California, became a chapter of the AIA. Under the boisterous and enthusiastic leadership of Charles Lummis the chapter soon had three hundred members, and was clamoring for work to be done in the Southwest. There was a similar surge of membership and interest in the Southwest in Salt Lake City, led by Colonel E. A. Wall and Byron Cummings, then a professor of classics at the University of Utah. Since votes in the Institute Council were determined by the size of chapter membership, and chapters could decide where donated monies for research were spent, Institute leaders paid heed.

In 1890, Alice C. Fletcher received a lifetime fellowship from the Thaw family of Pittsburgh, administered by Frederic Ward Putnam through the Peabody Museum at Harvard. Already well-known in Washington, D.C., for her work with American Indians, she settled there in 1891. Over the following decade she became a major figure in American anthropology and Indian affairs (Mark 1988:203–277). Hewett and Fletcher first met in Washington sometime between 1900 and 1902 (Chauvenet 1983:42), and developed their already mentioned close friendship in the following years.

Late in 1905, the AIA expanded its Americanist committee to include Jesse Walter Fewkes, Francis Kelsey, Alice Fletcher, and Charles Lummis. The Committee received $600 for a fellowship during 1906. The first candidate was Robert H. Lowie, a Boas protégé, but he declined. Hewett was the second choice and the Committee was to direct his work. His instructions were to help stimulate and develop western chapters of the Institute and to see to an archaeological survey of the Mesa Verde, in anticipation of its becoming a national park. In addition, in a February 8, 1906 letter to Hewett, Putnam sent the following instructions:

> You will begin work as soon as possible in the Pueblo region and carry on such researches as will enable you to make a comparative study of the culture,—especially of the art and architecture,—of the ancient Pueblo peoples with that of the ancient Mexicans, with the object of ascertaining whether there was any ethnical connection between the two regions. Then, according as circumstances may determine, you will either give all your time to productive work in some limited area of the Pueblo region, or you will make a preliminary survey of the region from the pueblos to ancient Mexico, carrying on such studies as you can during such a survey, all tending toward the solution of the problem of the connection between ancient Mexico and the ancient pueblos and between ancient Mexico and ancient Central America (ELHP).

From January to June, 1906, Hewett met with various AIA western chapters and got the survey of Mesa Verde underway, in addition to lobbying for the passage of the Lacey bill. He had begun his sometimes frantic pace of cross-country train trips that would characterize his life for the next three decades.

In June, 1906, Hewett set out from Casas Grandes, Chihuahua, to survey on horseback along the flanks of the Sierra Madre to the Valley of Mexico. He sent detailed monthly reports of his work to Bowditch (e.g., a December 26, 1906 letter [ELHP]). When he reached Mexico City, he spent a good deal of time with Alice Fletcher, who was visiting as a guest of Zelia Nuttall. Hewett, Fletcher, and sometimes Nuttall, visited Puebla, Cholula, Monte Alban, and Mitla. They had long talks about the direction American archaeology ought to take (Mark 1988:296–298, 305–307).

In December, 1906, after she returned to Washington, Fletcher presented a plan to the Americanist Committee of the AIA. Her stated aims were to stimulate work in the New World and to strengthen AIA ties with its burgeoning Western chapters:

> It is proposed that a basal plan for work under the American Committee of the AIA shall be the preparation of a map of the culture areas of the American continent, as a contribution to the world study of the human race.
>
> [Much already done, but,] it is believed that such a graphic tabulation will not only facilitate the task of correlating work already and now in progress, but will make it possible to direct the efforts of the various Societies of the Institute which desire to support active field work in our own country, that all the archaeological research undertaken will fit into the broad plan proposed, and thus help toward the

solution of some of the problems that confront the student of human culture.

A preparatory step toward the carrying out of this basal plan would be the appointment of an officer to be known as Director of American Archaeology, whose immediate duty would be to direct and coordinate all work undertaken by the affiliated societies of the Institute. This step should be followed by the establishment of a School of American Archaeology, in which graduate students should be received for instruction and employment in field research, and so fitted to be workers in the wide field opened by this basal plan.

Since culture areas do not correspond with political boundaries, international relationships and work will naturally follow (cited in Bowditch 1907:47–48).

On January 2, 1907, the Committee on American Archaeology accepted Fletcher's plan, and recommended Hewett to the AIA Council as Director of American Archaeology. He was duly elected two days later and also made a member of the Committee (Mark 1988:306–307).

Hewett now found himself in a position of strength. Francis Kelsey, a classicist from the University of Michigan, became AIA president in 1906. He was a Hewett fan. On the Americanist Committee, Hewett could count on Fletcher, Lummis, and, for the moment, Putnam. Bowditch was already getting irritated; Boas was waiting to see what Hewett would do.

### Santa Fe and the School of American Archaeology

When Hewett returned from Mexico at the end of 1906, he settled in Santa Fe. There he turned to his local network, led by Frank Springer, Judge John R. McFie, and Paul A. F. Walter, all prominent in Republican politics in New Mexico Territory. The four agreed that the venerable Palace of the Governors would be a splendid home for the proposed school and a museum. They moved on two fronts: first, to convince the New Mexico Territorial Legislature to let the AIA use the Palace for the school; second, to convince the AIA that there should *be* a school and that it should be located in Santa Fe.

As the complex maneuvering to these ends proceeded during 1907, Hewett accelerated his pace. In January and February, 1907, he lectured before AIA chapters in Cincinnati, Davenport, Dubuque, St. Louis, Kansas City, Lawrence, Topeka, Pueblo, Colorado Springs, Denver, Boulder, Salt Lake City, and San Francisco. During the long train rides he worked on revisions of the Uniform Rules and Regulations to implement the 1906 Antiquities Act (ASAR, Organic Act and Annual Reports, School of American Archaeology, 1907–1918:10–11).

The first AIA sponsored fieldwork under Hewett's coordination began in April, 1907, in Boone County, Missouri. The St. Louis chapter provided $1500 to support "mounds" excavation, directed by Gerard Fowke, who had been employed off and on for some years by the Bureau of American Ethnology. Hewett put in a token appearance and then left for Utah. In Salt Lake City, the Utah chapter put up $1000 of Colonel E. A. Wall's money "to be used in investigating the ancient ruins in the southeastern part of the state." Byron Cummings, with some students, took personal charge of the work. He had made his first horseback trip through southeastern Utah the previous year, and was entranced.

Hewett had advertised his first archaeological field school via a circular to Harvard and elsewhere. Three Harvard students, Alfred Vincent Kidder, Sylvanus Griswold Morley, and John Gould Fletcher, signed on. The adventures and misadventures of the three have become one of the primal legends of Southwestern archaeology (Givens 1992:11–24; Woodbury 1973). Hewett and his students met Cummings and his students, including Cummings's nephew, Neil M. Judd, in Bluff, Utah. On July 4, 1907, Hewett took his three neophytes to the confluence of McElmo and Yellowjacket canyons near the Utah-Colorado border. Hewett spent a few hours with them in the morning, and took them out onto a mesa top. According to Kidder, Hewett "waved an arm, taking in it seemed, about half the world, 'I want you boys to make an archaeological survey of this country. I'll be back in three weeks'" (Kidder 1957 III:39; cited by Givens 1992:100). Hewett proffered no further advice or training. He mounted his horse and rode away back toward Bluff, leaving the Crimson trio to their own devices.

Many years later, Hewett wrote that he had learned this pedagogical technique from a young waterfront ruffian in Chicago who taught kids to swim by "Pushing them off the pier" (Hewett 1943:149). The trio survived and did a credible job. Later in the season, Hewett and his now slightly seasoned students went to Mesa Verde to continue a survey of the ruins. There they met Jesse Nusbaum, a young photographer just graduated from Colorado Normal School whom Hewett had known for some time. Following some work on the mesa, Hewett took his three protégés to the Puyé site to begin excavations. By that time, John Gould Fletcher had had enough of Hewett's rough ways and Morley's incessant practical jokes. He left.[9] For Kidder and Morley, the summer was the beginning of a lifetime involvement in Southwestern, and later, Mayan archaeology as well as life-time friendships with Neil Judd and Jesse Nusbaum. The four would become major players in later rounds of Harvard vs. Hewett.

At some point during his busy summer of 1907, Hewett brought Alice Fletcher to see Santa Fe and the Pajarito country for the first time; she was enthralled. The two continued to plan for a school of American archaeology. But, discontent was ripening in Cambridge, Massachusetts. In the fall of 1907, Charles Bowditch resigned as chair of the AIA American Committee. He was weary of Hewett and Lummis and their bumptious western ways. He thought Alice Fletcher could keep them in check, since he believed Frederic Ward Putnam could keep *her* in check. But Putnam's "protégé" was nearing seventy and had ideas of her own that coincided with Hewett's. In December, 1907,

Fletcher pushed a proposal through the AIA annual meeting to create the School of American Archaeology. The location was to be determined, but it would likely be in the western United States. On December 30, 1907, the AIA Council adopted the following resolution:

> The School of American Archaeology is established to conduct the researches of the Institute in the American field and afford opportunities for fieldwork and training to students of archaeology. The School will direct exhibits of the local Societies in their respective fields, maintain archaeological research in the various culture areas of the American continent, direct the work of Fellows and collaborators with universities and other scientific organizations, both home and foreign, in the advancement of archaeological research. The School will provide field experience and training for students, but not to duplicate university offerings (ASAR, Organic Act . . . , 1907–1918:25–26).

A managing committee was established. It consisted of Alice Fletcher as chair, Franz Boas of Columbia University, Mitchell Carroll *ex officio* of George Washington University (Carroll was secretary of the council), Jesse Walter Fewkes, Mrs. John Hays Hammond of Washington, D.C., Francis W. Kelsey *ex officio* as president of the AIA, Charles Lummis, and Frederic Ward Putnam. On December 31, 1907, Hewett was appointed director of the School. After a brief period to get things organized, Hewett left for Europe and the Near East for eighteen weeks, including a stop at the University of Geneva to finish his doctorate.

Formal approval of the school by the AIA gave Hewett and his New Mexico allies ammunition to acquire the Palace of the Governors and establish the school in Santa Fe. Lummis and others from western chapters also pushed to have the school either in Santa Fe, or elsewhere in the west, preferably in Los Angeles. But, there were other viewpoints. Franz Boas had been nurturing plans for an International School of American Archaeology and Ethnology in Mexico City. He apparently hoped to include the AIA, and its funds, in the consortium of universities, research institutions, and governments he was putting together to support the school (Boas 1912, 1915; Godoy 1977). Establishing an AIA sponsored school in Santa Fe would cripple that support.[10]

In 1908 Hewett held another field school in Canyon de los Frijoles, with additional work at Mesa Verde. The Peabody Museum of Harvard put up $500, as did the New Mexico Archaeological Society, the University of Colorado, and the Colorado Historical Society (MVRC, Report on the Ruins of Mesa Verde, Colorado). The "field assistants" were Kidder, Morley, and John Peabody Harrington. Alfred Tozzer and Roland B. Dixon represented Harvard. Tozzer and Dixon did *not* hit it off with Hewett. They apparently thought Hewett's field methods (and persona) to be crude. Whatever Hewett did, by omission or commission (according to one legend it began when Hewett, ever frugal, denied Tozzer a second helping of bacon at breakfast), he made a lifetime enemy of Tozzer, who later became famous for his deeply felt and longlasting enmities toward those he disliked.[11] One example will suffice. In 1912, Tozzer wrote to Frederick Webb Hodge: "I still consider Hewett's influence over the young men under him bad, his methods of work unscientific and too extended, his methods of scattering propaganda undignified, and his assumption of omnipotence unexampled" (FWHP).

On his side, Hewett, in responding to concerns about criticisms of the School emanating from Harvard, wrote to A. L. Kroeber in July, 1909:

> . . . Professor Putnam is the only other person not in accord with my efforts, whose dissatisfaction need give me or the Institute any concern. His defection I profoundly regret, and I shall certainly accord to his views the highest respect and consideration in all things. I believe him to be sincerely friendly to the American work and desirous of its success. I only regret that so far as we are able to ascertain, after much earnest investigation, the trouble with both Mr. Bowditch and Professor Putnam is simply that they have been grievously imposed upon by an irresponsible young man [Tozzer] whom I invited to my camp last year with the sincere desire to afford him an opportunity for the fieldwork which he told me he greatly needed and to whom I showed every possible kindness and courtesy, but who, out of apparent pure wantonness, if not maliciousness, carried to those good friends of mine and of the American work, a bundle of tales so trifling in their absurdity, so malicious in their falsity, as to deserve the contempt of every thoughtful man. I am speaking in strong terms I know, but in a case like this I see no use in mincing matters. . . . I have no concession to make to falsity, and whatever compromise I enter into with reference to the conduct of our work in order to meet the views of our members . . . it is not to be interpreted as making any concession because of, or in the least being influenced by the lying attack of this young person, who, in my estimation, and in the estimation of others of calm and earnest judgment, has violated in a most reprehensible manner the fundamental principles of scientific ethics, merely out of pique or jealousy, or other motive equally unworthy and odious to a fair minded man (ELHP).

In November, 1908, five of the Americanist Committee—Bowditch, Boas, Putnam, Fletcher and Hewett—met in Cambridge, ostensibly to approve Santa Fe as the site for the School of American Archaeology. But Bowditch launched into a three-hour argument against Santa Fe; Putnam and Boas agreed. Fletcher and Hewett apparently lost, three votes to two. However, they sent mail ballots to the absentee members, Francis Kelsey, Mitchell Carroll, Mrs. John Hays Hammond, and Lummis. The recount made it six to three in favor of Santa Fe. Boas was apoplectic. Bowditch and Putnam sent Tozzer to the annual AIA meeting in Toronto in December, 1908, in an attempt to get the committee vote overturned. He failed (Mark 1988:320).

Hewett's Santa Fe allies now moved forward. They convinced the 1909 New Mexico legislature to establish the Museum of New Mexico. The legislation stipulated that both the Museum and the School would be housed in the

Palace of the Governors, and that the School would operate the Museum. Hewett was appointed director of the Museum. The legislature would provide operating expenses for the Museum, but the director's position carried no salary, a stipulation Hewett had requested.

The museum would be controlled by a board of regents, appointed by the governor of New Mexico. The school would be controlled by a managing committee, appointed by the AIA. The chairman of the Regents would sit on the School's managing committee. Hewett recommended the membership for both groups. He had learned his lesson about governing boards in Las Vegas: the majority of the members should be in your network and if possible, hand picked by you. The Museum's board of regents included Frank Springer, and a number of prominent New Mexicans favorably inclined to Hewett. The AIA committee was chaired by Alice Fletcher. Members included Hermon C. Bumpus of the American Museum, Byron Cummings, Jesse Walter Fewkes, Frederick Webb Hodge, William Henry Holmes of the Smithsonian, Charles Lummis, Congressman John Lacey, Francis Kelsey *ex officio* as AIA president, Mitchell Carroll *ex officio* as AIA secretary, and a number of potential donors, including Colonel E. A. Wall of Utah, and Mrs. John Hays Hammond of Washington, D.C. Frank Springer represented the Museum's board of regents. The executive committee consisted of Fletcher, Kelsey, Carroll, Fewkes, Hammond, Hodge, Lummis, McFie, and William Sloane, AIA treasurer (Fletcher 1910:1–3, 14–27).

Thus, by the late spring of 1909, Hewett was well-positioned, in terms of location, facilities, and organization. His salary came from the AIA, supplemented by lecture fees, and occasional earnings from Santa Fe real estate and other investments. Taking no salary as museum director was a political master stroke, since it removed the position from political porkbarreling, and allowed him to maintain a posture of altruism. He carried on a relentless schedule of lecturing around the country for the AIA. He continually widened his networks, and his carefully managed image made him seem to be "Doctor Archaeology," at least in the west and midwest. Like other politicians before and since, he had learned that an appeal to mid-America paid dividends.

All this incensed the Harvard crowd and its allies. Bowditch, Putnam, and Boas launched a counterattack throughout 1909. There was much talk of how "poor Alice" had been "deceived" and "hoodwinked" by Horrible Hewett. She was not personally criticized; it would have been extraordinarily impolitic to attack someone regarded by many as a living saint. Francis Kelsey, now firmly in control of the AIA, totally disagreed with suggestions that Fletcher was duped by Hewett. He called her "one of the most clearheaded and capable administrators that I have met" (cited by Mark 1988:321). Putnam, Boas and Bowditch carried their fight against Hewett to the December, 1909 annual meeting of the AIA. They lost, again, and thereupon resigned from the Institute (Mark 1988:323), but not from the fight.

Hewett did not take all the vituperation silently. At some point he apparently told Tozzer that he thought Roland Dixon did not share Tozzer's opinion of Hewett and his work. Dixon wrote a testy letter on September 1, 1910 informing Hewett that he did, indeed, share Tozzer's views (ELHP). Hewett also purportedly made some statements about Franz Boas's integrity late in 1910. This became one *cause celèbre* in the next round of Harvard vs. Hewett.

Before that round began, however, Hewett had three very successful years. He continued his field school in Frijoles Canyon. In 1909, he hired Jesse Nusbaum and Kenneth Chapman on the staff of the Museum of New Mexico, and Sylvanus G. Morley and John Peabody Harrington on the staff of the School. In 1910, he joined forces with Frederick Webb Hodge, recently appointed head of the Bureau of American Ethnology, to launch an interdisciplinary research program in the Rio Grande Valley. The program was designed to study the environment, archaeology, ethnohistory, ethnography, and linguistics of the region (ASAR, Organic Act . . . :23–25). Its most successful results were John Peabody Harrington's and others' (Harrington 1916; Henderson and Harrington 1914; Robbins, Harrington, and Freire-Marreco 1916) monographs on Tewa ethnogeography and ethnobiology.[12] Under Hewett's guidance, the Museum of New Mexico began acquiring major archaeological sites, including Pecos, Quarai, and Gran Quivira.

## Round Three: Harvard, Boas, and the Santa Fe Chamber of Commerce

In 1910, Bronson M. Cutting, a wealthy Harvard graduate from New York, moved to Santa Fe, seeking a cure for his tuberculosis (Lowitt 1992:19–46). He soon began dabbling in New Mexico politics, and convinced his mother to buy him a Santa Fe newspaper, *The New Mexican*, as a forum for his views. He was, according to a later biographer, "wealthy, simple, calculating, unpredictable, idealistic, ruthless, generous, self-centered and shy" (Campbell 1967; cited by Chauvenet 1983:98). With the exception of "wealthy," most of the adjectives would fit Hewett. Perhaps the similarity in temperament led to inevitable conflict. More likely was the fact that Cutting often supported the Democratic party (he was a personal friend of Teddy Roosevelt) and did battle with the Republicans. Hewett was closely aligned with several prominent Republicans.

Hewett and Cutting first clashed soon after the latter's arrival in Santa Fe. Cutting's sister, Justine Ward, asked Carl Lotave, an artist on the Museum of New Mexico staff, to paint her portrait. Hewett said he warned Cutting that Lotave was a "lady's man," and that his sister's reputation might be besmirched by the association. Cutting said Hewett was spreading malicious rumors about Mrs. Ward, and the two of them apparently told Hewett where to get off. Cutting thought Hewett a pretentious fool (Lowitt 1992:45–46). Thereafter, Cutting lost no opportunity to lambaste Hewett in *The New Mexican* and the halls of the legislature, where he came to have much cloakroom power. For twenty-five years he delighted in being a thorn in Hewett's side.

Cutting finally became a U.S. Senator in 1927. At his death in 1935, he was still making life uncomfortable for Hewett (Chauvenet 1983:97–98).

In the fall of 1911, Hewett was asked to become director of exhibits for the proposed California-Pacific Exposition to be held in San Diego in 1915 in celebration of the opening of the Panama Canal. The focus of the Exposition was to be anthropological in a broad sense. (Hewett used his Smithsonian connections to hire Aleš Hrdlička to develop major exhibits on human evolution.) Hewett convinced his boards that he could wear a third hat, to add to the other two. He thus became, simultaneously, director of the School of American Archaeology, director of the Museum of New Mexico, and director of exhibits at the San Diego Exposition. There were many in Santa Fe who thought Hewett already wore a plethora of fedoras.

The third hat provided an excuse for another try at discrediting Hewett. This time Franz Boas and the "Cambridge Crowd" from Harvard provided the ammunition. In November, 1911, Boas sent from Mexico a typeset "Open Letter" to Hewett asking him to affirm or deny statements Hewett was said to have made about Boas receiving "double or triple" payments from the Bureau of American Ethnology for work done by him. Since Boas's relationship with the Bureau had come under close and unfavorable scrutiny during a 1903 investigation that ousted W. J. McGee, Boas was undoubtedly very sensitive. William Henry Holmes, who had succeeded John Wesley Powell as head of the Bureau, was a staunch Hewett supporter. Holmes essentially cut off Bureau support of Boas's work when he took the Bureau reins in 1903 (Godoy 1977:229).

The gist of Boas's lengthy letter was that Hewett had alleged Boas was guilty of double- or triple-dipping in receiving payments for manuscripts from the Bureau of American Ethnology; and that Hewett had denied the allegations, but that Roland Dixon, Alfred Tozzer, Joseph Spinden, Francis Kelsey, and young Sylvanus Morley had, at various times, confirmed Hewett's statements. Therefore, Boas considered Hewett's denial "as at least a prevarication." Then, fumed Boas

> I should certainly test the questions between us in the courts, if I could do so without the prohibitive expense of taking the testimony of my witnesses to, and trying the controversy in, New Mexico, where you reside. I beg now to ask if you will not meet me in this matter, and authorize an appearance in your behalf and a trial in a court in an Eastern State, upon which our attorneys can agree. If you will not, I must be content with making public the facts.—Franz Boas (ELHP).

Boas attached copies of earlier letters to the AIA in which he castigated Hewett and impugned his work.[13]

Cutting published Boas's letters in *The New Mexican;* they were widely gossiped over in Santa Fe. Hewett maintained a stony silence, but his supporters generated a good deal of sympathy for him by appealing to regional chauvinism: us western good guys vs. those eastern snobs trying to tell us what to do.

## Hewett, San Diego, and the Maya

Hewett, meantime, accepted the position in San Diego and was soon deep in the development of the San Diego Exposition, particularly what would become the San Diego Museum of Man. He also received a grant of $3,000 from the St. Louis chapter of the AIA to begin work on Mayan archaeology, and would later receive funds from the Exposition to support additional work. With no real knowledge of Mayan archaeology, he chose the first site he encountered, Quiriguá in Guatemala. Conveniently, the site was on land belonging to the American Fruit Company, which later supported Hewett's work and turned the site into an archaeological park. Hewett brought along Jesse Nusbaum, and Sylvanus Griswold Morley. Hewett later hired Earl H. Morris, then a student at the University of Colorado, for a couple of seasons and in 1914, Neil Judd joined the team for a season to help make the papier-mâché squeezes used to produce replicas of the Quiriguá stelae shown at the San Diego Exposition, and then placed (where they remain) in the rotunda of the San Diego Museum of Man (Judd 1968:146–153). The work at Quiriguá and elsewhere, done primarily by Morley, Nusbaum and Morris is chronicled elsewhere (Brunhouse 1971:52–62).

On January 20, 1912, Hewett was in New York. In an interview in the *New York Times* (1912) he stated that Quiriguá "is believed to be the oldest city on the two American continents." He also promised to have the Maya glyphic system deciphered by June, 1912, stated that no one had been to Quiriguá from the time of John Lloyd Stephen's and Frederick Catherwood's visit in the 1840s until Hewett "rediscovered" it, postulated some connections between the Maya and the Zuñi, and drew an analogy between Maya glyphs and Southwestern dry paintings. Alfred Tozzer was outraged by such flummery, and vented his spleen to the *Times* (1912, copy in FWHP). On February 10, 1912, in a letter to F. W. Hodge he wrote, "We all feel here [Harvard] that something should be done, but what?" (FWHP). Hewett sailed blithely on to Guatemala.

The next step came in 1913. For some years, the Santa Fe Railway had been promoting the "romance" of the Southwest to stimulate tourism. In 1913, the Santa Fe Chamber of Commerce decided to join in. The Chamber declared that Santa Fe was the oldest city in United States, and had about 60,000 mailing envelopes printed so stating that claim in a logo. Hewett, citing Hodge and Adolph Bandelier, properly disagreed. Soon after, he evicted the Chamber of Commerce from the Palace of the Governors where it had maintained an office at Hewett's sufferance. This was too much for H. H. Dorman, president of the Chamber and a Bronson Cutting employee. Not only was he stuck with sixty thousand historically inaccurate envelopes, but also he had no office. The resulting brouhaha, carefully nurtured by Cutting, was truly marvelous. Letters from Tozzer to Dorman, dated October 11 and 13, 1913, gleefully printed in *The New Mexican* said (among other things):

> I rejoice that Santa Fe has at last risen to the occasion and has placed Hewett where he belongs. His methods of work serve as a laughing stock for a great many of us. . . . I think, with the exception of a few people in Washington, there is not an American archaeologist who stands for him.
>
> I think there are several men who would be willing to help you in showing up Hewett in his true light. Professor Franz Boas, of Columbia, is one these. . . .
>
> Hewett has always said that the "Cambridge Crowd" did not like him because they were jealous of him. You will find on investigation that it is more than Cambridge. I know of no one interested in scientific work along archaeological lines in America with the exception of two or three at Washington and a few personal friends who stand for Hewett. HIS SCIENTIFIC REPUTATION IS OF NO VALUE (copies in ELHP).

The uproar grew during October–November, 1913. Hewett stayed out of town, and let his local supporters handle the battles. There were numerous meetings. At a particularly heated Chamber of Commerce meeting Cutting stated "that he did not consider Dr. Hewett capable of being a director in the School of American Archaeology, nor did he consider the managing committee of the institute capable of selecting a director for this school or any other school" (*The New Mexican* 1913, clipping in ELHP). In response, sixteen organizations, from the New Mexico Archaeological Society to the Ladies Aid Society of the Methodist Church, as well as the Governor of New Mexico, issued formal resolutions of support for Hewett. Eventually, even the Santa Fe Chamber of Commerce passed a resolution by a 79 to 6 vote, repudiating its own director and supporting Hewett (Lowitt 1992:46–47; Resolutions 1913; Santa Fe Chamber of Commerce 1913, copy in ELHP).

Undaunted, Cutting and Dorman decided to develop their *own* plan of reorganization for the School of American Archaeology, and carry it to the AIA annual meeting in Montreal, even though neither of them were members. Dorman showed up in Montreal on January 2, 1914. He had the reorganization plan in hand, signed by fifteen Santa Feans. A telegram of support was sent by Roland B. Dixon, Pliny Earle Goddard, and Franz Boas, saying "[W]e know such plan to have approval of many serious anthropologists in Cambridge, New York, Chicago, California and urge you support it" (copy in ELHP).

The managing committee of the School rather thoroughly grilled Dorman. He retreated in apparent confusion, although he managed to obtain the stenographic transcript of the meeting; it was never seen again. The committee thereupon sent a resolution to the Santa Fe Chamber of Commerce, with copies of all the documents it had received. The resolution acknowledged

Dorman's appearance and the allegations against Hewett made in the reorganization plan, and included the following:

> WHEREAS, the aforesaid H. H. Dorman, upon request, stated that he was unable to furnish data and evidence upon which the statements in the communication were based. THEREFORE, Be it Resolved that this communication be laid upon the table (Letter and attachments from AIA Secretary to Santa Fe Chamber of Commerce, copy in ELHP).

Hewett undoubtedly enjoyed his triumph when he finally returned to Santa Fe later in January. But he paused only briefly; he was on his way to San Diego. There he and others opened the San Diego Exposition; it was a great success. As planned, the anthropology exhibits remained as permanent exhibits in the Exposition's California Building, which became the San Diego Museum of Man. Hewett became the director of the Museum; he also began teaching anthropology courses at San Diego State Teachers College and began dividing his year between San Diego and Santa Fe.

In 1917, Hewett and others opened the Museum of Art in Santa Fe, funded primarily by Frank Springer. Hewett took active steps to encourage artists to come to New Mexico, as well as to encourage Pueblo Indian arts and crafts. He and the Museum and School staffs were in the forefront of developing Fiesta and Indian Market in the 1920s and worked closely with the Santa Fe Railway and the Fred Harvey Company in promoting tourism (Thomas 1978; Dilworth 1996; Fowler in press:Chapter 6).

Also in 1917, the School of American Archaeology became the School of American Research. There were a number of reasons for the change, among them that the School was engaged in numerous non-archaeological activities. The central concern, however, was funding. The School was a function of the AIA, but had no legal status of its own. The AIA could not provide sufficient funds. To receive property and other endowments and otherwise generate income, the School needed to be incorporated, which provided the formal opportunity to take a new name. The articles of incorporation and by-laws for the School of American Research were adopted on February 3, 1917. The incorporators included W. H. Holmes, Alice Fletcher, Aleš Hrdlička, Mitchell Carroll, Francis Kelsey, and Frederick Shipley (all strong Hewett supporters from the AIA and the Smithsonian), as well as Frank Springer, Paul F. A. Walter, and John R. McFie (Hewett's stalwart allies in Santa Fe) (ASAR, Organic Act . . . :196–211, 214–217). The incorporation of the School and its name change seemed to Hewett to herald a new era (ASAR, Organic Act . . . :100). There were, however, young turks bent on mischief, lurking just over the horizon.

## Round Four: The Battle for Chaco Canyon

Although Hewett tried, he could not keep the Southwest as a private reserve for regional (i.e., the Four Corners states) archaeologists and anthropologists.

We previously noted that Hewett managed to have a number of major ruins placed under the control of the Museum of New Mexico, such as Pecos, Quarai, and Gran Quivira. He did cooperate with others when it was advantageous to do so, especially if others provided research funds. He had entered into a cooperative agreement with the Bureau of American Ethnology in 1910, as previously discussed.

Others soon came to work in the Southwest. Kidder, who maintained good relations with Hewett, at least until 1920, was at Pecos in 1915, 1916, and again after he returned from military duty in World War I (Givens 1992:29–76). The American Museum of Natural History sent Nels Nelson out to do his seminal stratigraphic work in the Galisteo Basin in 1914–15 (Nelson 1916). The Museum also began its long-term sponsorship of Earl Morris's work at Aztec Ruin in 1915 (Lister and Lister 1968, Lange and Leonard 1985), as well as Kroeber's (1916) and Spier's (1917) work at Zuñi.

Elsie Clews Parsons, a woman of independent means, began her ethnographic work in the Southwest in 1915. Through the Southwest Society, which she bankrolled, Parsons provided funds to support ethnographic work carried out by her mentor, Franz Boas, and a number of his students, especially Ruth Benedict, Ruth Bunzel, Esther Goldfrank, and Gladys Reichard (Hare 1985; Parezo 1993:63–75, 107–128, 157–188, 259–269; Zumwalt 1992).

Hewett had few objections to ethnographic research in the Southwest. But the continued influx of eastern archaeologists was troublesome. In 1920–21, some of the easterners staged an invasion of Chaco Canyon, which Hewett regarded as his private preserve since he had helped run out the Wetherills and the Hyde Expedition in 1902. The invasion was doubly offensive to Hewett because it was engineered by three of "his" former students, Neil M. Judd, A. V. Kidder, and Sylvanus Griswold Morley, aided and abetted by former employees Earl H. Morris and Jesse Nusbaum. Kenneth Chapman, a current employee of the Museum of New Mexico, helped from behind the scenes in Santa Fe. Furthermore, Hewett had in place an elaborate cooperative agreement in 1916 with the Smithsonian Institution and the Royal Ontario Museum of Toronto, Canada, to work in Chaco Canyon. The plan was delayed by World War I, but was ready to be implemented thereafter (ASAR, Organic Act . . . , 1907–1918:101–103), although the Smithsonian was forced to back out.

In order to set the scene, it is necessary to summarize the employment histories of the principal characters in the invasion. Morley and Kidder, having survived Hewett's tossing them off the pier, returned in 1908. Hewett hired Morley that year to head up the School's planned program of Mayanist research. Kidder returned to Harvard to finish his Ph.D. and then began his famous work at Pecos in 1915. Neil M. Judd, a nephew of Byron Cummings, met Kidder and Morley in 1907, as mentioned above, and was on Hewett's field school in Frijoles Canyon in 1910. Receiving a master's degree from the University of Utah, he was hired by the U.S. National Museum of the Smithsonian in 1911. In 1914, the Smithsonian "loaned" Judd to Hewett to direct the preparation of plaster casts of the Quiriguá stelae, as previously noted. In

1915–1917 he conducted archaeological research in Utah (Judd 1926, 1968:46, 61–72, 146–153), and by 1920, he was ready to take on much larger projects.

Earl H. Morris was raised in northwestern New Mexico. Keenly interested in archaeology since childhood (he and his father spent much time digging for artifacts), Morris chanced to meet Hewett on a train in 1911. Hewett sent Morris to work with Morley in the Maya country in 1912. Later Morris worked in the Galisteo Basin with Nels Nelson, learning stratigraphy and seriation from him. After receiving a master's degree from the University of Colorado, on Nelson's recommendation he joined the staff of the American Museum of Natural History in 1917 and began several years' work on the excavation and stabilization of Aztec Ruin which the Museum had purchased.

Kenneth M. Chapman, a brilliant artist, became associated with Hewett during the latter's days in Las Vegas and, as previously noted, joined him in Santa Fe when the Museum of New Mexico was created in 1909.[14] Chapman's central interest was Pueblo ceramics (Chapman 1933–36, 1938, 1970), and he was one of the founders of the Indian Arts Fund (see below). Jesse Nusbaum became Hewett's summer employee in 1908, and joined Hewett full-time when the Museum opened the following year. Chapman served as a curator in the museum; Nusbaum was photographer, field archaeologist, and general handyman.[15] In time, Hewett alienated Morley, Chapman, and Nusbaum (Brunhouse 1971:63–94, Chapman n.d., Nusbaum 1980:21–23), and apparently Morris as well. Morley escaped to the Carnegie Institution of Washington in 1914, although Hewett tried mightily to block his appointment. Morley's career as a preeminent Mayanist flourished from then on. He continued to live in Santa Fe until his death, and kept his hand in Southwestern archaeology as well as the roiling social and intellectual life of the community. Nusbaum escaped by enlisting in the armed forces in World War I. When he returned in early 1919, he joined Frederick Webb Hodge on the staff of the Museum of the American Indian in New York. (Hodge had been lured away from the Bureau of American Ethnology the previous year by George Heye.[16]) The next year Nusbaum married Aileen O'Bryan and in 1921, he became superintendent of Mesa Verde National Park.

Having introduced the principal characters, it is necessary to make note of the interlocking institutions through which they engineered their Chaco coup. The Carnegie Institution was endowed by Andrew Carnegie in 1902 (Carnegie Institution 1903). Some years earlier, Carnegie (1889) had propounded his "gospel of wealth." That is, that great personal fortunes should be stewarded and used for the good of humanity rather than squandered on personal possessions or enjoyment, in short the Protestant Ethic in action, à la Max Weber. For the next thirty years he practiced what he preached. When he died in 1919, it was reported that he had given away $350,695,653 for hundreds of libraries, the Carnegie Institute in Pittsburgh, the Carnegie Corporation, the Carnegie Institution, and a host of other organizations and activities (Bremner 1988:100–106).

Although the Institution organizers investigated the possibilities of anthropological research, little was accomplished for many years. Morley was hired in 1914, but the full blown Mayanist research program supported for decades was not established until 1924, when Earl Morris was hired and A. V. Kidder brought in to run it in 1929 (Givens 1992:77–119). Nonetheless, Morley's appointment gave him great prestige and brought him into the intellectual and research communities of Washington, centering on the Carnegie, the Smithsonian, the Cosmos Club, and various scientific societies.

The plan to develop a research program in Chaco Canyon led by Neil Judd had its inception in discussions between Judd, Kidder, Morley, and Morris in 1919. They were well aware that Hewett planned to restart the joint School of American Research and Royal Ontario Museum expedition (ROM). Hewett had ample research funds from the Museum of New Mexico and the ROM. Judd had no funds and was tied to his heavy curatorial responsibilities at the U.S. National Museum. But, he had direct access to, and was part of, the interlocking networks of the Washington science establishment. A key factor was Morley's appointment to the National Geographic Society's (NGS) research committee, created some years earlier to support exploration and research that could provide fodder for the magazine's successful mixture of gee-whiz cheesecake, beefcake, exploration and natural science reportage (Abramson 1987:143, Bryan 1987:90).

In April, 1920, championed by Morley, Judd was given a grant to conduct a reconnaissance of Southwestern ruins and Pueblo villages. An NGS photographer, Charles Martin, was sent along. Accompanied for part of the time by Kidder and Morris, Judd, Morley, and Martin made a grand tour, including a visit to Hodge at Hawikuh[17] and a trip by team and wagon into Chaco Canyon. In Chaco they encountered, as they knew they would, Hewett's crew (sans Hewett) digging in Chetro Ketl (Hewett 1921b:13). On September 7, 1920, Judd gave an interview in Santa Fe to a reporter from *The New Mexican,* in which he described the trip. The key part of the interview read: "[S]everal days were devoted to an examination of house remains within Chaco Canyon National Monument *where the National Geographic Society is contemplating the inauguration of intensive archaeological research* (*The New Mexican* 1920:2, emphasis added; clipping in NMJP). Having thrown the gauntlet at Hewett's feet, Judd left town the same evening. Morley remained to listen to the rumor mill and, if possible, negotiate with Hewett through intermediaries.

Judd and Morley faced several problems. First, as reported to Judd in a December 10, 1920 letter from Stephen T. Mather, Hewett held two valid permits from the Secretary of the Interior to "explore and excavate" in Chaco Canyon (NMJP). Gentlemanly protocol normally precluded one archaeologist invading another's domain. To exacerbate the protocol difficulty, Judd wanted to work on Chetro Ketl, the largest of the Chacoan ruins located just up-canyon from Pueblo Bonito and not yet fully excavated, but Hewett was already digging in Chetro Ketl. In a September 9, 1920 letter to Judd, Morley concluded that attempting to secure a permit to *literally* invade Hewett's archaeological space would be poor politics, at best; better to go after Pueblo Bonito and Pueblo del Arroyo (NMJP). Third, Hewett had arranged to use the Wetherill House and its water supply adjacent to the back wall of Pueblo Bonito, as well as three rooms actually in the ruin for photography and tool storage (Hewett 1921a:12–13).

Weighing all pertinent factors, Judd applied for a permit to excavate in Pueblo Bonito and Pueblo del Arroyo and submitted a proposal to the NGS Research Committee for a multi-year interdisciplinary program of research and ruins stabilization. The latter derived from several long talks with Stephen T. Mather, director of the National Park Service. In a follow-up exchange of letters, Judd (NMJP, October 18, 1920) and Mather (NMJP, December 10 and 22, 1920) agreed upon the need for high-level archaeological research in Southwestern sites, but research coupled with an extensive program of ruins stabilization. As Judd put it,

> . . . [I]n the major Chaco Canyon ruins—since they are of inestimable value not only to science . . . but to the American public as unparalleled examples of prehistoric Pueblo architecture—promiscuous collecting of specimens and haphazard excavations be prohibited if possible. Only research institutions of unquestioned standing, represented in the field by archaeologists of merited reputation, should be permitted to undertake investigations in this field and these institutions should have previously furnished satisfactory evidence of their ability to pursue such investigations to a proper conclusion. In addition, assurance should be exacted in advance that repair work, permanent in its nature, will accompany all excavations.

Learning that Judd's plans would likely succeed, Hewett counter-attacked on several fronts. First, he arranged for the immediate publication of a suite of profusely illustrated articles on Chaco Canyon (totaling sixty-one printed pages) in the January 1921 issue of *Art and Archaeology* magazine (Hewett 1921a, 1921b, Bloom 1921, Bradfield 1921, Chapman 1921). The articles laid out a detailed research plan, noting that work had been underway since 1916, thus establishing turf rights. Second was the critical matter of the Wetherills' six room stone house immediately behind Pueblo Bonito. After Richard Wetherill's murder in 1910, the house and the homestead passed into other hands (Gabriel 1992:230), and finally into those of a Mrs. H. B. Sammons of Farmington, New Mexico. She leased the house and land to a sheep rancher, who in turn sublet the property. Hewett had arranged to use the house as a laboratory and living quarters; Judd planned to use it for the same purposes. Earl Morris, acting for Judd, convinced Mrs. Sammons to lease the house to Judd. Hewett, however, managed through the lessees to raise various legal questions as to whether Mrs. Sammons had clear title, thus effectively blocking Judd. In the end, Judd was forced to build a tent camp and dig a well in the arroyo of Chaco Wash (NMJP, Judd letters to Morris, October 15, 1920, April 6 and May 30, 1921; Judd letter to Mrs. H. B. Sammons, October 14,

1920; Morris letters to Judd, December 17, 1920, February 8 and March 31, 1921).

On January 3, 1921, the Research Committee approved Judd's proposal and he set the machinery in motion to apply formally for an antiquities permit and for the Smithsonian to grant him several month's leave each year to direct the project (National Geographic Magazine 1921). But Hewett persevered. Through Frank Springer and various Washington contacts, he tried to stop the granting of the permits and argued that, since the Smithsonian as a public agency should never engage in anything "controversial," it should not let Judd participate in the project. (Hewett ignored the fact that the same argument might apply to his own public agency, the Museum of New Mexico, and therefore to him.) As indicated in Judd's May 30 letter to Morris (NMJP), it was even rumored that Hewett had a bill introduced in Congress giving effective control of key sites on federal lands to state institutions. The latter was, in fact, one of a series of attempts through state and federal legislation by both Byron Cummings and Hewett to achieve this sort of control (ELHP, Letter to Byron Cummings, February 3, 1928; ASAR, Preservation of the Scientific Resources of New Mexico, 1929). Meanwhile, Hewett suffered a reversal in Santa Fe. As reported in a March 31, 1921 letter by Morris to Judd (NMJP), the New Mexico Legislature learned of Judd's National Geographic grant and cut $4,000 from Hewett's budget—funds he had requested to continue at Chetro Ketl.

Judd arrived in Chaco Canyon in May, 1921, built a tent camp, dug a well, and proceeded to begin work at Pueblo Bonito. On August 3 he wrote to Morris:

> El Toro has yet to put in an appearance. He recently spent several weeks
> in Washington trying to convince those there that our dependency
> upon his water supply and especially the dust from our excavations ren-
> dered it absolutely impossible for him to proceed. Happily, the decision
> was held in abeyance until I had a chance to explain our point of view.
> A Park Service man came in to look the situation over . . . and was
> greatly disappointed to see the destruction caused at Chettro Kettle [sic]
> by this summer's rains. When the ditch east of the ruin was dammed it
> turned all the water into the newly excavated rooms with the result
> that many of the exposed walls have fallen. It is a sorry mess you may
> well believe. Our own work stood the test (NMJP).

After Judd left at the end of August, Hewett sent a crew to Chetro Ketl for a few weeks (Hewett 1922). But he did not return again until after Judd completed his project in 1927. In his 1922 annual report, Hewett rationalized his withdrawal from Chaco Canyon as follows:

> This would be a serious lapse were it not that in addition to the work of
> the School on the Chaco Canyon region during the last years, exten-
> sive operations are in progress under the National Geographic Society
> in the excavation and repair of Pueblo Bonito. With the excavations

conducted for several years past by the American Museum of Natural History at Aztec [Ruin] it would seem that probably an undue amount of attention is being paid to this section of the Southwest. It need not, therefore, be considered a serious loss if we reduce our activities in the Chaco Canyon for the present and increase in other sections equally important and less known (ASAR, Compiled Annual Reports of the School of American Research:77–78).

With these slightly sour grapes, Hewett moved on the following year to Gran Quivira, to begin excavations in cooperation with the National Park Service (ASAR, Compiled Annual Reports:87–88).

Judd, of course, continued in Chaco through the 1927 season, his work chronicled yearly in the *National Geographic Magazine* (e.g., Judd 1922a, 1923, 1925) and in technical reports (Judd 1922b). Judd's massive technical reports on Chacoan architecture and material culture finally appeared a quarter century and more later (Judd 1954, 1959, 1964). Hewett returned to Chaco Canyon and Chetro Ketl in 1929 after his appointment as professor of anthropology at the University of New Mexico. Among his graduate students were Florence Hawley (Ellis), Paul Reiter, Anna O. Shepard, Stanley Stubbs, and Gordon Vivian, all of whom would go on to make significant contributions to Southwestern archaeology. Hewett and his students continued to work in Chaco Canyon until 1940, although no final report was ever written (Lister and Lister 1981:96).

But Chaco Canyon still held many archaeological mysteries. In 1971, under the leadership of the late Robert H. Lister, and subsequently, W. James Judge, the National Park Service, in cooperation with the University of New Mexico, initiated a long-term study and re-study of the "Chacoan Phenomena" in the canyon and adjacent regions (see Lekson 1983, 1984; Mathien 1985; Windes 1987; Kincaid 1983; Nials, Stein, and Roney 1987). Yet much remains unknown about the enigma of Chaco Canyon, which has stirred Anglo curiosity since Lieutenant Simpson (1850) first described it in 1850.

The relative success of the eastern archaeologists against Hewett encouraged them in another round that followed in the 1920s, a battle for Rockefeller dollars and control of the Laboratory of Anthropology made possible by those dollars.

## Round Five: The Laboratory of Anthropology

The creation of the Laboratory of Anthropology in Santa Fe in 1928 was a unique event in Southwestern, indeed, American, anthropology; it was also a major defeat for Hewett. Stocking (1981, 1982) and others (Toulouse 1981a, 1981b; Peckham, Fox, and Lambert 1981) have reviewed the major outlines of the development and history of "The Lab," as it is still called, even though it has long been incorporated into the Museum of New Mexico system. However, the papers of Kenneth Chapman, Jesse Nusbaum and Frederick Webb Hodge cast some interesting additional light on the saga.

John D. Rockefeller, Jr. devoted much of his life to giving away to worthy causes at least the interest on the huge fortune founded by his father (Collier and Horowitz 1976; Harr and Johnson 1988). By the early 1920s Rockefeller's philanthropies included outdoor educationally oriented recreation in the broad sense, including national parks and historic preservation. At the same time that he was involved in Santa Fe and Mesa Verde, as discussed below, he was beginning to support the massive undertaking that became Colonial Williamsburg (Hosmer 1981, I:11–73).

In 1924, John D. Rockefeller, Jr. and his three oldest sons, John III, Nelson, and Laurence, went on an automobile tour of the Southwest and Yellowstone and Glacier national parks. They were accompanied by R. W. Corwin and another Rockefeller employee. Corwin was company physician for the Colorado Fuel and Iron Company—owned by the Rockefeller family. Corwin was born and raised in Greeley, Colorado, and was a lifelong friend of Jesse Nusbaum, also from Greeley; Corwin was also on the managing committee of the School of American Research.

The party first visited Santa Fe, touring the Palace of the Governors and meeting briefly with Hewett. Rockefeller suggested to Hewett that the Palace ought to be restored and furnished as an historic building. The museum collections and research areas, he suggested, ought to be housed in a new building. He also thought that a major library might be built that would house the collections of the School of American Research, the Museum and possibly the city and state libraries. In a 1954 memo to Freeman Tilden, Nusbaum said that Rockefeller told Hewett "he would appreciate receiving a report on the cost of carrying out such a program of proposals as he made and would give such a report very careful consideration" (MVRC). Amazingly, Hewett did nothing.

The Rockefeller party moved on to Taos and thence to Mesa Verde, arriving on July 3, 1924. Jesse and Aileen Nusbaum entertained them with personal tours of the ruins, a steak fry and a pageant—with Navajo workmen playing Anasazi roles! Rockefeller was entranced by the park and very taken by the Nusbaums. He donated $5,000 to match another $5,000 donated by Stella Leviston to build a museum at the park.

Rockefeller returned to Mesa Verde in 1926 with his wife, Abby Aldrich Rockefeller, and the three younger sons, Laurence, Winthrop, and David. They were again entertained by the Nusbaums. The Rockefellers invited the Nusbaums to visit them in New York. According to Jesse Nusbaum,

> They said of the thousands of people they met—sooner or later most of them asked for money—they actually had few true friends—those that never asked them for anything material—we were among those and they wanted to see more of us—have us in their home, etc. (MVRC, Nusbaum 1954 memo).

Rockefeller told Nusbaum about Hewett ignoring his earlier request. Nusbaum suggested that the Rockefellers see Kenneth Chapman in Santa Fe, who would show them the Indian Arts Fund collection. The collection had been started a few years earlier by Chapman, H. P. Mera, and others to gather the best examples of historic Pueblo pottery and stimulate a revival of ceramic manufacture among the Pueblos (KMCP, Chapman Memoirs, n.d.; Clark 1964). Chapman did indeed give them a tour of the collection, housed, at Hewett's sufferance, in the basement of the Art Museum. Hewett managed not to be in town, although he knew the Rockefellers were coming. The Rockefellers were very impressed with Chapman, the collection, and its purposes. On the spot, Rockefeller promised Chapman a minimum of $2,500 for future acquisitions. As stated in his letter to Rockefeller on September 9, 1926 (KMCP), and his memoirs (KMCP), Chapman put the funds in an Albuquerque bank and made no mention of the Rockefeller name to prevent price inflation.

Rockefeller also asked Chapman to write the sort of report he had previously requested from Hewett—that is, how to further develop and support local anthropological and historical organizations in Santa Fe. Chapman, with some help from Nusbaum, produced a report and proposal (KMCP, Chapman letter to Rockefeller, October 4, 1926). When Hewett found out, he averred that *he* would submit the report. Chapman countered that *he* also would submit a report, because Rockefeller had specifically asked him to so do.

Hewett did develop his own document—a major proposal to undertake massive anthropological research programs in Siberia and Latin America, but not in the Southwest. He also proposed to acquire the rest of the city block behind the Palace of the Governors for new laboratories and a library. With a cover letter in which Rockefeller's interest in Hewett's scheme was greatly magnified, Hewett channeled the proposal to Rockefeller through the current president of the AIA, Ralph V. D. Magoffin of New York University. Magoffin seems to have taken Hewett's hyperbole about Rockefeller's interest to mean possible general support for the AIA. Apparently, additional proposals for support of the Institute's overseas schools were prepared to be submitted with, or following, Hewett's proposal.

Hewett was to attend the International Congress of Americanists in Rome in September 1926. He tried to put together a "strong committee" of prominent AIA board members and himself to make a presentation to Rockefeller in New York City before Hewett sailed for Europe on September 8. But Rockefeller was still "out west," or so said his staff. It is probable that Hewett and Magoffin, through ignorance of Rockefeller's manner of doing business, badly misplayed their hand. From all accounts (Hosmer 1981, I:11–73, Harr and Johnson 1988:13–197, Collier and Horowitz 1976:77–178), Rockefeller worked either on a personal one-on-one basis, as with Nusbaum and Chapman, or strictly through his staff. Even if Rockefeller were in town, he probably would not have agreed to a hard-sell presentation by a committee of relative strangers. Further, the detailed staff work on which Rockefeller relied was not yet complete; matters were simply not mature enough for any sort of decision. Hewett and Magoffin did not see Rockefeller before September 8, nor thereafter.

There is some confusion about what happened next. Apparently, the entire AIA proposal package was sent to the Laura Spelman Rockefeller Foundation, another entity entirely, and was summarily rejected. Meanwhile, Rockefeller returned to New York to find Chapman's proposal, but not Hewett's. After much searching, the latter was found at the Foundation. Hewett's proposal was reviewed by Rockefeller and his staff. In a November 16, 1926 letter from Thomas B. Appelget (ELHP), Hewett was informed that "Mr. Rockefeller would not be inclined . . . to contribute toward the project". Rockefeller was still interested in doing something in Santa Fe; he turned to Chapman's proposals, for he had submitted two.

One of Chapman's proposals outlined an umbrella organization that would consolidate the Museum of New Mexico, the School of American Research, the New Mexico Historical Society, state and city libraries, and the Indian Arts Fund—a true mixture of apples, oranges, and persimmons. The proposal also requested funds to acquire land for expansion around the Palace. Chapman's second proposal requested an endowment to establish a museum for exhibiting the Indian Arts Fund collection, as well as funds for additional related fieldwork and collections. The museum was to be located on a choice piece of donated land south of Santa Fe.

Rockefeller called Jesse and Aileen Nusbaum to New York to review the entire matter (Nusbaum 1980:22). The three apparently had a long discussion on December 3, 1926. The next day, Jesse sent the following coded telegram to Chapman in Santa Fe:

> El Toro fell in crowding fence. Your big horse highly commended. Interests have selected trained man to thoroughly study situation. Your pet colt will receive separate consideration if big horse fails. Had most interesting conference. Mums the word . . . Jesse L. Nusbaum (KMCP, copy of telegram in Chapman n.d.:22).

The "trained man" was Hermon C. Bumpus, a zoologist and former director of the American Museum of Natural History, former president of Tufts College and a former member of Hewett's AIA managing committee. Since 1924, Bumpus had served with Rockefeller on the board of trustees of Brown University. He was also a former president of the American Association of Museums (AAM) and in 1926 was chair of its committee on "outdoor education." Rockefeller supported the committee and had helped fund the development of interpretive programs at Yosemite, the Grand Canyon, and elsewhere.

Bumpus's colleagues on the AAM committee were John C. Merriam, president of the Carnegie Institution of Washington; William de Chastignier Ravenel, assistant to the secretary of the Smithsonian and director of the Arts and Industries Museum; Robert S. Yard, founder and general secretary of the National Parks Association; and Clark Wissler of the American Museum of Natural History and Yale University. Wissler had chaired the Division of Anthropology and Psychology of the National Research Council through 1925 and then turned the chair over to A. V. Kidder.

By the mid-1920s there were anthropology programs at numerous major

American universities and several lesser ones as well. For several years there had been talk of the need for field schools, both archaeological and ethnographic. By 1925 the discussion had turned to an "intercollegiate" field school to provide training in one or both sub-disciplines. A model for the archaeological component was Fay-Cooper Cole's field school in Illinois. There, students dug and trowelled in the trenches and attended "trench-side" seminars (Guthe 1952:3). In contrast, Hewett's field schools, when he ran them, consisted of ladies with parasols and gentlemen in boater hats standing near the trenches while local hired laborers shoveled and trowelled. By 1925, the School of American Research "field schools" consisted primarily of tours of Puyé Ruins for the Fred Harvey Company Indian Detours (Thomas 1978).

Since field schools were clearly a form of "outdoor education," Wissler, Kidder, and Bumpus saw a way of promoting, through the AAM program, an intercollegiate field school, preferably in the Southwest. In the spring of 1926, a proposal for the support of graduate anthropological field training "at some suitable spot in the pueblo area of the Southwest" was submitted to the Laura Spelman Rockefeller Memorial Foundation (ALAB, Letter by Bumpus to Members of Executive Committee, February 11, 1927). John D. Rockefeller, Jr., as a trustee of the foundation, had read the proposal. Having heard the Nusbaums' views on the Chapman and Hewett proposals, and reviewing them in detail, Rockefeller now asked Bumpus to evaluate all the proposals and to travel to Santa Fe to investigate the situation personally and make a recommendation.

On December 10, 1926, Rockefeller (KMCP) wrote to Chapman at length, discussing the proposals and saying that Bumpus was on his way. Bumpus set out for Santa Fe *via* Cambridge, New York, Washington, and Chicago where he consulted "informally with anthropologists and other men of science of my acquaintance" (ALAB, Bumpus letter to Members of Executive Committee, February 11, 1927). He arrived in Santa Fe in early February 1927. There he was wined and dined by Hewett's allies and less ostentatiously by Chapman and the Nusbaums. Bumpus met the governor, as well as "many of those who might be classified as the local intelligentsia," but spent much of his time "very largely in examining the surrounding country" (ALAB, Bumpus letter to Members).

Bumpus and Hewett agreed, in principle, that the Palace of the Governors should become a "historical museum"; that land behind the palace should be acquired and a library placed there; "that, if a new and comprehensive Archaeological Laboratory and Museum should be constructed at Santa Fe . . . ," Hewett would cooperate, but that there should not be "unfriendly rivalry" for collections and sites. Finally, they agreed that if proper facilities were built, the Indian Arts Fund would place its collection there (ALAB, Bumpus letter to Members). From Chapman and Nusbaum, Bumpus learned that land for a *new* facility, *not* tied to Hewett's organizations, would be donated, if needed. The donors were Amelia Elizabeth White, Francis Wilson, and (behind the scenes) Hewett's old nemesis, Bronson Cutting (KMCP, Chapman Memoirs, n.d.).

Having gathered his data, Bumpus returned to New York and on March 21, 1927, submitted his report to Rockefeller (ALAB). Therein, he recommended that Rockefeller support a *new* entity: a "Museum and Laboratory of Anthropology" that would incorporate the Indian Arts Fund collection, and be placed on the donated land in Santa Fe. It would *not* be affiliated with the School of American Research nor the Museum of New Mexico.

Thus challenged, Hewett's feet and hands snapped figuratively into position and he made one final bid for control: he called a meeting of interested parties at the Cosmos Club in Washington, D.C.. Since its founding in 1879 by John Wesley Powell and others, many similar confrontations and collusions over who would control whatever pieces of scientific research pie was on the table or pieces of pork in the Congressional appropriations barrel had been played out in the club's rooms, as they continue to be. In an April 22, 1927 letter to Chapman, Kidder reported the following:

> I am in a state of complete nervous and physical collapse, following two days of more or less acrimonious sessions with Hewett, Bumpus, et al. How these blighters manage to sail through weeks on end of this sort of stuff, I cannot understand.
>
> Wednesday morning at the Cosmos Club reminded one of the lobby of a convention hall. Hewett was buzzing with Hrdlicka and Magoffin in corners; Bumpus with Hodge and Holmes in other corners. We met at two—the Executive Committee of the Museum Association, the members of Hewett's board who could be in Washington, Magoffin, and certain innocent [sic!] bystanders, like Judd and myself. [After much vituperation and posturing, there was] a sort of dog fight, which led nowhere but which eventually resulted in the appointment of a small conference group to attempt to get together on fundamentals. This group consisted of Bumpus, Hewett, Yard and myself; and we put in yesterday afternoon drawing up a declaration of principles, which is very sugary (KMCP).

The declaration said in so many words that if a new entity came into existence, everyone would cooperate. In short, a truce—for the time being.

Bumpus reported back to Rockefeller, again recommending an independent Museum and Laboratory of Anthropology. Rockefeller responded that he had requested information on existing institutions, but was now confronted with a "new situation." As quoted by Bumpus and Kidder in a June 6, 1927 statement to members of the Committee on Outdoor Recreation and others (ALAB), Rockefeller remained interested, but "could only consider a request tendered by an organization perfected and already in operation." Kidder and Bumpus thereupon proceeded to organize and formalize strands of their networks. On June 6, 1927, "there was held at the Yale Club, New York City, a meeting to organize an anthropological laboratory, museum and field station in Santa Fe, New Mexico" (ALAB, Bumpus and Kidder 1927 statement). On a motion by Franz Boas, those present became "the Committee on Organization of the Anthropological Laboratory." Kidder became temporary chair, with the power to appoint an Executive Committee, "of which K. M. Chapman shall be secretary," and the Executive Committee was charged to proceed to organize the laboratory (ALAB, Bumpus and Kidder, 1927 statement). The executive committee consisted of Kidder, Chapman, Clark Wissler, Roland B. Dixon, Frederick Webb Hodge, Silvanus Griswold Morley, and Neil Judd (FWHP, Letter from Kidder to Hodge, August 3, 1927). A quorum of the committee met in Santa Fe at the end of August 1927, formally incorporated a "Museum and Laboratory of Anthropology" in Santa Fe and named a board of trustees. The next day, they moved to Pecos to attend the first Pecos Conference (FWHP, Kidder letter to Hodge; Kidder 1927; Woodbury 1993:19–100).

The committee moved quickly. By November 1927, a preliminary statement was issued outlining the history of efforts to develop the Laboratory, as well as its aims and purposes (ALAB). On December 19, 1927, Kidder sent a lengthy letter with a proposal to Rockefeller (copy in ALAB). Both John D. Rockefeller, Jr. and the Rockefeller Foundation provided funds (over time about $270,000) and the "Museum and Laboratory of Anthropology" became a reality. In 1931, "Museum" was dropped from the title for political reasons, mainly related to Hewett and the Museum of New Mexico. Jesse Nusbaum, on leave from the National Park Service, was named director.

Despite his defeat, Hewett did not give up. He and Magoffin were named to the Lab's board of trustees, but soon found reasons to resign. However, both returned to the board, knowing too well that being *outside* the formal network was of little benefit. Being inside might help them gain their ends.

There was a good deal of skirmishing and rumor mongering on both sides in 1928 and 1929 (Zimmerman 1929). The central issue, as Stocking (1982) points out, remained regional chauvinism. Both Hewett and Byron Cummings strongly felt that local research and collecting should be done by local anthropologists and archaeologists, and that local collections should remain in local institutions. In 1927, as then president of the University of Arizona, Cummings pushed a law through the Arizona legislature mandating that archaeological collections made by anyone remain in Arizona. A federal court declared the law unconstitutional, and the U.S. Attorney General's office ruled that antiquities on federal lands were exclusively federal property (Cummings 1927).

Hewett (1929:12–14) got a similar law through the New Mexico legislature in 1929, but with a twist designed to gain control of The Lab. The law placed all institutions in New Mexico concerned with antiquities under a state commission headed by the director of the Museum of New Mexico; that is, Hewett! But the Lab's lobbyist, Francis Wilson, convinced the legislature to withdraw the bill before the governor signed it. He argued that the law violated the state constitution and Rockefeller would simply withdraw his support of the Lab (*The New Mexican* 1929, clipping in ELHP; *The Albuquerque*

*Journal* 1929a–b, clippings in ELHP; *The Albuquerque Journal* 1929c) if the law were signed. The Lab, independent of Hewett and his organizations, was a fait accompli.

The subsequent history of The Lab lies outside the scope of this study, but is discussed elsewhere (Toulouse 1981b; Peckham, Fox, and Lambert 1981; Stocking 1981, 1982). Because of the Depression and reduced funding by Rockefeller, the Lab never became what it creators hoped it would be. In many ways, its halcyon days were the few years from 1928 to 1934, when many of the future leaders of American anthropology came to Santa Fe to work under the then-leaders of the discipline in the several archaeological, cultural, and linguistic field schools held during those years.

Hewett moved on. He was nearing sixty-five in 1929. He finally shed his San Diego "hats," but took up a new one as professor of anthropology at the University of New Mexico. His appointment created the Anthropology Department there—and he returned, finally, to Chaco Canyon to conduct field schools. He continued to be active until his death in 1946. There were many other battles; some he won, some he lost; some were draws. The most remarkable thing about Hewett is that while he was engaged in the skirmishes discussed herein, he was also enmeshed in numerous other fracases over a wide range of issues. Chauvenet (1983) chronicles many of those skirmishes. They are all reflected in Hewett's collected papers. Unlike many others, Hewett kept all the bad things others wrote about him, as well as the good. They form a fascinating record.

Hewett, as noted at the outset, was a very stubborn man who pursued his goals relentlessly. He was an excellent politician, able to use the formal structures of, and the informal networks within, organizations and institutions to gain his ends. Only when his opponents adopted his tactics did they prevail. But they always knew that stepping into the ring with El Toro would prove a tough match. When the score cards are totted up, in my opinion, Hewett won more than he lost.

There are various monuments which Hewett helped to build, although certainly not to himself. They include the Museum of New Mexico, especially the Palace of the Governors and the Museum of Art; the School of American Research, which separated from the Museum of New Mexico after Hewett's death; the San Diego Museum of Man; and anthropology programs at San Diego State, the University of New Mexico, and the University of Southern California. In the 1920s, Hewett and his staff at the Museum and the School played central roles in the establishment of Indian Market and Fiesta—major annual economic and social events in Santa Fe.

In a wall of the interior courtyard of the Museum of Art in Santa Fe are two bronze commemorative plaques dedicated to Alice Cunningham Fletcher and Edgar Lee Hewett, who between them did much for Santa Fe and for American archaeology and anthropology. As one contemplates Hewett's plaque, Beatrice Blackwood's limerick comes to mind. But so do the words of

Edwin Ferdon, one of Hewett's students from the 1930s. Even now, in my own mind, as in Santa Fe itself, opinions about Hewett are split.

## Notes

1. The limerick is cited by Nusbaum (1980:23). Beatrice Blackwood, a prominent British anthropologist, visited Hewett and the School of American Research in 1927. Apparently, she was not impressed. The Ferdon quote is from Ferdon (1993:19).

2. Chauvenet (1983:33–96), Elliot (1987), Hinsley (1986), and Stocking (1982) have provided perspectives on portions of what is here called "Harvard vs. Hewett." To these perspectives I am adding another, gleaned from the personal papers of Edgar Lee Hewett, as well as those of Kenneth M. Chapman, Frederick Webb Hodge, Neil M. Judd, Earl H. Morris, Nels Nelson, Jesse Nusbaum, the Archives of the Laboratory of Anthropology, Santa Fe, and the Archives of the Research Center, Mesa Verde National Park, Colorado. Givens' (1992) recent biography of A. V. Kidder provides an additional dimension.

The Edgar Lee Hewett papers are in the archives of the History Division of the Museum of New Mexico, Santa Fe; the Kenneth Chapman papers are in the Indian Arts Collection archives of the School of American Research, Santa Fe; the Frederick Webb Hodge papers are at the Southwest Museum, Los Angeles; the Neil M. Judd papers are in the National Anthropological Archives at the Smithsonian Institution, Washington, D.C.; the Earl H. Morris and Nels Nelson papers are in the archives of the Department of Anthropology of the American Museum of Natural History, New York City; and some Jesse Nusbaum papers are in the files of the Laboratory of Anthropology, Santa Fe, and in the archives of the Research Center, Mesa Verde National Park, Colorado. The bulk of the Nusbaum papers are deposited in the National Anthropological Archives, Washington, D.C. The latter materials were not available at the time the research for this chapter was undertaken.

3. Hewett's dissertation, written by him in English, but rendered into excellent French by an unknown translator, was published in Geneva in 1908 in a small edition, as was the common practice among Continental universities. His course work at Geneva and his dissertation were for decades rather mysterious to Southwesternists. According to the Documents Librarian at the University of Geneva in 1985:

> Mr. Hewett only stayed briefly in Geneva. He registered for the summer
> session of 1904 in the Faculty of Letters, probably in order to make the
> necessary contacts for the preparation of his dissertation. The matter of
> his doctorate was brought up again during the session of March 10,
> 1907, when the Faculty Council decided to dispense with the prelimi-
> nary examination for the doctorate and named the committee for the
> defense of his dissertation.
>
> The discussion that took place in the Faculty Council on May 23, 1908,
> concerning the language in which the dissertation should be defended,

shows the difficulties with which Mr. Hewett handled French. I quote: "Mr. Hewett did not seem to be able to defend the dissertation in French." It was suggested that he be authorized to express himself in English. This favor was denied him, but in view of the exceptional quality of the dissertation, the council made the decision to dispense with the defence of the dissertation. . . .

To my knowledge, none of the three members of the committee for the defence of the dissertation was particularly interested in the archaeology of the Southwestern United States [Josette Wagner to Madeliene T. Rodack, 02/01/1985, cited in Schroeder 1993:xiii].

A retranslation into English of Hewett's dissertation, by Madeleine Turrell Rodack, appeared in 1993 (Hewett 1993).

4. The concepts and terms in the paper were lifted directly, and without credit, from a paper by John Wesley Powell (1898).

5. The saga of the Wetherill brothers in Southwestern archaeology, from their early work at Mesa Verde in the 1880s through their work as guides to various "expeditions" for four decades is chronicled in Atkins (1993), Fletcher (1977), Gabriel (1992), McNitt (1966), and Prudden (1906).

6. Lummis further claimed that he and Hewett met privately with President Theodore Roosevelt (an old Harvard classmate of Lummis's), seeking support for the bill. Roosevelt was convinced, according to Lummis, and used his influence to see the legislation through. A further Lummis assertion, that he and Hewett "nominated the scientific institutions of this country of recognized standing which should be given excavation permits. [And,] that list was made the official list of the Government" (cited by Gordon 1968:19) is arrant nonsense. Undoubtedly, Lummis was tweaking noses, one of his favorite activities.

7. For Bandelier's activities in the Southwest, see Lange and Riley (1996) as well as their editions of Bandelier's *Southwestern Journals* (Lange and Riley 1966; Lange, Riley, and Lange 1975–1984), and Bandelier's (1890–92) *Final Report*.

8. Earlier in the year, Tozzer had made his first field trip to the Southwest with William C. Farabee and Frederic Ward Putnam. The party dug for artifacts in Chaco Canyon (Anderson 1970) and Tozzer (1909) recorded a Navajo Night Chant held near the Wetherill Trading Post.

9. Fletcher fled not only Hewett, but his banker father and life in Arkansas. He went to Europe where he became associated with the Imagist poets centering around Amy Lowell and Ezra Pound. In later years, Fletcher returned to Arkansas where he wrote numerous books on agrarian themes, as well as more poetry, winning a Pulitzer Prize in Poetry in 1938. He committed suicide in 1950 (Fletcher 1988).

10. Boas, Tozzer, and others succeeded in establishing a cooperative International School of American Archeology [sic] and Ethnology in Mexico in 1910. It received support from the Mexican government and a variety of German, French, Spanish, and American universities and scholarly societies (Boas

1912, 1915; Tozzer 1915; Godoy 1977). Perhaps the School's most significant achievement was a clear demonstration of the value of stratigraphy and ceramic seriation for establishing culture history chronologies in the New World (Adams 1960; Boas 1915:385–386) just before Nels Nelson and A. V. Kidder began similar work in the Southwest. The School apparently fell victim to Mexican Revolutionary turmoil and World War I and ceased operations in 1915–16 (Stocking 1974:285).

11. According to Tozzer's obituary:

> In the summer of 1907 [sic], Tozzer, along with Dixon, Kidder, and Morley took part in a joint expedition of the Peabody Museum and the Archaeological Institute in the Rito de los Frijoles, New Mexico, under the direction of E. L. Hewitt [sic]. This collaboration with Hewitt marks the beginning of another cycle of Peabody Museum folklore. Tozzer's personal relationships were invariably characterized by an absolute and clear-cut integrity that resulted in the warmest kind of friendship or, less often, the exact reverse. . . . He invariably grasped the nettle; was never known to temporize or back away from a difficult situation. He had a saying: "See a head, hit it." In small matters this meant no more than "Do it now." In larger concerns it meant simply that he was not afraid to commit himself once and forever. His loyalty, both to friendships and enmities, has become traditional in the Peabody Museum (Phillips 1955:74, 76).

12. The principal result of the agreement in the end was to get John Peabody Harrington onto the Bureau of American Ethnology staff, thus giving him a permanent base for his obsessive life-long quest to record dying Indian languages (Laird 1975).

13. Boas's "Open Letter" read as follows:

I beg leave to send you the following open letter to Mr. Edgar L. Hewett, and two documents relating to his work.

Yours very truly,
FRANZ BOAS

Mr. Edgar L. Hewett,
Santa Fe, N.M.
Dear Sir:

On the 27th of April, 1911, Mr. Nelson S. Spencer of New York, acting as my attorney, asked whether you acknowledged the truth of certain statements said by Professor Roland B. Dixon of Cambridge, Mass., to have been made by you at Christmas, 1910, to the effect that you had in your possession information of a damaging character about me, relative to "the Walcott matter;" that you were prepared to use this information against me, and intended to do so under certain circumstances. Dr. Dixon believes that you also said that you had affidavits in connection with the affair.

On May 11, 1911, you replied to this letter as follows:

"I am just now in receipt of your note of the 27th ult. In reply I beg leave to state that you have been misinformed. The statements attributed to me were not made."

(Signed) Edgar L. Hewett

Inquiry on my part, dated May 20, brought a reply from Dr. Alfred M. Tozzer, Cambridge, Mass., dated May 29, stating that you had made the same statements to him. He added that Mr. Morley, who has been closely associated with you for several years, had spoken to several people, Dr. Tozzer among the number, of the charges "we [i.e., yourself and those around you] have against Boas."

He also writes, "I am informed by another man who is entirely reliable, but does not want his name used, that Hewett spoke very strongly against you, and stated that he had affidavits which were sufficient to bring much dishonor upon you."

Sending for still further rebuttal of your denial, I received a letter from Dr. J. H. Spinden of New York, dated June 2, 1911, who assures me that Mr. Morley had told him that "Dr. Hewett had an abundance of legal proof, including affidavits and Government records," showing that I had received payment doubly or triply for the same work from the Bureau, and that I had diverted funds from their proper use. He continues: "My memory is somewhat uncertain on details, but it seems to me that something was said concerning a manuscript or book which was purchased by you with Government money, and either the money not forwarded to the owner of the manuscript or the document not turned over by you to the Bureau. As I remember, there was an affidavit from the man who had owned the manuscript or book."

On June 3 I wrote to Mr. Morley at Santa Fe, repeating these statements, and asking whether these statements had been made, and who his informants were. This letter has remained without reply.

Professor Francis Kelsey, who has acknowledged, in a letter written to my attorney, to have spread the same report, "that I had received payment two or three times for the same work for the Bureau of Ethnology" without taking the trouble to inform himself as to its truth, gives as his source of information "a former Government officer." Considering your personal relation to Mr. Kelsey, your former connection with the Government, and the identity of the wording of the charge, this also points to you.

Considering all these facts, I believe the testimony of three gentlemen of irreproachable character, and consider your answer of May 11, addressed to my attorney, as at least a prevarication.

I should certainly test the questions between us in the courts, if I could do so without the prohibitive expense of taking the testimony of my witnesses to, and trying the controversy in, New Mexico, where you reside. I beg now to ask if you will not meet me in this matter, and authorize an appearance in your behalf and a trial in a court in an Eastern State, upon which our attorneys can agree. If you will not, I must be content with making public the facts.—Franz Boas

The two enclosed letters read as follows:

New York, Dec. 24, 1909
To the President and Council of the Archaeological Institute of America
MR. PRESIDENT, GENTLEMEN OF THE COUNCIL:

I herewith beg to tender my resignation as a member of the Managing Committee of the American School and of the Archaeological Institute of America,
for the reason that I am unable to indorse the scientific and administrative
policies of the American School.

It is my conviction that a school of American archaeology must stand for
the development of broad and careful scientific method. Instead of this, the
policy of the American School has been to encourage superficial work, to carry
on a few detailed investigations that may have been technically satisfactory if
it so happened that good men were in charge of it, but without any attention
to the general development of the broad aspects of American archaeology. I
cannot conscientiously remain affiliated with an institution whose prime aim
is to cater to the public taste for constant expansion of work without heeding
the needs of science.

My objections to the administrative methods of the School are equally
strong. When the opinions of the Committee did not agree with those of its
executive officer, * [*Mr. E. L. Hewett] the composition of the Committee was
modified by the appointment of new members. When, after serious discussion, a decision was reached not in conformity with the wishes of the executive officer of the Committee, votes by letter, without opportunity for discussion, and on matters not previously brought before the committee, were taken.
When a proposition like that of establishing a school of archaeology in Boulder did not seem desirable to the executive officer of the Committee, the question was not brought before the Committee at all. When a minority report for
presentation before the Archaeological Institute was handed in, it was not presented. Under these conditions, membership on the Committee appears to me
unprofitable and undignified.

Yours very respectfully,
FRANZ BOAS

Mexico, D. F. Dec. 16, 1910
Professor Francis M. Kelsey, Ann Arbor, Mich.
MY DEAR PROFESSOR KELSEY:

I have received your letter in which you ask my opinion in regard to Mr. Edgar
Hewett's scientific work. . . .

In my letter of resignation from the American Committee of the Archaeological Institute . . . I expressed my disapproval of both the scientific and administrative methods of Mr. Hewett.

My specific objection is based on his lack of appreciation of what constitutes scientific work. So far as I know, Mr. Hewett is capable of conducting an
excavation of a local archaeological site, but he has never succeeded in convincing me that he has a knowledge of the objects of archaeological and, in
general, anthropological research. His paper, "On the Groundwork of American Archaeology," may be cited to substantiate this point.

. . . I consider his method of work highly objectionable from the point of view of thoroughness. Instead of husbanding his forces, he covers so much ground—from a purely geographical point of view—that thoroughness is impossible. No man can conduct a school in Santa Fe, excavations in the same region, in Guatemala, in Mexico, and work in Colorado, Dakota and so on, for local societies. Since the organization of these enterprises is his work, he alone is to blame for this dissipation of energy, which, from a scientific point of view, is inexcusable. The criticism which I make in this respect is a fundamental one: the progress of science requires slow and steady work by well trained observers, and forbids work by local talent that requires supervision. The artificial stimulation of local interests, without the possibility of insisting on and providing for scientific work, appears to me little short of criminal, because the remains are much safer where they are, under ground, where they may await the time when competent men will save them.

   . . . I have emphasized for more than twenty years the need of slow and careful work and of good preparation; and for this reason Mr. Hewett's everextending schemes and attempts at work for which he is not prepared are extremely distasteful to me.

   Equally undesirable seems to be the type of publications which he produces, all of which are insignificant, or premature. They give the impression of having been written under pressure. . . .

   Yours very truly,
   FRANZ BOAS [Boas 1911]

   14.  Kenneth Chapman is best known for his brilliant studies and renderings of Southwestern Pueblo pottery designs, carried out over many years. Less known, but equally important is his scientific illustration work for Frank Springer. Chapman and Springer met when Hewett hired Chapman at New Mexico Normal School. Springer was a highly successful attorney, businessman, and man of affairs, but his avocation was paleontology, especially crinoids. For over twenty years, Chapman worked half-time for Springer, drawing hundreds of intricate technical illustrations for Springer's publications (1901, 1911, 1926). This support apparently made it possible for Chapman to survive at the Museum of New Mexico on the small salary Hewett paid him (Chapman n.d.).

   15.  Among Nusbaum's "handyman" creations were the redoing of the facade of the Palace of the Governors in what became an integral part of the "Santa Fe" architectural style which Morley (1915) helped create (Brunhouse 1971: 61–62). Others included supervision of construction of the New Mexico Building at the 1915 San Diego Exposition (the building still stands), the Painted Desert Exhibit also at the Exposition, the Museum of Art in Santa Fe in 1917 (patterned after the New Mexico Building, which in turn was patterned by the architect George Rapp after the church at Acoma Pueblo), the original museum building at Mesa Verde National Park, and the first road onto the Mesa (Nusbaum papers and photo archives, MVRC).

   16.  George Heye had founded the Museum of the American Indian in 1916, after years of ardent collecting. In 1919, using his funds and those of New York philanthropists Archer Huntington and Harmon W. Hendricks, Heye embarked on a great period of expansion. He hired Hodge, Nusbaum, George

Pepper and George Dorsey in 1918–19. Under the museum's auspices, and with funds from Hendricks, Hodge undertook his well-known excavation and ethnohistory of Hawikuh (Hodge 1937; Smith, Woodbury, and Woodbury 1966). Heye, Hodge, Hendricks and the others had an exuberant good time building the Museum and partying during the Prohibition Twenties, as reflected in many informal letters in the Hodge papers (FWHP). In 1931, Hodge became director of the Southwest Museum in Los Angeles, where he remained until his death.

17. There is a famous photograph of this visit, which has been published many times (e.g., Smith, Woodbury, and Woodbury 1966:Plate 34).

### References Cited

ALAB: Archives, Laboratory of Anthropology, Museum of New Mexico, Santa Fe.

ASAR: Archives, School of American Research, Santa Fe.

ELHP: Edgar Lee Hewett Papers, Division of History, Museum of New Mexico, Santa Fe.

FWHP: Frederick Webb Hodge Papers, Southwest Museum, Los Angeles.

KMCP: Kenneth M. Chapman Papers, Indian Arts Collection, School of American Research, Santa Fe.

MVRC: Archives of the Research Center, Mesa Verde National Park, Colorado.

NMJP: Neil M. Judd Papers, National Anthropological Archives, Smithsonian Institution, Washington D.C.

Abramson, Howard S. 1987. *National Geographic: Behind America's Lens on the World*. New York: Crown Publishers.

Adams, Richard. 1960. "Manuel Gamio and Stratigraphic Excavation." *American Antiquity* 26: 99.

*Albuquerque Journal*. 1929a. "The Scientific Conservation Bill Said to Jeopardize Rockefeller Gift of Laboratory to State." *Albuquerque Journal* (March 6).

———. 1929b. "State Relics Bill Recalled by the House." *Albuquerque Journal* (March 7).

———. 1929c. "Wise Action." *Albuquerque Journal* (March 8).

Altherr, Thomas L. 1985. "The Pajarito or Cliff Dwellers' National Park Proposal, 1900–1920." *New Mexico Historical Review* 60 (3): 271–294.

Anderson, Anthony. 1970. "The 1901 Expedition to Chaco Canyon, New Mexico. Account of the Expedition and Analysis of the Material." MS 2128J, Chaco Center Archives, Maxwell Museum, University of New Mexico, Albuquerque.

Atkins, Victoria M., ed. 1993. "Anasazi Basketmaker. Papers from the 1990 Wetherill-Grand Gulch Symposium." Bureau of Land Management Cultural Resource Series, no. 24. Salt Lake City: Bureau of Land Management.

Bandelier, Adolph F. 1881a. *Historical Introduction to Studies Among the Sedentary Indians of New Mexico*. Papers of the Archaeological Institute of America, American Series 1 (1): 1–33.

———. 1881b. *A Visit to the Aboriginal Ruins in the Valley of the Rio Pecos*. Papers of the Archaeological Institute of America, American Series 1 (2): 34–133.

———. 1890–1892. *1890–92 Final Report of Investigations among the Indians of the Southwestern United States, Carried on Mainly in the Years from 1880 to 1885, Parts I–II,* pp. 1–319 and 1–591. Papers of the Archaeological Institute of America, American Series, III and IV. Cambridge, Massachusetts.

Baum, Henry. 1904a. "Pending Legislation for the Protection of Antiquities on the Public Domain." *Records of the Past* 3 (4): 99–116.

———. 1904b. "Pending Legislation for the Protection of Antiquities on the Public Domain." *Records of the Past* 3 (5): 143–150.

Bingham, Edwin R. 1955. *Charles F. Lummis. Editor of the Southwest.* San Marino, California: Huntington Library.

Bloom, Lancing B. 1921. "The Emergence of Chaco Canyon in History." *Art and Archaeology* 11 (1–2): 29–35.

Boas, Franz. 1912. "International School of American Archaeology and Ethnology in Mexico." *American Anthropologist* 14: 192–194.

———. 1915. "Summary of the Work of the International School of American Archeology and Ethnology in Mexico, 1910–1914." *American Anthropologist* 17 (2): 384–391.

Bowditch, Charles. 1907. "The Work of the Institute in American Archaeology." *American Journal of Archaeology* 11: 47–48.

Bradfield, Wesley. 1921. "Economic Resources of Chaco Canyon." *Art and Archaeology* 11 (1–2): 36–38.

Bremner, Robert H. 1988. *American Philanthropy,* 2nd ed. Chicago: University of Chicago Press.

Bruce, Robert V. 1987. *The Launching of American Science, 1846–1876.* Ithaca: Cornell University Press.

Brunhouse, Robert L. 1971. *Sylvanus G. Morley and the World of the Ancient Maya.* Norman: University of Oklahoma Press.

Bryan, Charles D.B. 1987. *The National Geographic Society: 100 years of Adventure and Discovery.* New York: H. N. Abrams.

Campbell, John. 1967. "The Decline of the Republican Party 1910–1925." Typescript of lecture in Santa Fe Historical Society, Santa Fe.

Carnegie, Andrew. 1889. "Wealth." *North American Review* 148: 653–664.

Carnegie Institution of Washington. 1903. Yearbook no. 1, 1902. Washington, D.C.: Carnegie Institution of Washington.

Chapman, Kenneth M. 1921. "What the Potsherds Tell." *Art and Archaeology* 11 (1–2): 39–44.

———. 1933–36. *Pueblo Indian Pottery.* 2 vols. Nice, France: Szwedzicki.

———. 1938. "The Pottery of Santo Domingo Pueblo: a Detailed Study of Its Decoration." *Laboratory of Anthropology Memoirs 1.* (Reprinted 1977 by School of American Research, Santa Fe and the University of New Mexico Press, Albuquerque.)

———. 1970. *The Pottery of San Ildefonso Pueblo.* Santa Fe: University of New Mexico Press for the School of American Research.

———. n.d. Memoirs. KMCP.

Chauvenet, Beatrice. 1983. *Hewett and Friends. A Biography of Santa Fe's Vibrant Era.* Santa Fe: Museum of New Mexico Press.

Clark, Ann N. 1964. "From Basement to Basement. A History of the Indian

Arts Fund" (with annotations by Kenneth M. Chapman). Santa Fe: Indians Arts Research Center, School of American Research.

Collier, Peter and David Horowitz. 1976. *The Rockefellers. An American Dynasty.* New York: Holt, Rinehart, Winston.

Cummings, Byron. 1927. Letter to E. L. Hewett 12/18/27. ELHP.

Dilworth, Leah. 1996. *Imagining Indians in the Southwest: Persistent Visions of a Primitive Past.* Washington, D.C.: Smithsonian Institution Press.

Elliott, Clark A. and Margaret W. Rossiter, eds. 1992. *Science at Harvard University. Historical Perspectives.* Bethlehem: Lehigh University Press.

Elliot, Malinda. 1987. *The School of American Research, the First Eighty Years.* Santa Fe: School of American Research.

Ferdon, Edwin N., Jr. 1993. "Introduction. Edgar L. Hewett: the Nature of the Man." In *E. L. Hewett, Ancient Communities in the American Desert,* 11–19. Archaeological Society of New Mexico Monograph Series, no. 1.

Fiske, Turbesé L. and Keith Lummis. 1975. *Charles F. Lummis. The Man and His West.* Norman: University of Oklahoma Press.

Fletcher, Alice C. 1910. Third Annual Report of the Managing Committee of the School of American Archaeology. Boston: Archaeological Institute of America.

Fletcher, John G. 1988[1937]. *The Autobiography of John Gould Fletcher,* edited by L. Carpenter. Fayetteville: University of Arkansas Press.

Fletcher, Maurine S., ed. 1977. *The Wetherills of the Mesa Verde. Autobiography of Benjamin Alfred Wetherill.* East Rutherford: Fairleigh Dickinson University Press.

Fowler, Don D. 1986. "Conserving American Archaeological Resources." In *American Archaeology Past and Future,* edited by David J. Meltzer, Don D. Fowler, and Jeremy A. Sabloff, 135–162. Washington, D.C.: Smithsonian Institution Press.

——. In press. *A Laboratory for Anthropology. Science and Romanticism in the American Southwest, 1846–1930.* Albuquerque: University of New Mexico Press.

Fowler, Don and Catherine S. Fowler. 1991. "The Uses of Natural Man in Natural History." In *Columbian Consequences,* vol. 3. *The Spanish Borderlands in Pan-American Perspective,* ed. by D. H. Thomas, 37–71. Washington, D.C.: Smithsonian Institution Press.

Gabriel, Kathryn, ed. and compiler. 1992. *Marietta Wetherill. Reflections on Life with the Navajos in Chaco Canyon.* Boulder: Johnson Books.

Givens, Douglas R. 1992. *Alfred Vincent Kidder and the Development of Americanist Archaeology.* Albuquerque: University of New Mexico Press.

Godoy, Ricardo. 1977. "Franz Boas and his Plans for an International School of American Archaeology and Ethnology in Mexico." *International Journal of the History of the Behavioral Sciences* 13: 22–42.

Gordon, Dudley C. 1968. "Lummis and the Lacey Act." *Masterkey* 42: 17–19.

Green, Jesse. 1990. *Cushing at Zuni: The Correspondence and Journals of Frank Hamilton Cushing, 1879–1884.* Albuquerque: University of New Mexico Press.

Guthe, Carl E. 1952. "Twenty-five Years of Archaeology in the Eastern United

States." In *Archeology of Eastern United States,* edited by J. B. Griffin, 1–12. Chicago: University of Chicago Press.

Hare, Peter H. 1985. *A Woman's Quest for Science: Portrait of Anthropologist Elsie Clews Parsons.* New York: Prometheus Books.

Harr, John E. and Peter J. Johnson. 1988. *The Rockefeller Century.* New York: Charles Scribner's Sons.

Harrington, John P. 1916. "The Ethnogeography of the Tewa Indians." Twenty-ninth Annual Report of the Bureau of American Ethnology, pp. 29–618. Washington, D.C.

Henderson, Junius and John P. Harrington. 1914. "Ethnozoology of the Tewa Indians." *Bureau of American Ethnology Bulletin* 56.

Hewett, Edgar L. 1898 "The Study of Anthropology." *The Crucible* 6 (8): 237–240.

———. 1903. "Archaeology [of New Mexico]." Report of the Governor of New Mexico to the Secretary of the Interior, 370–374. Washington, D.C.: U.S. Government Printing Office.

———. 1904a. "Archaeology of Pajarito Park, New Mexico." *American Anthropologist* 6: 629–659.

———. 1904b. "Government Supervision of Historic and Prehistoric Ruins." *Science* 20 (517): 722–727.

———. 1904c. Memorandum Concerning the Historic and Prehistoric Ruins of Arizona, New Mexico, Colorado and Utah, and their Preservation. General Land Office Circular Relating to Historic and Prehistoric Ruins of the Southwest and their Preservation. Washington, D.C.: U.S. Government Printing Office. (Reprinted 1905 as "A General View of the Archaeology of the Pueblo Region." Smithsonian Institution Annual Report for 1904, 583–605.)

———. 1905. "Preservation of Antiquities." *American Anthropologist* 7: 164–166.

———. 1906. "Preservation of American Antiquities: Progress during the Last Year; Needed Legislation." *American Anthropologist* 8: 109–114.

———. 1921a. "The Chaco Canyon and Its Ancient Monuments." *Art and Archaeology* 11 (1–2): 3–28.

———. 1921b. "The Excavation of Chettro Kettle [sic], Chaco Canyon, 1920." *Art and Archaeology* 11 (1–2): 45–62.

———. 1922. "The Chaco Canyon in 1921." *Art and Archaeology* 14 (3): 115–131.

———. 1929. *Preservation of Scientific Resources.* Santa Fe: School of American Research.

———. 1943. *From Cave Dwelling to Mount Olympus.* Albuquerque: University of New Mexico Press.

———. 1946. *Campfire and Trail.* Albuquerque: University of New Mexico Press.

———. 1993. "Ancient Communities in the American Desert. Archaeological Research on the Distribution and Social Organization of the Ancient Populations of the Southwestern United States and Northern Mexico." Archaeological Society of New Mexico Monograph Series, no. 1. (Originally

published in 1908 as "Les Communautés Anciennes dans le Désert Améri-
can . . . ," Librairie Kündig, Genéve.)

Hinsley, Curtis M., Jr. 1981. *Savages and Scientists: The Smithsonian Institution
and the Development of American Anthropology, 1846–1910.* Washington,
D.C.: Smithsonian Institution Press.

———. 1986. "Edgar Lee Hewett and the School of American Research in Santa
Fe, 1906–1912." In *American Archaeology Past and Future,* edited by David
J. Meltzer, Don D. Fowler, and Jeremy A. Sabloff, 217–236. Washington,
D.C.: Smithsonian Institution Press.

Hodge, Frederick W. 1937. "History of Hawikuh, New Mexico, One of the So-
called Cities of Cíbola." Hodge Anniversary Fund, Publication no. 1, Los
Angeles.

Holsinger, S. J. 1901. Report on Prehistoric Ruins of Chaco Canyon, New Mexico. Ordered by General Land Office Letter "P," December 18, 1900. General Land Office files, National Archives, Washington, D.C.

Hosmer, Charles S., Jr. 1981. *Preservation Comes of Age.* 2 vols. Charlottesville:
University Press of Virginia.

Judd, Neil M. 1922a. "The Pueblo Bonito Expedition of the National Geographic Society." *National Geographic Magazine* 41 (3): 323–331.

———. 1922b. "Archaeological Investigations at Pueblo Bonito, New Mexico."
*Smithsonian Miscellaneous Collections* 72 (15): 106–117.

———. 1923. "Pueblo Bonito, the Ancient." *National Geographic Magazine* 44
(2): 99–108.

———. 1925. "Everyday Life in Pueblo Bonito." *National Geographic Magazine*
48 (3): 227–262.

———. 1926. "Archaeological Observations North of the Rio Colorado." *Bureau
of American Ethnology Bulletin* 82.

———. 1954. "The Material Culture of Pueblo Bonito." *Smithsonian Miscellaneous Collections* 124.

———. 1959. "Pueblo del Arroyo, Chaco Canyon, New Mexico." *Smithsonian
Miscellaneous Collections* 138.

———. 1964. "The Architecture of Pueblo Bonito." *Smithsonian Miscellaneous
Collections* 147 (1).

———. 1968. *Met Men Along the Trail: Adventures in Archaeology.* Norman: University of Oklahoma Press.

Kidder, Alfred V. 1924. *An Introduction to the Study of Southwestern Archaeology.*
New Haven: Yale University Press.

———. 1927. "Southwestern Archaeological Conference." *Science* 66(1716).

———. 1957. Unpublished Memoirs, 3 vols. Harvard University, Peabody Museum Archives. Portions reproduced in Givens (1992).

Kincaid, Chris, ed. 1983. Chaco Roads Project, Phase I. A Reappraisal of Prehistoric Roads in the San Juan Basin, 1983. New Mexico Bureau of Land
Management, Albuquerque.

Kroeber, A. L. 1916. "Zuñi Potsherds." *American Museum of Natural History Anthropological Papers* 18 (1): 1–37.

Laird, Carobeth. 1975. *Encounter with an Angry God. Recollections of my Life
with John Peabody Harrington.* Banning, California: Malki Museum Press.

Lange, Charles H. and Carroll L. Riley, eds. 1966. *The Southwestern Journals of Adolph F. Bandelier, 1880–1882.* Albuquerque: University of New Mexico Press; Santa Fe: School of American Research and Museum of New Mexico Press.

Lange, Charles H., Carroll L. Riley, and Elizabeth M. Lange, eds. 1970–84. *The Southwestern Journals of Adolph F. Bandelier, 1883–84, 1885–1888, 1889–1892,* 3 vols. Albuquerque: University of New Mexico Press; Santa Fe: School of American Research.

Lange, Charles H. and Carroll L. Riley. 1996. *Bandelier: The Life and Adventures of Adolf Bandelier, American Archaeologist and Scientist.* Salt Lake City: University of Utah Press.

Lange, Frederick W. and Diana Leonard, eds. 1985. *Among Ancient Ruins. The Legacy of Earl H. Morris.* Boulder: Johnson Books.

Lee, Ronald F. 1970. "The Antiquities Act of 1906." Washington, D.C.: U.S. Department of the Interior, National Park Service.

Lekson, Stephen H., ed. 1983. "The Architecture and Dendrochronology of Chetro Ketl." Reports of the Chaco Center, no. 6, Albuquerque.

———. 1984. "Great Pueblo Architecture of Chaco Canyon, New Mexico." Publications in Archaeology 18B. National Park Service, Albuquerque.

Lister, Robert H. and Florence C. Lister. 1968. *Earl Morris and Southwestern Archaeology.* Albuquerque: University of New Mexico Press.

———. 1981. *Chaco Canyon, Archaeology and Archaeologists.* Albuquerque: University of New Mexico Press.

Lowitt, Richard. 1992. *Bronson M. Cutting, Progressive Politician.* Albuquerque: University of New Mexico Press.

McNitt, Frank. 1966. Rev. ed. *Richard Wetherill: Anasazi. Pioneer Explorer of Southwestern Ruins.* Albuquerque: University of New Mexico Press.

Mathien, Frances Joan, ed. 1985. "Environment and Subsistence of Chaco Canyon." *National Park Service Chaco Canyon Studies Publications in Archaeology* 18E, Santa Fe.

Mark, Joan. 1988. *A Stranger in Her Native Land: Alice Fletcher and the American Indians.* Lincoln: University of Nebraska Press.

Morgan, Lewis H. 1877. *Ancient Society.* New York: Henry Holt.

———. 1881. "Houses and House Life of American Aborigines." *Contributions to North American Ethnology* 4. Washington, D.C.

Morley, Sylvanus G. 1915. "Santa Fe Architecture." *Old Santa Fe Magazine* 2: 278–301.

National Geographic Magazine. 1921. "A New National Geographic Expedition." *National Geographic Magazine* 39 (6): 637–643.

Nelson, Nels. 1916. "Chronology of the Tano Ruins, New Mexico." *American Anthropologist* 18: 159–180.

*New Mexican.* 1913. "Animated Debate. Special Meeting of the Chamber of Commerce. Dr. Hewett is Discussed." November 19.

———. 1920. "Archaeologists Cover 2,000 Miles in Twenty Days." September 8, p. 2.

———. 1929. "Alleges Bill Would Bar Great Rockefeller 'Lab' from State." March 2.

*New York Times.* 1912. "Uncovering an Ancient City. Oldest in America is that of Quirígua, Guatemala, it is Thought—Dr. Hewitt [sic] Expects to Discover its Secret Next Summer" (January 21).

Nials, Fred, John Stein, and John Roney. 1987. "Chacoan Roads in the Southern Periphery: Results of Phase II of the BLM Chaco Roads Project." *New Mexico Bureau of Land Management Cultural Resources Series,* no. 1, Albuquerque.

Nusbaum, Rosemary, ed. 1980. *Tierra Dulce. Reminiscences from the Jesse Nusbaum Papers.* Santa Fe: Sunstone Press.

Oleson, Alexandra and John Voss, eds. 1979. *The Organization of Knowledge in Modern America, 1860–1920.* Baltimore: Johns Hopkins University Press.

Parezo, Nancy. 1993. *Hidden Scholars: Women Anthropologists and the Native American Southwest.* Albuquerque: University of New Mexico Press.

Patterson, Thomas C. 1995. *Toward a Social History of Archaeology in the United States.* Fort Worth: Harcourt Brace College Publishers.

Peckham, Stewart, Nancy Fox, and Marjorie Lambert. 1981. "The Laboratory's Modern Era: 1947–1981." *El Palacio* 87 (3):32–42.

Phillips, Philip. 1955. "Alfred Marsten Tozzer—1877–1954." *American Antiquity* 21: 72–80.

Powell, John W. 1898. Report of the Director [the Five Categories of Human Activities—Esthetology, Technology, Sociology, Philology and Sophiology]. Sixteenth Annual Report of the Bureau of American Ethnology, 1894–95, xv–xcix.

Prudden, T. Mitchell. 1906. *On the Great American Plateau.* New York: G. P. Putnam's Sons.

Resolutions. 1913. List of Santa Fe Organizations Supporting E. L. Hewett against Charges made by Chamber of Commerce. Manuscript in ELHP.

Robbins, Wilfred W., John P. Harrington, and Barbara Freire-Marreco. 1916. "Ethnobotany of the Tewa Indians." *Bureau of American Ethnology Bulletin* 55.

Santa Fe Chamber of Commerce. 1913. Resolution to AIA Regarding School of American Archaeology, November 11.

Schroeder, Albert H. 1993. "Preface to this Edition." In *E.L.Hewett, Ancient Communities in the American Desert.* Archaeological Society of New Mexico Monograph Series, 1: xi–xvii.

Simpson, James H. 1850. Journal of a Military Reconnaissance from Santa Fe, New Mexico to the Navajo Country. Report of the Secretary of War, 31st Congress, 1st Session, Senate Executive Document 64.

Smith, Watson, Richard B. Woodbury, and Nathalie F. S. Woodbury. 1966. "The Excavation of Hawikuh by Frederick Webb Hodge. Report of the Hendricks-Hodge Expedition, 1917–1923." Contributions from the Museum of the American Indian, Heye Foundation, vol. 20, New York.

Spier, Leslie. 1917. "An Outline for a Chronology of Zuñi Ruins." *American Museum of Natural History Anthropological Papers* 18 (3): 207–331.

Springer, Frank. 1901. "Uintacrinus: Its Structure and Relations." Memoirs of the Museum of Comparative Zoology at Harvard College, 25 (1).

———. 1911. "Some New American Fossil Crinoids." Museum of Comparative Zoology, Harvard University, Cambridge.

———. 1926. *American Silurian Crinoids*. Washington, D.C.: Smithsonian Institution.

Stocking, George W., Jr. 1981. "Anthropological Visions and Economic Realities." *El Palacio* 87 (3): 14–17.

———. 1982. "The Santa Fe Style in American Archaeology: Regional Interest, Academic Initiative and Philanthropic Policy in the First Two Decades of the Laboratory of Anthropology." *Journal of the History of the Behavioral Sciences* 18: 3–19.

Stocking, George W., Jr., ed. 1974. *The Shaping of American Anthropology, 1883–1911. A Franz Boas Reader*. New York: Basic Books.

Thomas, Diane H. 1978. *The Southwest Indian Detours*. Phoenix: Hunter Publishers.

Toulouse, Betty. 1981a. "Prelude: Founding of the Laboratory." *El Palacio* 87 (3): 4–6.

———. 1981b. "The Laboratory's Early Years: 1927–1947." *El Palacio* 87 (3): 6–13.

Tozzer, Alfred. 1909. "Notes on Religious Ceremonials of the Navaho." In *Putnam Anniversary Volume. Anthropological Essays Presented to Frederic Ward Putnam in Honor of his Seventieth Birthday, April 16, 1909*, edited by Franz Boas, et al., 299–343. New York: G. E. Stechert and Co.

———. 1912. "Letter to the Editor, The New World's Oldest City?" *New York Times*. January 25.

———. 1915. "Report of the Director of the International School of Archaeology and Ethnology in Mexico for 1913–14." *American Anthropologist* 17 (2): 391–395.

Wilder, Marshall P. and Edmund F. Slafter. 1882. Petition Regarding Indian Antiquities. Congressional Record (1882) 47th Congress, First Session, p. 3777.

Windes, Thomas C. 1987. "Investigations at the Pueblo Alto Complex, Chaco Canyon, New Mexico, 1975–1979." 2 vols. *National Park Service Chaco Canyon Studies Publications in Archaeology* 18F. Santa Fe.

Woodbury, Richard. 1973. *Alfred V. Kidder*. New York: Columbia University Press.

———. 1993. *Sixty Years of Southwestern Archaeology. A History of the Pecos Conference*. Albuquerque: University of New Mexico Press.

Zimmerman, J. F. 1929. Letter to A. V. Kidder 1/3/29. ALAB.

Zumwalt, Rosemary L. 1992. *Wealth and Rebellion: Elsie Clews Parsons, Anthropologist and Folklorist*. Urbana and Chicago: University of Illinois Press.

# 12

## Women in Southwestern Archaeology

## 1895–1945

Jonathan E. Reyman

### Introduction

Anthropology has long been considered "the welcoming science" (Parezo 1993b:3).

> Of all the sciences anthropology has the reputation for being the most open to women scholars . . . Openness has a long history in the discipline. Scholars in the nineteenth century realized that anthropology, as a fieldwork endeavor, could not be successfully undertaken without women (Parezo 1993b:3).

Despite the perception, and to a lesser extent, the reality that women have a place within anthropology, women nonetheless have experienced discrimination from "subtle marginalization" (Parezo 1993a:37) to the most blatant exclusion (e.g., Babcock and Parezo 1988:*passim*); Dincauze 1992; Nelson, et al. 1994:*passim*; Parezo 1993a:*passim*; Reyman 1989:49–51, 1992, 1994).

> . . . [F]or women to become archaeologists in an historically male-dominated profession, in and of itself signifies that they are special; they have survived and achieved success in a profession where numerous obstacles have been erected to full participation by women (Reyman 1992:72).

The result of this discrimination has been significant in terms of the loss of people from the profession and in the loss of important information.

This essay, then, focuses on four points relevant to the issues of discrimination and marginalization: certain women's accomplishments in southwestern archaeology prior to World War II; the apparent, systematic exclusion of their accomplishments from most histories of southwestern and American archaeology; selected implications of this exclusion, especially its detrimental consequences in terms of our understanding of southwestern archaeology, with specific reference to the archaeology of Chaco Canyon, New Mexico; and the importance of unpublished archaeological records as critical resources for a better understanding of both the history of archaeology and archaeological history. Increased attention must be paid to and greater use made of the unpublished archaeological record because these materials are often major sources of *primary* data that cannot be replicated or otherwise obtained. The failure to make better use of these unpublished records deprives archaeologists of valuable information and thus handicaps their efforts to do and to write better archaeology.

## Historical Background

Women have been major contributors to all subdisciplines within American anthropology and especially to cultural anthropology and archaeology. Ruth Benedict and Margaret Mead were pivotal figures in the development of American anthropology, as was Elsie Clews Parsons, although in a less public way. In fact, Parsons, through her financial support of student field workers, most notably students of Franz Boas (e.g., Ruth Bunzel and Esther Goldfrank), may have been the most influential of all. Her financial support and the training it provided were critical to the early development of what might be called anthropology's "infrastructure" as opposed to its public image where Mead and Benedict were clearly more visible and influential.

All three women served as President of the American Anthropological Association (Parsons in 1941, Benedict in 1947, and Mead in 1960); other women have served since in the same office, but only Laura Bohannan (1971–1973), Janet Dixon Keller (1990–1994), and Barbara Tedlock (1994–1998), have served as editor of the *American Anthropologist* since the *New Series* began in 1898.

Women have also been prominent in American archaeology, but recognition and acknowledgment of their contributions have similarly lagged behind that accorded their male counterparts.[1] Of the 31 original signers of The Society of American Archaeology constitution (December 29, 1935), six were women: Emma Reh, Helen Roberts, Dorothy Schulte, Ellen Spinden, Sallie Wagner, and Gene Weltfish. Among the first 42 elected fellows of the SAA (December 29, 1935) were four women: Katherine Bartlett, Frederica de Laguna, Anna Gayton, and Florence Hawley. However, no women were among the first officers and council members of the SAA or on the first editorial staff of *American Antiquity* (Griffin 1985:266–267). Founded December 28, 1934, the SAA waited 34 years (1968) to elect its first woman president, H. Marie Wormington; and not until 1981 did Dena Dincauze become the first woman to serve as editor of *American Antiquity.* Whatever the reasons for the dearth of women officers, council members, and editors, it was not for a lack of suitable, qualified women. Bertha Dutton, Florence Hawley Ellis, Madeline Kneberg, Betty Meggers, and Marian White, among others, were certainly capable.

Historically, the American Southwest can be viewed as a microcosm of American archaeology. Almost from the earliest days, women have been part of archaeology in the Southwest. Some, such as Alice Eastwood, were excavators. Eastwood, a botanist by training, worked with the Wetherill brothers at

Mesa Verde in the 1880s and 1890s and introduced Nordenskiöld to them. The Wetherill-Nordenskiöld collaboration was short but important and productive (Nordenskiöld 1893).

Most women, however, were assigned to field laboratories where they cleaned, catalogued, and restored artifacts, "which work anthropologist Clark Wissler saw as fitting for women since it resembled housekeeping" (Babcock and Parezo 1988:4). A. V. Kidder thought young women an "unreliable element" on field crews because of the likelihood of marriage (Babcock and Parezo 1988:v), a view that did not prevent him from employing his own wife, Madeleine Kidder, as a field assistant at Pecos. Indeed, among married couples, wives often worked as unpaid assistants, and were expected to do so. Examples are Ann Axtell Morris at Aztec Ruin and the La Plata sites, and Hattie Cosgrove at Swarts Ruin and Awatovi. Even when trained as field workers, women were usually relegated to laboratory work that was generally considered menial labor.

Despite these obstacles, women managed to produce significant and lasting contributions to southwestern archaeology. Two notable examples from this period include Anna Shepard's collaborative book on Pecos ceramics and her volume on other prehistoric New Mexican pottery (Kidder and Shepard 1936; Shepard 1942). These and other research eventually resulted in her monumental work, *Ceramics for the Archaeologist* (Shepard 1956). There were also a few men such as Franz Boas, Dean Byron Cummings at Arizona, and Edgar Lee Hewett at New Mexico who accepted and encouraged women in the field. However, most men did not, and Hewett, especially, was criticized for his support of women field workers.[2]

During the 1920s, women continued to be relegated mostly to minor field roles, but by the 1930s, a few women were excavating sites or major features, although usually under the direction of a male supervisor. Chaco Canyon was a major center for such activity (Mathien 1992) where Florence Hawley excavated sections of Tseh So (Bc50), Bc51, and Chetro Ketl and its trashmound (Brand, Hawley, Hibben, et al. 1937; Hawley 1934, 1939); Nan Glenn (1939) dug sections of Bc50; Dorothy Luhrs (1935) excavated Kin Nahasbas, a Chacoan Great Sanctuary; Bertha Dutton (1938) dug Leyit Kin (Bc26) and several other Chacoan sites, although she is better known for her 1930s work at Kuaua (Dutton 1963); Janet Woods (1934) dug the Court Kiva at Chetro Ketl, as well as other architectural features; and Margaret Woods (Janet Woods' sister) excavated Talus Unit 1 with its platform mound (Woods 1935).

Elsewhere in the Southwest, Marjorie Lambert excavated Paa-ko and also dug at Kuaua (Lambert 1935, 1937, 1938, 1954), and Dorothy Keur (1941) excavated a series of sites on Big Bead Mesa. Yet even in the 1930s, women were still assigned mostly to lab work.[3]

As in other areas of American society where women, at best, were considered secondary contributors, most male archaeologists, if they accepted women on field crews, regarded them as nonessential participants. Male archaeologists typically opposed women's participation in the field, a situation that continued into the 1950s (Dincauze 1992:131). Furthermore, with few exceptions, women's archaeological contributions were not regarded as highly as men's accomplishments, and women were often specifically discouraged from pursuing careers in archaeology (Babcock and Parezo 1988:4; cf. Gero 1983, 1985; Thomas 1989:138–142).

This denial, or at least neglect of women's contributions persists today. As discussed previously (Reyman 1992:76–77), a recent survey of about two dozen archaeology textbooks plus five to six dozen books and a like number of articles on the history of American archaeology and southwestern archaeology in particular indicates that women's contributions are undervalued or ignored. In *A Study of Archeology* (Taylor 1948), for example, only three women (Mary Butler, Madeline Kneberg, and Anna Shepard) are mentioned in terms of archaeology, although Taylor had worked with Bertha Dutton, Florence Hawley, and other women at Chaco Canyon in the 1930s. No women are cited in the archaeological papers in *One Hundred Years of Anthropology* (Brew 1968), and few are cited in the other papers in the volume. Willey and Sabloff (1980) mention several women (e.g., Madeline Kneberg, Dorothy Keur, Anna Shepard, Tatiana Proskouriakoff, Betty Meggers, Joyce Marcus, and Winifred Gladwin), a slight improvement over the first edition (1974). None of these women is discussed at length except Meggers and, to a lesser extent, Winifred Gladwin, although Anna Shepard pioneered technical ceramic studies (Kidder and Shepard 1936; Shepard 1942, 1956). Furthermore, Dorothy Keur (1941) published the first Society of American Archaeology monograph, in which she was among the first to study acculturation archaeologically, research that predated, in part, Steward's (1942) "direct historical approach" (which Steward must have known but never acknowledged in print). Finally, Florence Hawley (1936, 1950) compiled one of the first and best pottery manuals for the Southwest, developed the cross-dating method combining masonry, ceramics, and dendrochronology (Hawley 1934), and she was one of the first to test dendrochronology outside the Southwest (Hawley 1941). The deliberate omission of women's accomplishments, or at least the oversight and lack of discussion of their research and contributions and those of other women archaeologists within the context of the history of American archaeology, are both revealing and regrettable.

This same lack of recognition of women's contributions is characteristic of books on southwestern archaeology, per se, from the two editions of *Southwestern Archaeology* (McGregor 1941, 1965) to more recent works such as *Prehistoric New Mexico* (Stuart and Gauthier 1981). One exception is *Prehistory of the Southwest* (Cordell 1984), which might be explained by the fact that the author is a woman archaeologist. However, female authorship, itself, does not ensure adequate coverage of women's research. Archaeology texts written or co-authored by women, such as Robert Sharer and Wendy Ashmore (1987), are not much better in their coverage of women's research than the other books cited above. One of the few texts with sections highlighting women archaeologists' contributions is *Archaeology* (Thomas 1989). Finally, of the eleven authors in *Dynamics of Southwest Prehistory* (Cordell and Gumerman 1989), only one is a woman (Linda Cordell).

More recently, a woman colleague experienced such constant discrimination, both overt and covert, that she resigned her tenured associate professorship. Despite her excellent teaching, her award-winning book, and superb administrative skills, the university made no effort to retain her after she submitted her resignation (Reyman 1994:87–89). Similar situations are present in a number of cases discussed by various authors in Parezo, ed. (1993) and Nelson, et al. (1994).

How can this be explained? Others have dealt with this issue in greater depth and with more understanding (e.g, Gero 1983, 1985; Nelson, et al. 1994; Wylie 1993); I see it simply as another example of men excluding women from what men perceive as a traditional male domain, despite the fact that women have been active participants in and contributors for a century or more. In my experience, male archaeologists, like men in general, all too often are uncomfortable with women as colleagues and intellectual partners, and thus try to exclude them.[4] Worse, Dena Dincauze notes (personal communication) that some men literally do not recognize women as colleagues but rather treat them as invisible nonpersons—as if by ignoring or excluding them from their visual perception and cognitive domain women archaeologists will simply disappear. Men ought to realize by now that this won't happen, but unfortunately, in today's parlance, "they still don't get it."

Such behavior is insensitive and cruel; it is also bad scholarship to exclude or ignore scholarly contributions because of scholars' gender. Women have been active in southwestern archaeology for 100 years; they still are, and in increased numbers. To continue to ignore their contributions is intellectually dishonest.

Another example follows, although not from the Southwest:

> My first field season, in 1955, was spent with River Basin Surveys teams in South Dakota . . . that Fall I wrote to inquire about prospects for the next season . . . a letter came . . . The writer rejected my application on the grounds that women want to join field crews only to seduce the men (Dincauze 1992:131).

Unfortunately, such discrimination and sexual harassment are still common within anthropology. As the administrator of an anthropology program, I frequently dealt with women students' complaints about sexual harassment from archaeological field crews and faculty (Reyman 1994:86–89; cf. Nelson, et al. 1994).

This discrimination has had unfortunate consequences, both for individuals and for archaeology as a discipline. Valuable people have been lost to the profession, and by ignoring women's contributions, valuable data have been overlooked and serious errors of fact and interpretation have been made. Two brief historical examples are offered below to support this argument (and a third is provided in footnote 5). Readers, however, should consult Babcock and Parezo (1988), Dincauze (1992), Gero (1983, 1985), Mathien (1992), Nelson, et al. (1994), Parezo (1993a, 1993b), and Reyman (1989, 1992, 1994) for additional data and case studies on this issue.

## Historical Examples

In 1909, Matilda Coxe Stevenson wrote to George H. Pepper informing him that some seeds he had found and sent to her for identification were milkweed (*Asclepias incarnata Engelm*). Had Pepper accepted and used this information, he would have avoided misidentifying as cotton a series of prehistoric Basketmaker and Pueblo textiles he had excavated. It is unclear why Pepper did not use Stevenson's information, especially given that he had asked her for the identifications. However, from his correspondence on file at several institutions such as the American Museum of Natural History and the former Heye Foundation-Museum of the American Indian, one can reasonably infer that Stevenson's sex was a factor in his decision (cf. Parezo 1993a). If so, Pepper was hardly unique in his attitude. Indeed, Boas, Cummings, and Hewett, as noted earlier, are remarkable precisely because they were *atypical* for their time in their willingness to accept and sponsor women as field anthropologists and archaeologists.

A second and more important example is the case of Marietta Palmer Wetherill. A review of her recorded observations in light of more recent research indicates that the consistent disregard of her statements, among other factors, has adversely affected our understanding of Chaco Canyon archaeology (Reyman 1989).

It is easy, at first, to ignore Marietta Palmer Wetherill. Born in 1876, schooled in music, married at nineteen to Richard Wetherill, and widowed with five children at thirty-three following Richard's murder in 1910, she was not a trained archaeologist. However, neither were any of the Wetherill brothers nor, initially, were Harold Colton, Harold Gladwin, William Shirley Fulton, Lyndon Hargrave, George Pepper, Leslie Spier, Alfred Kroeber, and many others. In the case of the Wetherill brothers—and this came much later—the lack of formal archaeological training does not seem to have hampered acceptance of their work. While it is true that some of the above earned the Ph.D. which conferred academic and intellectual credibility, not all did. George Pepper (b. 1873), for example, was but a year past his belated high school graduation (1895) and little more than an archaeological novice when, at age twenty-three, his mentor, Frederick Ward Putnam, put him in charge of the Hyde Exploring Expedition fieldwork at Chaco Canyon. In fact, prior to World War I, and to a lesser extent World War II, trained archaeologists were hardly legion. Most field archaeologists gained their training through participant observation. Robert Lister, for example, started as a "camp boy" at Chaco Canyon in 1936. Marietta Wetherill, then, was not unusual in her lack of formal archaeological training; moreover, she had spent a good deal of time working with Richard and the other Wetherill brothers, both at Chaco Canyon and on the

1897 Grand Gulch Expedition (McNitt 1966). In retrospect, she proved to be a careful observer; archaeologists have erred in disregarding her observations on Chaco Canyon.

Gordon Vivian (1948) summarized these observations following a lengthy conversation with Marietta Wetherill. For example, Wetherill (and others) long ago noted the presence of a prehistoric road at Chaco Canyon: "North of [Pueblo] Alto in certain lights you can still see what appears to be a wide roadway running down to the Escavada. In the old days . . . it could be traced clear to the San Juan" (Vivian 1948:3). Her statement was generally ignored until the late 1960s and early 1970s when the Chacoan road system was confirmed by archaeological field tests. The Chacoan roads are now widely known and generally recognized as important integrative features in the Chacoan regional political and socioeconomic systems.

Marietta Wetherill also correctly identified the remains of prehistoric irrigation systems on the canyon floor (Vivian 1948:2). Therefore, it is curious that, when these observations were confirmed empirically, her other recorded observations continued to be ignored or disregarded. For example, Wetherill related

> the story of the wall between Pueblo Bonito and Chettro Kettle [sic] . . . [I]t was about 4 feet high and extended all the way between the two pueblos . . . Dick wouldn't let the Navajo use stone from the ruin so when they built some of the post and private residence the Navajo went out and hauled in this wall and now it's in the buildings (Vivian 1948:3).

In 1982, I examined a series of aerial photographs at the Chaco Center, then at the University of New Mexico; a "linearity" extending from Chetro Ketl to Pueblo Bonito (generally east to west) is clearly visible in the photographs. Later that summer, C. Randall Morrison, then Park Archaeologist at Chaco Canyon, and I carried out very brief field reconnaissance in the space between the two sites using the photographs and Marietta Wetherill's description as guides. There is no question that there are remnants of a masonry wall in the area between the two pueblos, as she noted in the above citation. Thus we have preliminary confirmation for the existence of the wall, although a full field test is necessary and remains to be done.[5]

If such a wall existed, as appears to be the case, there are significant implications. At the very least, the presence of the wall *suggests* the possibility that Chetro Ketl and Pueblo Bonito were physically linked; that sometime after the construction of each pueblo, they might have ceased being the independent architectural and sociopolitical units that most archaeologists commonly assume they were. Of greater significance is that this wall, taken in conjunction with Chetro Ketl, Talus Unit 1, Hillside Ruin, the Northeast Foundation Complex, and Pueblo Bonito, raises the *possibility* that the Chacoan Anasazi planned to merge Chetro Ketl and Pueblo Bonito into a single large town site or great house more than 1200 meters long.

Although the detailed construction sequence chronology for these five architectural units has yet to be worked out, and perhaps never will be, the best evidence on hand (e.g., Hawley 1934; Judd 1954, 1964; Lekson, et al. 1984) indicates that there is substantial and significant overlap among the tree ring dates and the corresponding masonry styles to infer contemporaneity among the five, that is, the western portion of Chetro Ketl, Talus Unit 1, Hillside Ruin, the Northeast Foundation Complex, and the eastern portion of Pueblo Bonito were all built within the same general construction period(s). All five, plus other sites, can be considered part of "downtown Chaco" (Lekson, et al. 1984:5–7, 272–273). Therefore, if there were an overall plan for the expansion of the central portion of Chaco Canyon, or even a generally recognized need for more architectural space at the various large town sites or great houses, then the *possibility* cannot be ruled out that these five units were to be combined into one "megasite" via the construction of the wall between Chetro Ketl and Pueblo Bonito, and the subsequent construction of room blocks behind or to the north of it. That this construction was never finished—as is indicated by the state of the Northeast Foundation Complex—does not negate the hypothesis; it means only that one must explain *why* it was left incomplete. It must be noted, however, that the extent of the construction between the two sites is greater than that which appears on any map or site plan. We do not know the full extent of the Northeast Foundation Complex because, as Judd (1964:144) states with regard to the walls of the structure, "We followed them in both directions—west to their point of beginning and eastward [toward Chetro Ketl] until we *tired* of the pursuit" (emphasis mine).

The possible development of such a large structure runs counter to the argument apparently favored by most former Chaco Center personnel, that is, that Chaco Canyon had only a small resident population (Judge 1989; Judge and Schelberg 1984; Toll 1985; Windes 1984; cf. Reyman 1987, 1989). On the contrary, it seems that, at some point in time, the Chacoans perceived the need for a great deal more architectural space, presumably one result of a large and *growing* population. Recently rediscovered burial data (Reyman 1989; also see below) support this argument while helping to refute the hypothesis that the resident population was small.

Why was Marietta Wetherill's statement regarding the wall disregarded? In some cases it seems that a few archaeologists believe she meant that the wall extended in a general north-south direction from the canyon wall to the (now) arroyo, thus *dividing* the space between Chetro Ketl and Pueblo Bonito (Robert Lister, personal communication). In other cases, as with her other observations, archaeologists simply considered this observation inaccurate and ignored it.

Significantly, to the best of my knowledge, no one bothered to examine aerial photographs for evidence to support or refute her statement, and no one performed any field checking until we did.

Marietta Wetherill also noted that, "there used to be vast quantities of timbers exposed at Chettro Kettle [sic]. The Navajo hauled away wagon loads of them for fire wood" (Vivian 1948:3). This observation helps to explain the physical deterioration of Chetro Ketl between the late 1890s and the 1920s.

One of the ongoing and perplexing problems in Chacoan archaeology is the *apparent* paucity of burials. For more than seven decades, Chacoan archaeologists assumed that a large population was needed to construct the thousands of sites and features in the canyon and its environs, and thus searched for the remains of that population.

Where are they buried? The answer has not been forthcoming (e.g., Hewett 1936; Judd 1954:325–342; Akins 1986). This apparent paucity of skeletal remains is one of the factors, and probably the major one, that has led to the recent downward revision of the prehistoric population estimates along with the concomitant argument that Chaco was basically a deserted ceremonial center (Judge 1989; Judge and Schelberg 1984; Toll 1985; Windes 1984; cf. Reyman 1987, 1989).

Here, again, Marietta Wetherill's observations are pertinent. First, there is a photograph, now at the Western Archaeological and Conservation Center in Tucson, on which she wrote: "This is a burial mound near Pueblo Bonito" (Vivian 1948:3). Second is her observation that, "There are a lot of these mounds and most of them are about 20 feet high. The wind has blown all the sand and ashes off the bones and there are bones and skulls and pottery all over the mounds. Some are very large and *acres* in extent" (Vivian 1948:3).

Most archaeologists have assumed that she was wrong, that she had confused trashmounds and the mounds formed by the collapse of the small house sites (the so-called Bc or Hosta Butte Phase sites) with burial mounds, and that there were no burial mounds, *per se,* at Chaco Canyon. The recent rediscovery of photographs and field notes made by Richard Wetherill and George Pepper confirms the accuracy of her statements (Reyman 1989).[6] One mound was about 20 feet high, or perhaps higher judging from the height of nearby Pueblo del Arroyo. While not "*acres* in extent" (my best guess is that *this* part of her statement actually refers to cemeteries rather than mounds), we now have evidence for these cemeteries, which appear to be quite large. This mound was large enough so that a grid system of 64, 8' x 8' squares did not cover its entire surface (Reyman 1989:51). Other burial mounds are visible in the photographs and are described in the field notes; there are also photographs of the burials themselves. In one case reported by Pepper and Wetherill, more than 40 burials were excavated in a single trench, and more than 30 came from another trench. Digging stopped only because the men became bored with the work owing to the lack of what they considered to be unusual or interesting grave goods (see Reyman 1989:49–51 for a summary). These field notes support Marietta Wetherill's observations about the numbers of burials and the presence of such things as sand and ashes in the burial sites. The data also raise the intriguing possibility that Richard Wetherill was buried in one of these mounds following his murder in 1910, as I have speculated (Reyman 1989:51).

The implications are clear and important. The lack of burials is apparent, not real; thus, the downward revision of population estimates is unwarranted to the extent that it is based on the supposed scarcity of burials.

This, in turn, refutes the hypothesis that, for most of the year, the Chaco Canyon pueblos constituted what was essentially a deserted ceremonial center; this hypothesis is no more valid for Chaco than it was for the Mayan area where it was also discarded once a more complete understanding was achieved of Mayan population and settlement patterns.

Finally, Marietta Palmer Wetherill must now be regarded as an accurate observer. The Vivian memorandum and other records containing her observations are on file at the Chaco Canyon library, the Chaco Center archives at the University of New Mexico, and elsewhere, and have been known by and available to archaeologists for more than 40 years. In the mid-1970s, I asked several Chaco Center archaeologists, male and female, why they gave no credence to her stated observations about the burials, especially considering that her observations had been confirmed with regard to the roads, irrigation systems, and other architectural features. In addition to the response noted earlier, they also answered to the effect of "what did she know?" After all, she was only Richard Wetherill's wife, and much of what he reported was not accurate. Given the recent rediscovery of his notes and photographs, their comment about her requires re-evaluation. So both men and women must share responsibility for ignoring Marietta Wetherill's observations, although the greater supervisory role of men in the Chaco Center (see Mathien 1992) means that they must bear the larger share of the consequences. Indeed, their failure to pay closer attention to her stated observations has adversely affected our understanding of Chacoan archaeology and has wasted both time and money.

## Summary and Conclusions

The examples from Stevenson and Wetherill cited above are neither isolated nor unique, but they are instructive; it also should be noted that similar materials exist for other areas of the American Southwest (Reyman 1989), and probably for every area of the world where archaeology has been conducted. There are substantial amounts of significant unpublished materials collected by many women field workers, both well-known and obscure (e.g., Florence Hawley Ellis and Alice Eastwood, respectively). There are also substantial and significant unpublished materials collected by men such as Neil Judd, Warren Moorehead, George Pepper, Frank Roberts, and Richard Wetherill, but these latter materials are often better organized (e.g, Glenn 1982; Saquet 1983), better known, and more often used than the women's whose work is more likely to be ignored.

Regardless of who did the work, these unpublished materials contain important *primary* data that can neither be replicated nor otherwise obtained. These records must be read and used, though not uncritically. One consequence of continuing to ignore these records is to handicap archaeological research which, in turn, adversely affects our understanding of specific sites as well as regional and areal archaeology in terms of both the excavated materials and the history of the fieldwork. At the very least, the archaeological picture is less complete than it should be; even worse is that serious errors of fact and interpretation occur, as noted above. In a discipline where data are often scarce and hard to obtain, such ignorance is inexcusable. The same careful consideration must be given to the unpublished archaeological records that we give to the published materials. Furthermore, the accomplishments of women archaeologists, as described in the above examples, must be given the same consideration as those of male archaeologists.

Unfortunately, although some materials are easily accessible, many, perhaps most, are often in obscure places, scattered among several or many institutions, and difficult to locate. The research is also hampered by difficulty in obtaining financial support. Neither archival research nor the publication of archival research is a priority with the National Science Foundation (John Yellen, personal communication); and it is often necessary to submit several proposals to the National Endowment for the Humanities for the same project because its programs either overlap or cover only part of the proposed research program. Finally, few private foundations support such archival research, and those that do such as Wenner-Gren and The American Philosophical Society provide only relatively small grants. Perseverance is necessary, especially because the results in terms of primary data are invaluable. Archaeology is too important for us to neglect the treasure in our midst that is the unpublished record. Better archaeological history and a better history of American archaeology require that more attention be paid to these materials, as well as to the people who produced them, especially our long overlooked and ignored women colleagues.

## Acknowledgments

This chapter is a revised and expanded version of two earlier papers, "Women in Southwestern Archaeology: 1895–1945" (First Joint Archaeological Congress, Baltimore, 6 i 89), and "Women Archaeologists in the American Southwest, 1895–1945: Review and Reflection" (22nd Annual Chacmool Conference, Calgary, 11 xi 89). It also includes and builds upon materials previously published in Reyman (1989, 1992, 1994). The research into the Wetherill and Pepper materials was supported by NSF Grant BNS87–01657, Wenner-Gren Grant-in-Aid 4012, the Andrew W. Mellon Foundation, and Illinois State University.

## Notes

1. I am not familiar with the situation in Europe and elsewhere, but I suspect that it is similar. In England, for example, a few women such as Jaquetta Hawkes and Kathleen Kenyon achieved recognition for their work, but women's names and accomplishments are conspicuously absent from standard archaeological histories such as Daniel (1950).

2. Nancy Parezo (personal communication) states that although Hewett employed significant numbers of women on field projects and in laboratories, at least some of the women felt exploited in terms of position/title and salary. They were paid less than lower ranking men or men with less responsibility.

3. Of course, one should neither underestimate nor denigrate the importance of laboratory work, especially artifact analyses. It is essential to the final goal of fieldwork—publication of results. Good lab work makes or breaks site reports and syntheses. Nevertheless, in the minds of most archaeologists then and, perhaps, now, it is fieldwork that is the "real" archaeology. Note how many archaeologists dig season after season but spend little time in the lab, thus publishing little, if at all, and thus rendering their fieldwork relatively useless to the discipline.

4. Documentation of discrimination is difficult to obtain and harder to publish (but see Nelson et al. 1994, a significant compendium of research on the subject). As both an undergraduate and graduate student, I heard male professors tell women students in classes that women usually didn't have what it took to be archaeologists. In one case, a professor told a student that she would never become an archaeologist as long as she continued to "think like a woman" (whatever that meant). Written documentation is even harder to obtain; where it does exist, there are ethical issues involved in publication, as well as legal ones. For example, some years ago I discovered several student evaluations from a 1930s Chaco Canyon field school. These were among the papers (probably forgotten) deposited by another archaeologist in a national archive. In evaluating one student, the male supervisor gave her "excellent" ratings in all areas of field and laboratory work, then downgraded her overall performance because she was female. To the best of my knowledge, this woman never completed a degree in anthropology nor became an archaeologist.

Should this material be published? The archaeologist is deceased, so he is no longer in a position to harm other women's academic careers. To publish the material, although probably not illegal because it is now in the public domain, might be unethical (although not as unethical as his behavior, which was not illegal at the time). As important, perhaps, is that the publication could be hurtful or embarrassing to the woman, assuming she is still alive.

I am also mindful of the reaction to Taylor (1948) as a lesson in personalizing criticism. The aftermath of *A Study of Archeology* is still with us at the personal level, although lessened by the passage of more than fifty years (Reyman forthcoming).

5. The National Park Service turned down a proposal to conduct field tests to verify or refute Pepper's, the Wetherills', and Moorehead's observations, as reported in the Hyde Exploring Expedition field notes, Vivian's 1948 memorandum, and other unpublished records. The observations to be tested include the Pueblo Bonito—Chetro Ketl wall, architectural features in the South Gap, several mounds, and a number of features at outlying sites such as Pueblo Pintado and Kin Bineola.

6. Funds are currently being sought to publish the materials from the Hyde Exploring Expedition.

## References Cited

Akins, Nancy J. 1986. *A Biocultural Approach to Human Burials from Chaco Canyon, New Mexico*. Reports of the Chaco Center, no. 9. Santa Fe: National Park Service.

Babcock, Barbara A. and Nancy J. Parezo. 1988. *Daughters of the Desert: Women Anthropologists and the Native American Southwest, 1880–1980*. Albuquerque: University of New Mexico Press.

Brand, Donald D., Florence M. Hawley, Frank C. Hibben, et al. 1937. *Tseh So, A Small House Ruin, Chaco Canyon, New Mexico*. Bulletin 308, Anthropological Series, vol. 2, no. 2. Albuquerque: University of New Mexico.

Brew, John Otis, ed. 1968. *One Hundred Years of Anthropology*. Cambridge: Harvard University Press.

Cordell, Linda S. 1984. *Prehistory of the Southwest*. Orlando: Academic Press.

Cordell, Linda S. and George J. Gumerman, eds. 1989. *Dynamics of Southwest Prehistory*. Washington, D.C.: Smithsonian Institution Press.

Daniel, Glyn. 1950. *A Hundred Years of Archaeology*. London: Gerald Duckworth and Company.

Dincauze, Dena F. 1992. "Exploring Career Styles in Archaeology." In *Rediscovering Our Past: Essays on the History of American Archaeology*, edited by Jonathan E. Reyman, 131–136. Aldershot: Avebury Press.

Dutton, Bertha P. 1938. *Leyit Kin, A Small House Ruin, Chaco Canyon, New Mexico*. Monographs of The School of American Research, no. 7, Santa Fe.

———. 1963. *Sun Father's Way: The Kiva Murals of Kuaua*. Albuquerque and Santa Fe: University of New Mexico Press, The School of American Research, and The Museum of New Mexico.

Gero, Joan. 1983. "Gender Bias in Archaeology: A Cross-Cultural Perspective." In *The Socio-politics of Archaeology*, edited by Joan Gero, David Lacy, and Michael L. Blakey, 51–57. Anthropological Research Report, no. 23. Amherst: The University of Massachusetts.

———. 1985. "Socio-politics and the Woman-at-Home Ideology." *American Antiquity* 50 (2): 342–350.

Glenn, James R. 1982. *Register to the Papers of Neil Merton Judd*. Washington, D.C.: National Anthropological Archives.

Glenn, Nan. 1939. "Appendix B—Bc50, Substructures." In *Preliminary Report on the 1937 Excavations, Bc50–51, Chaco Canyon, New Mexico*, edited by Clyde Kluckhohn and Paul Reiter, 166–174. Bulletin 345, Anthropological Series, vol. 3, no. 2. Albuquerque: University of New Mexico.

Griffin, James B. 1985. "The Formation of The Society for American Archaeology." *American Antiquity* 50 (2): 261–271.

Hawley, Florence M. 1934. *The Significance of the Dated Prehistory of Chetro Ketl, Chaco Cañon, New Mexico*. Santa Fe: Monographs of The School of American Research, no. 2.

———. 1936. *Field Manual of Prehistoric Southwestern Pottery Types*. Bulletin 291, Anthropological Series, vol. 1, no. 4. Albuquerque: University of New Mexico.

———. 1939. "Section A—Culture Complexes and Succession in the Refuse

Mound." In *Preliminary Report on the 1937 Excavations, Bc50–51, Chaco Canyon, New Mexico,* edited by Clyde Kluckhohn and Paul Reiter, 10–17. Bulletin 345, Anthropological Series, vol. 3, no. 2. Albuquerque: University of New Mexico.

———. 1941. *Tree-ring Analysis and Dating in the Mississippi Drainage.* University of Chicago Publications in Anthropology, Occasional Series, no. 2. Chicago: University of Chicago.

———. 1950. *Field Manual of Southwestern Pottery Types.* Rev. ed. Bulletin 291, Anthropological Series, vol. 1, no. 4. Albuquerque: University of New Mexico.

Hewett, Edgar Lee. 1936. *The Chaco Canyon and its Ancient Monuments.* Albuquerque and Santa Fe: University of New Mexico and The School of American Research.

Judd, Neil M. 1954. *The Material Culture of Pueblo Bonito.* Smithsonian Miscellaneous Collections, vol. 124. Washington, D.C.: Smithsonian Institution.

———. 1964. *The Architecture of Pueblo Bonito.* Smithsonian Miscellaneous Collections, vol. 147, no. 1. Washington, D.C.: Smithsonian Institution.

Judge, W. James. 1989. Chaco Canyon—San Juan Basin. In *Dynamics of Southwest Prehistory,* edited by Linda S. Cordell and George J. Gumerman, 209–261. Washington, D.C.: Smithsonian Institution Press.

Judge, W. James and John D. Schelberg, eds. 1984. *Recent Research on Chaco Prehistory.* Reports of the Chaco Center, no. 8. Albuquerque: National Park Service.

Keur, Dorothy L. 1941. *Big Bead Mesa: An Archaeological Study in Navaho Acculturation, 1745–1812.* Memoir No. 1. Menasha: The Society for American Archaeology.

Kidder, Alfred V. and Anna O. Shepard. 1936. *The Pottery of Pecos,* Vol. II. Papers of the Phillips Academy Southwestern Expedition, no. 7. New Haven: Yale University Press.

Lambert, Marjorie J. 1935. "The Material from Kuaua." *El Palacio* 38 (21–23): 119–122.

———. 1937. "A Preliminary Account of the Excavations of Paako, San Antonio, New Mexico." *New Mexico Anthropologist* 1 (5): 73–77.

———. 1938. "The Kivas of Paako and Kuaua." *New Mexico Anthropologist* 2 (4–5): 71–80.

———. 1954. *Paa-ko: Archaeological Chronicle of an Indian Village in North-central New Mexico.* Monographs of The School of American Research, no. 19. Santa Fe: The School of American Research.

Lekson, Stephen H., William B. Gillespie, and Thomas C. Windes. 1984. *Great Pueblo Architecture of Chaco Canyon, New Mexico.* Publications in Archaeology 18B. Albuquerque: National Park Service.

Luhrs, Dorothy L. 1935. "The Excavation of Kin Nahasbas, Chaco Cañon, New Mexico." Typescript. Chaco Culture National Historic Park library, Chaco Canyon, New Mexico.

Mathien, Frances Joan. 1992. "Women of Chaco: Then and Now." In *Redis-*

*covering Our Past: Essays on the History of American Archaeology,* edited by Jonathan E. Reyman, 103–130. Aldershot: Avebury Press.

McGregor, John C. 1941. *Southwestern Archaeology.* New York: John Wiley & Sons.

———. 1965. *Southwestern Archaeology.* 2nd ed. Urbana: University of Illinois Press.

McNitt, Frank. 1966. *Richard Wetherill: Anasazi.* Rev. ed. Albuquerque: University of New Mexico Press.

Nelson, Margaret C., Sarah M. Nelson, and Alison Wylie, eds. 1994. *Equity Issues for Women in Archeology.* Archeological Papers of the American Anthropological Association, no. 5. Washington, D.C.: American Anthropological Association.

Nordenskiöld, Gustaf. 1893. Translated by D. Lloyd Morgan. *The Cliff Dwellers of the Mesa Verde, Southwestern Colorado, Their Pottery and Implements.* Stockholm: P. A. Norstedt and Stöner.

Parezo, Nancy J. 1993a. "Matilda Coxe Stevenson: Pioneer Ethnologist." In *Hidden Scholars: Women Anthropologists and the Native American Southwest,* edited by Nancy J. Parezo, 38–62. Albuquerque: University of New Mexico Press.

———. 1993b. "Anthropology: The Welcoming Science." In *Hidden Scholars: Women Anthropologists and the Native American Southwest,* edited by Nancy J. Parezo, 3–37. Albuquerque: University of New Mexico Press.

Parezo, Nancy J., ed. 1993. *Hidden Scholars: Women Anthropologists and the Native American Southwest.* Albuquerque: University of New Mexico Press.

Reyman, Jonathan E. 1987. "Review of 'Recent Research on Chaco Prehistory,' edited by W. James Judge and John D. Schelberg." *The Kiva* 52 (2): 147–151.

———. 1989. "The History of Archaeology and the Archaeological History of Chaco Canyon, New Mexico." In *Tracing Archaeology's Past: The historiography of Archaeology,* edited by Andrew L. Christenson, 41–53. Carbondale: Southern Illinois University Press.

———. 1992. "Women in American Archaeology: Some Historical Notes and Comments." In *Rediscovering Our Past: Essays on the History of American Archaeology,* edited by Jonathan E. Reyman, 69–80. Aldershot: Avebury Press.

———. 1994. "Gender and Class in Archeology: Then and Now." In *Equity Issues for Women in Archeology,* edited by Margaret C. Nelson, Sarah M. Nelson, and Alison Wylie, 83–90. Archeological Papers of the American Anthropological Association, no. 5. American Anthropological Association, Washington, D.C.

———. In press. "Walter W. Taylor." In *Archaeologists: A Biographical Encyclopedia,* edited by Tim Murray. New York: ABC-Clio Books.

Saquet, Janette. 1983. *Register to the Papers of Frank Harold Hanna Jr.* Washington, D.C.: National Anthropological Archives.

Sharer, Robert J. and Wendy Ashmore. 1987. *Archaeology: Discovering Our Past.* Palo Alto: Mayfield Publishing.

Shepard, Anna O. 1942. *Rio Grande Paint Ware*. Publication 528. Washington, D.C.: Carnegie Institution of Washington.

———. 1956. *Ceramics for the Archaeologist*. Publication 609. Washington, D.C.: Carnegie Institution of Washington.

Stevenson, Matilda Coxe. 1909. Letter to George H. Pepper. Typed. National Anthropological Archives, Washington, D.C.

Steward, Julian H. 1942. "The Direct Historical Approach to Archaeology." *American Antiquity* 7 (4): 337–343.

Stuart, David E. and Rory P. Gauthier. 1981. *Prehistoric New Mexico: Background for Survey*. Santa Fe: Historic Preservation Bureau.

Taylor, Walter W. 1948. *A Study of Archeology*. Memoir 69. Menasha: American Anthropological Association.

Thomas, David Hurst. 1989. *Archaeology*. 2nd ed. New York: Holt, Rinehart, and Winston.

Toll, H. Wolcott. 1985. "Pottery Production, Public Architecture, and the Chaco Anasazi System." Ph.D. diss. University of Colorado, Boulder.

Vivian, Gordon R. 1948. Memorandum for Superintendent McNeill, Chaco Canyon. Typed. Chaco Culture National Historic Park library, Chaco Canyon, New Mexico.

Willey, Gordon R. and Jeremy Sabloff. 1974. *A History of American Archaeology*. San Francisco: W. H. Freeman and Company.

———. 1980. *A History of American Archaeology*. 2nd ed. San Francisco: W. H. Freeman and Company.

Windes, Thomas C. 1984. "A New Look at Population in Chaco Canyon." In *Recent Research on Chaco Prehistory*, edited by W. James Judge and John C. Schelberg, 75–88. Reports of the Chaco Center, no. 8. Albuquerque: National Park Service.

Woods, Janet. 1934. Excavation of the Court Kiva, Chetro Ketl. Typescript. Chaco Culture National Historic Park library, Chaco Canyon, New Mexico.

Woods, Margaret. 1935. Report on Talus Unit No. 1, Chaco Canyon. Handwritten manuscript, Chaco Canyon, New Mexico.

Wylie, Alison. 1993. "Chilly Climate Issues for Women in Archaeology." In *Women in Archaeology: A Feminist Critique*, edited by Hilary du Cros and Laurajane Smith, 245–258. Occasional Papers in Prehistory, no. 23, Department of Prehistory, Research School of Pacific Studies. Canberra: The Australian National University.

# Contributors

Alice Beck Kehoe taught as Professor of Anthropology, Marquette University, until her 1999 retirement, and is author of *The Land of Prehistory: A Critical History of American Archaeology* (1998, Routledge). She co-edited *Powers of Observation: Alternative Views in Archaeology* with Sarah M. Nelson (Archaeological Papers No. 2, American Anthropological Association, 1990) and contributed to *Rediscovering Our Past: Essays on the History of American Archaeology* (Jonathan Reyman, editor, Avebury, 1992) and to *Tracing Archaeology's Past: The Historiography of Archaeology* (Andrew Christenson, editor, Southern Illinois University Press, 1989).

Mary Beth Emmerichs holds a Ph.D. in history, specializing in social contexts of modern history. She is on the faculty of the University of Wisconsin-Sheboygan.

Elin C. Danien is a Resarch Associate of the University Museum, University of Pennsylvania; her dissertation included extensive inquiry into Robert Burkitt and his affairs.

Donald McVicker is Professor of Anthropology at North Central College, Illinois. His researches focus on Mesoamerican ethnohistory, archaeology, and the history of anthropology in American museums.

Neil Asher Silberman is author of several books on Near Eastern archaeology, contributing editor to Archaeology Magazine, and co-author, along with Mark Leone, of *Invisible America: Unearthing Our Hidden History* (Henry Holt, 1995).

Lawrence G. Desmond published a full-length study of the Le Plongeons, *A Dream of Maya* (University of New Mexico Press, 1988), and is presently employed in cultural resource management archaeology. His expertise in photography led him to appreciate the Le Plongeons' work.

William G. Dever is Professor, Department of Oriental Studies, University of Arizona, Tucson. He has held national office in the Archaeological Institute of America and published extensively in the area of Biblical archaeology.

Stephen L. Dyson is Professor of Classical Archaeology, SUNY-Buffalo. His leadership in Classical archaeology of the Mediterranean earned him the honor of President of the Archaeological Institute of America.

James W. Halporn held the position of Professor of Classical Studies and Comparative Literature, Indiana University, Bloomington, and presently is a research scholar in Cambridge, Massachusetts.

Mary Ann Levine earned the Ph.D. in American archaeology from the University of Massachusetts-Amherst. She contributed to the section "Women in Archaeology" in the 1996 *Cambridge Illustrated History of Archaeology* (Paul G. Bahn, editor), and to *Women in Archaeology* (edited by Cheryl Claassen, University of Pennsylvania Press, 1994). She is now a faculty member at Franklin and Marshall College, Pennsylvania.

Susan J. Bender is Professor of Archaeology, Skidmore College. Her publications include a contribution to the Christenson-edited *Tracing Archaeology's Past,* and like Levine, to the Claassen-edited *Rediscovering Our Past.*

Jonathan E. Reyman is on the staff of the Ilinois State Museum. He contributed to the Christenson-edited *Tracing Archaeology's Past,* and edited *Rediscovering Our Past.*

# Index